# ESSAYS ON THE LAW AND PRACTICE OF GOVERNMENTAL ADMINISTRATION

# Essays on the Law and Practice of Governmental Administration

A Volume in Honor of

## FRANK JOHNSON GOODNOW

*President Emeritus, The Johns Hopkins University*

Contributed by His Students in Grateful Acknowledgment
of His Scholarly Inspiration and Counsel

Edited by

CHARLES G. HAINES

and

MARSHALL E. DIMOCK

GREENWOOD PRESS, PUBLISHERS
NEW YORK                                          1968

# FRANK J. GOODNOW

Since Frank Johnson Goodnow, the first president of the American Political Science Association, began teaching at Columbia University in 1883, scores of students have received lasting inspiration from his personality and scholarship, while countless others in the field of social science research have been greatly influenced indirectly by his work. The present volume has been contributed by his former students at Columbia University and at Johns Hopkins University, who, since the completion of their graduate study, have specialized in the fields of administrative law or public administration. Were it not for the desire to keep the essays in honor of President Goodnow within the general confines of public administration and administrative law, others of Dr. Goodnow's students would have been asked to participate in this project. In view of the fact that Frank J. Goodnow's influence was so great in the study of municipal government, practical politics, constitutional reform, and other fields of political science, the advisability of limiting the scope of the contributions may be questioned. However, because of the desire to emphasize the aspect of government in which Dr. Goodnow made his outstanding contributions (he has been frequently referred to as "the father of American administration") and because of the necessity of limiting the number of essays in the testimonial volume, the present volume in honor of President Goodnow has been restricted primarily to the administrative aspects of government.

It has not been the desire of those who have contributed essays to this volume to attempt to add luster to the reputation of one who has already distinguished himself so widely and so permanently. The intention of the

v

present essays is to acknowledge in a small way the appreciation and admiration of those of Dr. Goodnow's students who have since devoted themselves to governmental administration and to the administrative aspects of public law. Our tributes should be paid, whenever possible, while a great man is still among us.

No finer summary of Frank J. Goodnow's contributions and accomplishments could be prepared than the one which was read by Dr. Charles A. Beard at the luncheon in honor of President Goodnow at the New Orleans meeting of the American Political Science Association in 1929. On this occasion Dr. Beard spoke as follows:

Nothing could be more fitting on the twenty-fifth anniversary of the founding of the American Political Science Association than a tribute to Frank J. Goodnow from his former students, a legion in number, and from the larger fellowship that has come within the range of his influence through the written word. No doubt it is perilous to attempt to fix beginnings in the wide and everlasting flow of human thought, but it may be safely said that Mr. Goodnow was the first scholar in the United States to recognize the immense importance of administration in modern society and to sketch the outlines of the field. This was in itself an achievement large enough to give his work a secure place in the rising structure of American political science. He did more. Not content with the law of his subject, he went behind the scenes to explore the nature and operations of politics in relation to administration—thus setting tasks significant and challenging enough to occupy a whole generation of successors. This, too, was an intellectual performance sufficient for the morning and evening of one man's life. But ever inquiring, Mr. Goodnow carried his analysis over into the amazing jurisprudence of constitutional law and disclosed in that mysterious domain (once generally supposed to be mathematical) the operation of sentiments, intuitions, and opinions. His volume on Social Reform and the Constitution finished paying his debt, if there was any balance against him. When his books are listed like landmarks, the story is not yet told. With study, Mr. Goodnow combined practice. His services on President Taft's efficiency and economy commission, revealed Mr. Goodnow as a scholar interested in the application of his science and as a leader, in the rationalization movement, associated with institutes for administrative research, which has been perhaps the most striking development in American political science. For all these things the appreciation of students is forthcoming in heaping measure. With a record of work struck off at Mr. Goodnow's forge, we could close. Yet this is not enough.

We must also bear witness to his personal qualities, his unfeigned simplicity, as natural as the rain and sun, without pride or pique of office or authorship, his careless generosity in scattering aid to students without hope of reward here or hereafter, his unfailing humor flowing up out of a knowledge that all are born to trouble, folly, and joy, as the sparks fly upward. Those whose paths cross his find a new mellow light in their ways. Let us say these things now while it is yet day and we stand with our hands to the plow in the furrow.

Certainly the high lights of Goodnow's career and of his personal influence were brought out by Dr. Beard with keen insight. The details of Dr. Goodnow's activities and scholarly contributions would fill a much more extensive treatise than we are able to present here. However, building upon the outline which Professor Beard supplied in 1929, the editors desire to record other facts regarding Goodnow's life and contributions.

Frank Johnson Goodnow, who was born in 1859, completed his undergraduate work at Amherst in 1879 and received the LL. B. degree from Columbia in 1882. Following this, he studied at the École Libre des Sciences Politiques, Paris, and at the University of Berlin where he specialized in administrative law. He began his academic career at Columbia University, where, between 1883 and

1887, he was instructor of history and lecturer on the administrative law of the United States; between 1887 and 1891 he was the Adjunct Professor of History and Administrative Law; while between 1891 and 1903 he was Professor of Administrative Law; between 1903 and until he assumed the presidency of Johns Hopkins University in 1914 he held the Eaton Professorship of Administrative Law and Municipal Science, and during the years 1906-1907 was the Acting Dean of Political Science. When the American Political Science Association was founded in 1904, Goodnow became its first president. Accepting the presidency of Johns Hopkins University in 1914, he guided the destinies of that institution until his retirement in 1929. In recognition of the eminence which he achieved as a scholar and as an administrator, the following honorary degrees were awarded to Dr. Goodnow: LL. D., Amherst, 1897, Columbia, 1904, Harvard, 1909, Brown, 1914, Princeton, 1917, Johns Hopkins, 1930, and J. D., University of Louvain, 1927.

Not many men who have served as presidents of major universities for fifteen years have been able to distinguish themselves by their writings and by their activities outside of the University. Although President Goodnow wrote only two books after becoming president of Johns Hopkins University, he had completed what is ordinarily regarded as a lifetime's activity in research before becoming a university president. Moreover, he found time to engage in services to national, state, and local governments in addition to a continuing interest in and service to the cause of education generally. During 1913-1914, Dr. Goodnow was the legal adviser to the Chinese government. Soon after going to the state of Maryland, he was called upon to take a leading part in framing for the state government a budget system which met legislative sanction and has proved of inestimable value in safeguarding the expenditure of public funds. Goodnow was also one of the leading members of President Taft's Commission on Efficiency and Economy. He was also made a member of the Permanent International Commission established according to the terms of the treaty between the United States and China. He served as a member of the Board of School Commissioners in Maryland, a duty which drew heavily on his time and strength while president of Johns Hopkins University. President Goodnow was also a member of the Advisory Board of the Citizens' Military Training Camps. In the field of education and research his contacts were numerous and his influence was great; he was one of the leading members of the board of the Brookings Institution and of the board of the Institute of Government Research; a regent of the University of Maryland; a trustee of the Peabody Institute and of the Tome Institute; one of the founders of the Institut Internationale de Droit Public; a fellow of the American Academy of Arts and Sciences; an advisory editor of the Encyclopaedia of Social Sciences; a member of the National Council of the Foreign Policy Association; and a member of the American Committee on Rights of Religious Minorities. These were merely some of the more important of President Goodnow's affiliations and interests during the period of his presidency at Johns Hopkins University.

While serving as President of Johns Hopkins University, Mr. Goodnow continued to teach constitutional and administrative law and to supervise the dissertation work of students who desired particularly to work under his guidance. As a colleague of Professors W. W. Willoughby and W. F. Willoughby, he found his teaching duties extremely pleasant and he looked upon his relations with students as an indispensable part of his academic life.

As a university administrator, President Goodnow made an outstanding success. The total assets of the University, which, in 1914, were slightly under $9,000,000, had been increased to $35,000,000 at the time of Dr. Goodnow's retirement, and the student body, which, in 1914, numbered 1,471 had grown in 1929 to 5,794. Moreover, the so-called Goodnow plan, which carried even further Johns Hopkins' traditional emphasis upon research, will long be remembered as evidence of President Goodnow's forward-looking policies with reference to higher education. However, the multitudinous duties and concerns of a university presidency never succeeded in forcing President Goodnow to withdraw from the teaching and research field and his knowledge of, and enthusiasm for, social science research were as great on the last day that he met his classes in Gilman Hall as they were when he assumed the presidency of Johns Hopkins University in 1914.

Prior to his going into the field of university administration, Dr. Goodnow had already gained renown as a scholar and writer, the best known of his contributions being *Politics and Administration* (1900), *Social Reform and the Constitution* (1911), *Principles of the Administrative Law of the United States* (1905), and *Comparative Administrative Law* (1893). However, the full extent of Mr. Goodnow's influence upon the future of American political science is not discoverable in a mere enumeration of the books which he wrote.

Frank J. Goodnow is properly called "the father of American administration." With the commencement of formal instruction in political science, the field of government was considered merely that of constitutional powers and limitations. It was Goodnow who emphasized for the first time the importance of administration; it was he

who staked out the field which the study of public administration was to occupy for over a generation, and it was
he who first directed attention to the operations and techniques of the governmental mechanism. In the words of
Professor Oliver Field, "Professor Goodnow seems to
have realized that administrative law to be really intelligible and useful must be thought of as the law of governmental administration." By far the largest number of
Goodnow's writings pertain to administrative law and
public administration. Thus we find his *Comparative
Administrative Law* (1893), *Municipal Home Rule* (1895),
*City Government in the United States* (1904 and 1908),
*Principles of the Administrative Law of the United States*
(1905), *Selected Cases on the Law of Officers* (1906),
*Municipal Government* (1909), and, in collaboration with
Frank G. Bates, *Municipal Government* (1919).

Although it is true that Goodnow emphasized primarily
the theory of the separation of powers, the relation of the
executive to other branches of government, the territorial
distribution of administrative functions, the powers of the
executive under the American constitutional system, the
place of local administration in government, the law of
officers and the methods of control over administration,
and although it is admittedly a fact that the materials dealt
with where largely judicial decisions, sight should not be
lost of the fact that Goodnow laid a great deal of stress
upon the methods and forms of administrative action. As
a matter of fact, it is not too much to state that the general
content of Goodnow's course on administrative law did
not differ substantially from the usual substance of a
course on public administration today. The principal differences in scope and emphasis today are that legal materials are not utilized to any great extent and that modern

public administration emphasizes much more finance and non-legal techniques.

Goodnow's best known and most greatly admired book is unquestionably his *Politics and Administration*. This challenging treatise, which caused considerable controversy among political scientists at the time, pointed out that all of government is divisible into the making of law and policy, which Goodnow designated as politics, and the execution of the will of the state which is the general content of administration. Not only did this brilliant analysis emphasize the dual division as compared with the tripartite division of governmental powers, not only did it show the inescapable relation between the formulation and the execution of the law, but it also gave public administration the emphasis and the dignity which it had never received before and which it is only now beginning to acquire in full measure. In this book, Goodnow progressed much further toward the present emphasis in administration upon management and actual ways of doing things in contrast with the legal rule relative to the subject.

Out of Goodnow's original research on comparative and American administrative law, there also grew the interest in municipal administration and local government generally. A very large part of Goodnow's course on administrative law was devoted to a consideration of municipal government and as a result, several of his most promising students afterwards specialized in the field of municipal government and administration. In his attention to municipal government, more than at any other point perhaps, Goodnow evidenced the essential realism and spirit of practical reform with which he approached governmental problems generally. As one of those who was outstanding in the movement for reform in New

York City, for the establishment of the merit system and the elimination of spoils from public office, and as one of those who was instrumental in the establishment of the Bureau of Municipal Research, Goodnow exerted a personal influence on his students and on the cause of municipal improvement which has had a far-reaching effect. Professor Goodnow was constantly telling his students that government could not be understood and lasting improvements could not be made unless the political behavior and the political motivation underlying and eventually controlling constitutional and administrative law were properly mastered.

As Charles A. Beard has said, " Mr. Goodnow carried his analysis over into the amazing jurisprudence of constitutional law and disclosed in that mysterious domain (once generally supposed to be mathematical) the operation of sentiments, intuitions and opinions." His *Social Reform and the Constitution* is almost as widely known and as deeply admired as his *Politics and Administration*. In this book we find, par excellence, Goodnow the liberal and the practical idealist. Turning in his *Social Reform and the Constitution* to the very matrix of American political science, Dr. Goodnow dispelled the notion that constitutional law is merely a matter of precedent and strict legal rules and inspired a study of pressures and motivations and social consequences. In 1916, Goodnow published a volume entitled *Principles of Constitutional Government* in which he dealt with the problem of constitutional growth in the principal countries of the world.

Still another group of books resulted from Dr. Goodnow's experience as legal adviser to the Chinese government and as one who was thoroughly schooled in the theory and practice of the state. In 1914, there appeared *The Amended Provisional Constitution,* a document which the Columbia Professor had drafted for the Chinese government. In 1916, also as a result of his residence in and his knowledge of Chinese problems, Goodnow published a book entitled, *China, an Analysis*. In the same year there also appeared a short monograph of Goodnow's entitled *The American Conception of Liberty and Government*.

These books, more than a dozen in number, constituted the principal evidences of Mr. Goodnow's research and scholarship, but in addition there are to be found several articles in professional journals which added greatly to the knowledge and thinking in the field of political science. It is truly remarkable that in half of a professional lifetime, one man should have contributed so much, but it goes without saying that the real value of Dr. Goodnow's contributions are by no means to be found in the quantity of his writings but in the new interpretations, fresh emphases, and new vistas which he presented to his students and to the younger political scientists throughout the country. A significant expression of their real worth is found in the words of Professor Field who has said of Professor Goodnow, " His work . . . now seems much more substantial and penetrating than it did twelve or fifteen years ago."

Anyone who was brought into association with Goodnow as a student appreciates the fact that personal contact with him was as inspiring as any relationship between instructor and student could be, that it was primarily his character, personality and intellect that left a lasting mark and affection in the lives of those who were fortunate enough to study under him. It would be impossible to say which of Goodnow's qualities impressed his students most. Everyone who came in contact with him could not help but be imbued with his enthusiasm for social studies and be inspired with his spirit of practical idealism. Another class room characteristic was the keen, cutting edge of his mind and the penetrating logic of his statements and of his interrogations. His logic was always crystal clear and after an exposition of a subject, obscurities and uncertainties seldom remained. While interrogating his students, he was merciless, but behind it there was always that good humor and sympathetic concern which marked him a great character and one of the greatest of teachers. Finally, he was admired as a man for his broad, sociological approach to governmental problems and for his liberal and public-spirited views on social problems. He attacked the most contentious issues of society with the utmost fearlessness and insisted upon analyzing the implications and social effects of constitutional decisions and of governmental policies.

For such a man, no group of essays could constitute a fitting tribute and it is only to be hoped that what is lacking in the merit of the following contributions will be more than offset by the profound admiration and deep feeling entertained for Dr. Goodnow by his former students who have participated in this modest enterprise.

# CONTENTS

# PART I

# ORIGIN AND MEANING OF PUBLIC ADMINISTRATION

# PUBLIC ADMINISTRATION AND ADMINISTRATIVE LAW

BY

## JOHN A. FAIRLIE

It is only since the last decade of the nineteenth century that the terms "public administration" and "administrative law" have come to receive extended recognition in English-speaking countries. In this recent development Professor Frank J. Goodnow was the first important leader; and it seems appropriate in this volume to consider the origin and development of these terms and their application.

The word administration is derived from the Latin; and similar terms are to be found in the Romance languages—Provençal, French, Italian, and Spanish. In its broadest sense, as applying to the management of any kind of business, it is to be found in English as early as Chaucer. By the sixteenth century the word had come to be used in a special sense in English law for the management of the estates or property of deceased persons. Towards the end of the seventeenth century it was being used for the management of public affairs; and early in the next century for the work of the executive (or non-legislative) part of government.[1]

That the use of the term "administration" in these later senses was known in America towards the end of eighteenth century may be seen from the clear definition by Alexander Hamilton in one of the Federalist papers (No. 72):

[1] Murray's Dictionary of the English Language; Littleton's *Tenures* (1574); Nevile, *Plato Rediv.* (1681); *Gentleman's Magazine* (1731). Worcester's Dictionary gives quotations from Burnet and Swift.

The administration of government, in its largest sense, comprehends all the operations of the body politic, whether legislative, executive, or judiciary; but in its most usual, and perhaps its most precise significance, it is limited to executive details and falls particularly within the province of the executive department. The actual conduct of foreign negotiations, the preparatory plans of finance, the application and disbursement of the public moneys, the arrangement of the army and navy, the direction of the operations of war; these, and other matters of a like nature, constitute what seems to be most properly understood by the administration of government.

Public administration on a considerable scale developed in ancient times in Assyria, Egypt, Persia, and Northern India; and reached a maximum, until modern times, in the Roman empire.[2] Modern administrative systems may be said to begin in England, after the Norman conquest, with the development of a centralized system of royal courts; and until the eighteenth century there was no sharp distinction between judicial and executive administration. On the continent of Europe, with the growth of royal power, France took the lead in the development of a centralized executive administration.[3] During the seventeenth and eighteenth centuries descriptive works on government and on special phases of governmental activity were published; but even in France the terms administra-

---

[2] Cf. J. J. F. Bilhon, *Principes d'administration et d'économie politique des anciens peuples appliquées aux peuples modernes* (Paris, 1819); Denis Serrigny, *Droit public et administratif romain* (Paris, 1862); K. J. Marquardt, *Römische Staatsverwaltung* (Leipzig, 1881-85); W. J. Arnold, *Roman Provincial Administration* (1914); W. Liebenam, *Städteverwaltung im römischen Kaiserreiche* (1900); Germaine Rouillard, *L'Administration civile de l'Égypte byzantine* (1923); R. J. Bonner, *The Administration of Justice from Homer to Aristotle* (1931).

[3] Thomas Frederick Tout, *Chapters in the administrative history of Medieval England* (1920-33); Jean Brissaud, *A History of French Public Law* (trans. by J. W. Garner, 1915), pp. 82, 87, 218, 400, 516, 556.

tion and administrative law were not in common use until early in the nineteenth century.[4]

## Continental Europe

The development of a distinct body of administrative law on the continent of Europe was promoted by the French interpretation of the doctrine of separation of powers, under which it was held that the judiciary should not interfere with the legislative or executive agencies. This view led to the creation of separate administrative courts, such as the Council of State in France (1800), a mixed court in Prussia in 1847, an appellate *Verwaltungsgerichtshof* for the Grand Duchy of Baden in 1863, and a supreme administrative court in Prussia in 1875. The existence of such courts served to demarcate more clearly the law governing public administration.

Some idea of the scope and content of French administrative law may be indicated by reference to some of the treatises on this subject. The second edition of Dufour's

---

[4] Th. Ducrocq, *Droit administratif* (1897-1905), 7th ed., p. viii. Before 1800 works on public administration were published under the term "police." Cf. Nicolas de La Mare, *Traité de la police*, 4 vols. (1719-38); Dessarto, *Dictionnaire universel de police* (1786-90); V. Justi, *Grundsätze der Polizeiwissenschaft* (1782); Jung-Stilling, *Lehrbuch der Staats-Polizei-Wissenschaft* (1788); J. Necker, *Du pouvoir exécutif dans les grands états* (1792); Franz Arnold Von der Becke, *Von Staatsämtern und Staatsdienern* (1797). Cf. Ogburn and Goldenweiser, *The Social Sciences* (1927), pp. 280-81.

For early works using the terms administration and administrative law, cf.: J. Necker, *De l'administration des finances de la France* (1784); M. Fleurigeon, *Code administratif* (1809); W. J. Behr, *Die Verfassung und Verwaltung des Staates* (1812); C. J. B. Bonnin, *Principes d'administration publique* (ed. 3, 1812); E. V. Foucart, *Précis du droit public et administratif* (1814); Louis Macarel, *Élémens de jurisprudence administrative* (1837); M. de Cormenin, *Questions de droit administratif* (1822); Köstlin, *Ueber Verwaltungsjustiz* (1823); K. A. Malchus, *Politik der innern Staatsverwaltung* (1823); J. L. E. Ortolan et L. Ledeau, *Le ministère public en France* (1831).

*Traité Générale de Droit Administratif* (published in 1854) consisted of seven volumes, and the third edition (1868-70) had eight volumes, with a four volume supplement in 1901; Batbie's *Traité Théorique et Pratique du Droit Public et Administratif* (1st edition, 1861-68) comprised seven volumes; the second edition (1885-94) is in nine volumes. Ducrocq's *Droit Administratif,* first published in 1861 in one volume, in the seventh edition (1897-1905) had seven volumes.

Dufour's treatise has two main divisions. The first, on the public authorities (in two volumes), deals with the chief of the state, ministers, prefects, sub-prefects, mayors, councils of prefecture, the court of accounts, and the council of state, with special chapters on Algeria and the colonies. The second major division (in six volumes) deals with the various administrative services in thirty-five chapters, in alphabetical order, from *ateliers insalubres* to *la voirie,* with chapters on the several local councils. Batbie's work considers the administrative areas and their legal status, the administrative services (such as public lands, property, works, and finance), and the system of administrative courts. Ducrocq gives one volume each to administrative agents and councils, administrative tribunals, and principles of public law; and three volumes to civil persons, including the state (with sections on the public domain, public debt and taxation), public establishments (departmental and communal), and establishments of public utility (scientific and educational, religious, charitable, etc.).

In one of the most widely used recent works on French administrative law, Professor H. Berthélemy (Dean of the Faculty of Law in the University of Paris) defines the terms " administrative " and " administrative law " in these words:

All the services which concur in the execution of the laws, the services of justice excepted, are administrative services, and administrative law is the totality of the principles according to which their activity is exercised. It is one of the branches of public law, which includes also constitutional law, criminal law, and the law of nations (public international law).[5]

Rather less than one-fourth of this work deals with administrative organization. Nearly two-thirds are given to administrative action, with sections and chapters on police, national defense, public domain, and optional services of the state (including economic services, education, and charities). A third main division deals with administrative justice.

Another important recent work on the *General Principles of Administrative Law,* by Professor Gaston Jèze, assumes a knowledge of administrative organization, and is mainly a study of juridical principles, based largely on decisions of the court of cassation, the council of state and the tribunal of conflicts. The first volume of the third edition deals with the general principles of judicial powers and judicial control of legislative and administrative acts. The second volume considers " the notion of public service " (including public services operated by concessionaries and establishments of public utility), and " the individual in the public service " (a discussion of the status and problems of public functionaries). The third volume deals with the functioning of the public services, including the powers of surveillance and control of higher officials, and the methods of coordinating particular services.[6]

[5] H. Berthélemy, *Traité élémentaire de droit administratif* (1st ed., 1900, 12th ed., 1930).

[6] Gaston Jèze, *Les principes généraux du droit administratif* (1st ed., 1904, 2nd ed., 1914, 3rd ed., 3 vols., 1925-30) ; L. Rolland, *Précis de droit administratif* (4th ed., 1932).

8    JOHN A. FAIRLIE

In addition to the general treatises on French administrative law, there are more specialized works on the administrative courts, and on other phases.[7] Important articles in English on French administrative courts and administrative law have been published by Professor Léon Duguit of the University of Bordeaux, Professor J. W. Garner of the University of Illinois, and others.[8]

Laws and decrees relating to public administration are published; also reports of administrative decisions of the Council of State since 1800. There are several dictionaries and encyclopedias. The leading periodicals dealing with administrative matters are the *Revue Générale d'Administration* (1878) and the *Revue du Droit Public et de la Science Politique* (1894).[9]

An Italian work on the *Fundamental Principles of Administrative Law*, by Giandomenico Romagnosi, was pub-

[7] Rodolphe Dareste de la Chavanne, *La justice administrative en France* (1862, 2nd ed., 1898); L. F. J. La Ferrière, *Traité de la juridiction administrative* (2nd ed., 1896); René Jacquelin, *Les principes dominant du contentieux administratif* (1899); André Thiers, *Administrateurs et administrés* (1919); Jean Appleton, *Traité élémentaire du contentieux administratif* (1927); Roland Maspetiol, *La tutelle administrative* (1930).

[8] L. Duguit, in 29 *Political Science Quarterly* (1914), p. 385; Walton, in 13 *Illinois Law Review* (1918), p. 63; J. W. Garner, in 9 *American Political Science Review* (1915), p. 657; 38 *Yale Law Journal* (1924), p. 597; *Political Science and Government* (1928), ch. 24; 7 *New York University Law Quarterly Review* (1929), p. 387; cf. also 3 *Cambridge Law Journal* (1929), p. 355; 12 and 13 *Journal of Comparative Legislation* (3rd series, 1930 and 1931), pp. 44, 213, 56; 17 *American Bar Association Journal* (1931), p. 133; and 1932 *Scottish Law Times*, pp. 166, 221.

[9] Alfred Pierre Blanche, *Dictionnaire général d'administration* (nouv. ed., 1904); M. Block, *Dictionnaire d'administration française* (5th ed., 1905, supplement, 1907); Dalloz, *Code Administratif* (1928); *Jurisprudence générale*; Joseph Delpech, *Code administratif avec supplement* (1927); *Recueil des arrètes du Conseil d'État*; Maurice Hauriou, *Notes d'arrètes sur decisions du Conseil d'État et du Tribunal des Conflits . . . de 1892-1928* (1929); *Répertoire du droit administratif*, 28 vols. (1882-1914); Sirey, *Recueil générale des lois et decrets*; G. W. Stromberg, *Guide to the Law and Legal Literature of France* (1931), pp. 210-216.

lished as early as 1814. Later works were published by
G. Manna, G. Rocco, G. Gianguinto, F. Persico, De
Gioannis, Enrico del Guerra, and more recent works by
Victor E. Orlando, Enrico Presutti, Antonio Salandra, and
S. Romano.[10] Orlando's comprehensive treatise has nine
substantial volumes, by different authors, the ninth dealing with public finance. Salandra's work, after an introductory chapter, is divided into three parts: the first a
general treatment of government by law, including several chapters on administrative justice; the second part on
the organization of public administration, general, central,
and local; and the third part on administrative legislation.

In Spain the recognition of administrative law is shown
by digests of judicial decisions on administrative cases
and treatises on the subject published since the middle of
the nineteenth century.[11] One of the more recent works,

[10] G. Romagnosi, *Principi fondamentali del diritto amministrativo*
(1814); G. Manna, *Il diritto amministrativo* (1839-45); G. Rocco,
*Corso di diritto amministrativo* (1850-56); G. De Gioannis Gianquinto,
*Nuovo diritto amministrativo d'Italia* (1864); *Corso di diritto publico
amministrativo* (3 vols., 1877-8); F. Persico, *Principii di diritto amministrativo* (1866); Enrico del Guerra, *L'ammistrazione publica in Italia*
(1893); V. E. Orlando, *Primo trattato completo di diritto amministrativo
italiano* (1897); *Principii di diritto amministrativo italiano* (5th ed.,
1925); Enrico Presutti, *Instituzioni di diritto amministrativo italiano*
(2nd ed., 1917-20); Antonio Salandra, *Corso di diritto amministrativo*
(1921); Silvio Trentin, *Les Transformations récentes du droit public
italien* (1929); S. Romano, *Corso di diritto amministrativo* (1930);
*Archivo guiridico* (1877); *Revista di diritto publico* (1909); *Rivista
italiana per la scienze giuridiche.*

[11] E. M. Borchard, *Guide to the Law and Legal Literature of Spain*
(1915), pp. 12, 16, 88, 111-114; *Biblioteca juridica de la Revista general
de legislation y jurisprudencia. Sección de jurisprudencia administrativa*
(1850); Carlos M. Sanguinet, *Diccionairio juridico-administrativo*,
5 vols. (1858-64); John M. Panitoja, *Repertorio de la jurisprudencia
administrativa 1846-68* (1869); Jose Gallostia y Frau, *Jurisprudencia
del Consejo de Estado sobre la procedienca de las demandas administra-
tivas* (1867); *Lo contencioso-administrativo* (1881); Santos Alfaro
y la Fuente, *Tratado completo de lo contencioso-administrativo* (1875);

by Vincente Santamaria de Paredes, presents the subject in two main divisions: Part One on administrative organization—in general, ministers, the council of state, provincial and municipal administration; and Part Two on the various administrative functions, classified as those relating to purposes and to methods, with a section on administrative proceedings in litigated matters.

Public administration in South America began in the Spanish and Portuguese colonies; and a general ordinance of Spain for the administration of the colonies was published at Madrid in 1783. Works on administrative law were published in Brazil, Argentine, Chile, and Cuba before 1860; and later works have appeared in these and other South American countries.[12]

In Germany the *Reichskammergericht* of the medieval empire (established in 1495) exercised some control over the activity of the administration in the particular territories. But with the decline of central authority after the

Fernun Abella y Blanc, *Derecho administrativo provincial y municipal*, 6 vols. (1887); *Tratado de derecho administrativo español*, 3 vols. (1886-88); Manuel Colmeiro, *Elementos del derecho politico y administrativo de Espana* (7th ed., 1887).

Among more recent works may be noted: Adolfo Posada, *Tratado de derecho administrativo* (1897-8, 4th ed., 1930); Vicente Santamaria de Paredes, *Curso de derecho administrativo* (8th ed., 1914); Gascon y Marin, *Droit administratif*.

[12] E. M. Borchard, *Guide to the Law and Legal Literature of Argentina, Brazil and Chile* (1917), pp. 138, 324, 420; *Ordenanza general para el gobierno de Intendentes, subdelegados y demas empleados de Indias* (1783); J. M. Marilla, *Breve tratado de derecho administrativo español general del reino y especial de la esta de Cuba* (Habana, 1847?); Vicente Pereira do Rego, *Elementos de direito administrativo brasileiro* (1857); P. G. R. Veiga Cabral, *Direito administrativo brasileiro* (1859); Santiago Prado, *Principios elementales de derecho administrativo Chileno* (1859); Ramon Ferrara, *Derecho administrativo general y Argentino* (1865); J. S. Quintiros, *Derecho administrativo* (Bolivia, 1894); L. V. Lopez, *Derecho administrativo Argentina* (1902); H. J. Quiro y R. P. Emiliani, *Derecho administrativo* (1902); Rafael Bielsa, *Derecho administrativo y legislación administrativa* (Buenos Aires, 1921).

Reformation, the increasing power of the lesser governments, and the development of the absolute police state, the very existence of any " law of police " controlling public officials was questioned and denied at the beginning of the nineteenth century.[13] But the recognition and differentiation of administration began soon after 1800; and with the establishment of administrative courts in several states beginning about 1850, the development of a distinct body of administrative law became more clear and was recognized in the writings of Robert von Mohl, Ludwig von Rönne, Lorenz von Stein, Rudolf Gneist, A. von Sarwey, Karl von Stengel, and many others.[14]

Von Rönne described, in one volume, the organization of the Prussian state and local administration, the judicial powers of administrative officials, the ordinary courts and special courts, and the legal relations of public officials.

[13] G. H. von Berg, *Handbuch des deutschen Polizeirechts* (2nd ed., 1802); Gonner, *Deutschen Staatsrecht* (1804); quoted in F. Fleiner, *Les principes généraux du droit administratif allemand*, pp. 25, 26. Cf. D. G. Struben, *Grundlicher Unterricht von Regierungs und Justizsachen* (1733); Johann Stephan Pütter, *Anleitung zum deutschen Staatsrecht* (1792).

[14] E. M. Borchard, *Guide to the Law and Legal Literature of Germany* (1912), pp. 171, 178-186; W. J. Behr, *Die Verfassung und Verwaltung des Staates* (1812); Carl von Pfizer, *Ueber die Grenzen zwischen Verwaltungs und Civil Justiz* (1828); G. von Weber, *Ueber Verwaltung und Justiz* (1830); G. L. Funke, *Die Verwaltung in ihren Verhältniss zur Justiz* (1838); Karl P. Heinzen, *Die preussische büreaukratie* (1845); Robert von Mohl, *Die geschichte und literatur der staatswissenschaften*, 3 vols. (1885); *Die polizei-wissenschaft nach den grundsätzen des rechtstaates* (3rd ed., 1866); Ludwig von Rönne, *Das Staatsrecht der preussiche Monarchie* (1856, 4th ed., 4 vols., 1881, 5th ed., 1899); F. F. Mayer, *Grundsätze der Verwaltungsrechts* (1862); Lorenz von Stein, *Das Verfassungsmässige Verwaltungsrecht* (1869); *Die innere Verwaltung* (1883); Rudolf Gneist, *Der rechtstaat und die verwaltungsgerichte. in Deutschland* (2nd ed., 1879); O. von Sarwey, *Das öffentliche recht und die verwaltungsrechtspflege* (1880); *Allgemeines verwaltungsrecht* (1884); Edgar Loening, *Lehrbuch des deutschen verwaltungsrechts* (1884); Karl von Stengel, *Die organization der preussischen verwaltung* (1884); *Lehrbuch des deutschen verwaltungsrecht* (1886).

A second volume dealt with the various fields of public administration in four main divisions: law, police, material and intellectual interests, and finance.

George Meyer's *Lehrbuch* has been called the first attempt at a complete presentation of the administrative law of Germany. This deals with: (1) general doctrine and internal affairs, including public welfare measures; (2) external affairs, or foreign relations; (3) military matters; and (4) finance.[15]

*Deutsches Verwaltungsrecht* by Otto Mayer, has been considered the leading work on this subject in Germany. This includes a general part on historical development, the foundations of administrative law, and legal protection in administrative matters, but does not give a detailed account of the organization of administrative agencies. A special part deals with the police power, finance, the law of public property (*öffentliche sachenrecht*), public obligations (official relations, contracts, damages), and the law of juristic persons (corporations).[16]

A recent work of importance is that of Fritz Fleiner, now of the University of Zurich. The general part discusses fundamental notions (the separation of powers, historical development, the task and sources of administrative law); the subjects of public administration (the state, autonomous administration, and new forms of organization in economic matters); relations between the public administration and the citizen; and judicial protection. The second part deals with administrative activities (public services and public property) and the adminis-

---

[15] Georg. Meyer, *Lehrbuch des deutschen verwaltungsrecht* (1883, 4th ed., 1913).

[16] Otto Mayer, *Deutsches Verwaltungsrecht* (1895-6, ed. française, 4 vols., 1903-06; 3rd ed., 1924), Bibliography, pp. 267-9.

trative obligations of citizens (police regulations and taxation).[17]

A widely used text is Hue de Grais' *Handbuch,* which has been used in many editions. Another recent work is that of Walter Jellinek. Recent developments are noted in the *Preussisches Verwaltungsblatt* (1879), the *Zeitschrift für Verwaltungsrecht und Verwaltungsgerichtsbarkeit* (1893), the *Jahrbuch des öffentlichen Recht* (1907), and the *Jahrbuch der Rechtsprechung zum Verwaltungsrecht.* Decisions of the higher administrative courts of Baden, Bavaria, Prussia and Saxony are published.[18]

There is also an extensive literature on administrative law in Austria, Hungary, Belgium, Switzerland, and other continental European countries. In Belgium there are no administrative courts. The new constitutions of Germany and Finland provide for administrative courts, while Poland has a tribunal of conflicts. The constitution of Czechoslovakia declares that the judicial power shall be

[17] Fritz Fleiner, *Institutionen des deutschen verwaltungsrecht* (1911, 8th ed., 1921, ed. française, 1933).

[18] Hue de Grais, *Handbuch der Verfassung und Verwaltung in preussen und der deutschen Reich* (25th ed., 1930); Walter Jellinek, *Verwaltungsrecht* (1928, 3rd ed., 1931); Herman G. James, *Principles of Prussian Administration* (1913); F. F. Blachly and M. E. Oatman, *The Government and Administration of Germany* (1928); *Preussisches Verwaltungsblatt* (1879) — since 1928 the *Reichsverwaltungsblatt and preussisches Verwaltungsblatt; Zeitschrift für Verwaltungsrecht und Verwaltungsgerichtbarkeit* (1893); *Jahrbuch der Rechtsprechung zum Verwaltungsrecht* (1907-8); *Jahrbuch des offentlichen Rechts der Gegenwart* (1907); *Die Rechtsprechung des badischen Verwaltungsgerichthof* (1864-1910), 3 vols.; *Entscheidungen des preussischen Obererwaltungsgericht* (1877); *Sammlung von Entscheidungen des bayrischen Verwaltungsgerichtshof* (1880); *Jahrbücher des königlichen sachsischen Obververwaltungsgerichts* (1902); Joseph von Grassman, *Die Staatsverwaltung* (Bavaria, 1913); Roger Dryoff, *Bayrisches Verwaltungsgerichtsgestez* (1828, 6th ed., 1920); Rudolf von Bitter, *Handwörterbuch der preussischen Verwaltung* (2nd ed., 1911; 3rd ed., 1928).

separated from the administrative power and a supreme administrative court has been established.[19]

## Great Britain

In Great Britain and the United States the general use of the terms administration and administrative law came later than on the continent of Europe. Bouvier's *Law Dictionary* (first published in 1839), at the end of its article on the administration of estates, gives a brief definition of the administration of government: " The management of the affairs of the government; the word is also applied to

[19] Stratis Andréades, *Le contentieux administratif des états modernes* (1934); J. W. Garner, *Political Science and Government*, pp. 785-6; Budwinski, *Sammlung der Erkenntnisse des k. k.* (Oesterreichisches) *Verwaltungsgerichtshofs* (1876); Ernst Mayrhofer, *Handbuch für den politischen verwaltungsdienst* (Wien, 7 vols. and Index, 1895-1903); Supplements (1909, 1913); Josef Ulbrich, *Lehrbuch der österreich.schen Verwaltungsrecht* (1904); Mischler and Ulbrich, *Oesterreichisches Staatswörterbuch* (2nd ed., 4 vols., 1909); Friedrich Tezner, *Die rechtsbildende Funktionen der österreichischen verwaltungsgerechtlichen Rechtsprechung* (1925); Ludwig Adamovitch, *Grundriss des österreichischen Staatsrechtes* (1928); Rudolf Herrnritt, *Oesterreichisches Verwaltungsrecht* (1925); " La nouvelle procédure administrative austrichienne," *Annuaire de l'Institut internationale de droit public* (1932); *Zeitschrift für Verwaltung*; Nemethy, " Die Grundzüge und die actuellen Probleme der inneren Verwaltung," *Ungarisches Jahrbuch* (1929); Desider Márkus, *Ungarisches verwaltungsrecht* (1912); Zoltan de Magary, *Synopsis of the Public Administration of Hungary* (1932); Publications of the Hungarian Institute of Public Administration; H. K. Steffens, *Den norske centraladministrations historie 1814-1914* (1914); Johann Jacob Schollenberger, *Grundriss des Staats-und Verwaltungsrechts des schweizerischen Kantone*, 3 vols. (1898-1900); Naum Reichesberg, *Handwörterbuch der schweizerischen Volkswirtschaft, Socialpolitik und Verwaltung*, 4 vols. (1903); Fritz Fleiner, *Schweizerisches Bundesstaatsrecht* (1923); R. Kranenberg, *Het nederlandsch staatsrecht* (1928-30); Maurice Capart, *Droit administratif élémentaire* (Bruxelles, 1922, 3rd ed., 1930); A. Giron, *Le droit administratif de la Belgique* (1881); Paul Errera, *Traité de droit public belge* (1909, 2nd ed., 1916-18); M. Vauthier, *Précis du droit administratif de la Belgique* (1928); *Entscheidungen des obersten Verwaltungsgerichtes* (Czechoslovakia); George Hoetzel, " Le contentieux admin-

the persons entrusted with the management of public affairs." The first edition of Poole's *Index to Periodicals* (covering the period from 1802 to 1881), lists only five articles in English periodicals under the caption administrative—the earliest on " Administrative reform in England, 1854," in the *Eclectic Review* for that year. In the first volume of the American *Index to Legal Periodicals* (1899) a number of articles on the Administration of Justice are listed, but the rubric " Administrative Law " first appears for isolated articles in 1893 and 1903 and includes a considerable list only in the fourth volume (1908-1922).[20]

Austin seems to have been the earliest English writer to recognize adminstrative law as a distinct topic. Dividing his major division of the law of persons into the three classes of private conditions, political conditions, and mis-

istratif en Tchechoslovaquie," *Revista de drept public* (1926) ; J. Prãzák, *Rakvuské právo správeni* (Praga, 1905) ; John W. Wuorinen, *Le Finlande*; *aperçu de l'organisation politique et administrative* (1921) ; P. Negelescu, *Tratat de drept roman* (Bucharest, 1930) ; V. Onison, *Traité de droit administratif roumain* (1930) ; E. A. Poulopol, " La justice administrative roumain," *Bulletin de la Société de Législation comparée* (1931) ; G. Angelopoulos, *Système de droit administratif* (1885-88) ; G. Papastathopoulos, *La jurisdiction administrative* (Athens, 1932) ; S. Andréadès, *Le contentieux administratif des états modernes et la juridiction administrative en Grèce* (Paris, 1932) ; N. Handjeff, *Organisation der Staatsund Selbstverwaltung in Bulgarien* (1931).  Some account of public administration in Russia under the present régime may be found in the *Soviet Union Year Book*; Chase, Dunn and Tugwell, *Soviet Russia in the Second Decade* (1929) ;  and Judah Zelitch, *Soviet Administration of Criminal Law* (1931).

[20] Cf., *The Undue Administration: or the usual management of the customs considered, etc.* (London, 1718), p. 30; *Administration dissected: In which the grand national culprits are laid open for inspection* (London, 1779), p. 302; *The Administration of the Affairs of Great Britain, Ireland, and Their Dependencies* (4th ed., 1823), p. 207; *Opinions as to the real state of the nation, with strictures on a pamphlet entitled " The Administration of the Affairs of Great Britain, etc."* (2nd ed., 1823).

3

cellaneous conditions, he says: "The law of political conditions, or public law (with the strict and definite meaning) is frequently divided into constitutional and administrative law"; and he defines the latter in these words: "Administrative law determines the ends and modes to and in which the sovereign powers shall be exercised: shall be exercised directly by the monarch or sovereign number; or shall be exercised directly by the subordinate political superiors to whom portions of those powers are delegated or committed in trust." [21] He notes, however, that constitutional and administrative law are not mutually exclusive, and also finds it difficult to describe the boundary by which the conditions of political subordinates are severed from the conditions of private persons.

A recent English writer criticizes Austin's definition " in that it does not recognize the overlapping of the province of Administrative Law into that of Constitutional Law as essential in the nature of things, but treats it rather as accidental." [22]

Sir George Cornwall Lewis, in his *Essay on The Government of Dependencies* (1841), discusses and defines administrative powers. He first classifies the powers of government into legislative, executive, arbitrary, and inquisitorial, and then comments as follows:

Executive commands or acts may, in general, be divided into the two classes of judicial and administrative. . . . An administrative proceeding is for the purpose of carrying a law into effect where there is no question about the legal culpability, or dispute about a legal right or obligation of a person. . . . In an administrative proceeding the government functionary acts or

---

[21] *Province of Jurisprudence* (1832); *Lectures on Jurisprudence* (1861-3, 3rd ed., 1869), pp. 73, 772-3.
[22] F. J. Port, *Administrative Law* (1929), p. 5.

may act spontaneously; in a judicial proceeding he does not act until he is set in motion by an accusation or plaint addressed to him . . . an administrative proceeding may take place without the necessity of allowing any . . . opportunity of explanation to the persons whom it may affect. . . . Hence, the term administrative may be properly confined, in accordance with the ordinary usage, to executive acts not judicial. . . . It should be observed, however, that functionaries whose business is principally judicial sometimes perform administrative acts, and that functionaries, whose business is principally administrative, sometimes perform judicial acts.[23]

An early step towards the systematic study of British administrative services was the publication of *Notes of materials for a history of public departments* (1846) by F. S. Thomas, a permanent official. Walter Bagehot, in essays on Sir William Pitt and Sir Robert Peel, classed both of these as great administrators, and discussed the qualities necessary for such. He noted that administration in its most enlarged sense includes legislation, and he also said: " A great deal of what is called legislation is really administrative regulation: it does not settle what is to be done, but *how* it is to be done; it does not prescribe what our institutions shall be, but directs in what manner existing institutions shall work and operate." [24]

In *The Institutions of English Government* (1863) Homersham Cox treats the subjects in three books—legis-

---

[23] 1891 ed., pp. 13-20. A footnote calls attention to much inconsistency in the use of these terms. " The term executive is sometimes used in a specific sense and is opposed to judicial, instead of comprehending it. As so used, its meaning nearly agrees with that of administrative, as defined in the text. . . . The term administrative is sometimes used in a general sense, and includes judicial, instead of being opposed to it. Thus we speak of the ' administration of justice,' and generally of the ' administration of a government.' "

[24] *The Works of Walter Bagehot* (Hartford, 1911), III, 18, 40, 126, 158; *The National Review*, July, 1856; July, 1861.

lation, jurisdiction, and administrative government. His primary classification of governmental functions is into legislative and executive; the executive he subdivides into judicial and administrative, and defines the latter in these words: " The administrative bodies discharge those functions of executive government which do not require for their performance authority to interpret laws."

About this time a German writer, Professor Rudolf Gneist, began a series of studies of English government, in which he applied the continental terms of administrative law and administrative courts.[25]

Holland, in his treatise on *Jurisprudence* (first published in 1880), recognized administrative law as a branch of public law. According to his analysis:

The various organs of the sovereign power are described by Constitutional law as at rest; but it is also necessary that they should be considered as in motion, and the manner of their activity should be prescribed in detail. The branch of law which does this is called Administrative Law, " Verwaltungsrecht " in the widest sense of the term.

Different views are taken as to the topics which are included under this very wide conception. It may be fairly said to include the making and promulgation of laws, the action of the government in guiding the state as a whole, the administration of justice, the management of the property and business transactions of the state, and the working in detail by means of subordinates entrusted with a certain amount of discretion, of the complex machinery by which the State provides at once for its own existence and for the general welfare.

Administrative law, as thus conceived, is not a coherent body

[25] Rudolf Gneist, *Geschichte und heutige Gestalt der englischen Communalverfassung oder der Self-government* (1863); *Self-government, Communalverfassung und Verwaltungsgerichte in England* (1879); *History of the English Constitution* (1882), ch. 48. " The Development of the Administrative Jurisdiction "; *Das englische Verwaltungsrecht* (1883-4).

of doctrine, and it is convenient so to specialize the use of the term as to apply it only to two of the five above-mentioned topics.

He then assigns four of the topics to other fields, leaving for administrative law " the working . . . of the complex machinery by which the State provides . . . for its own existence and for the general welfare." In this specific sense it deals with such matters as revenue, armed forces, dependencies, état civil, and the promotion of material, intellectual, and moral welfare. He also notes the existence in continental Europe of special administrative courts to deal with questions of administrative law, which in England are brought before justices of the peace and the superior courts.

In Maitland's opinion, Holland's idea could be expressed in the statement that " while Constitutional Law deals with structure, Administrative Law deals with function"; but he held that this distinction can scarcely be carried to a logical conclusion and that Holland was forced to abandon it for the sake of convenience. Frederick Port emphasizes the need for including the organization of the administrative agencies and also objects to Holland's express exclusion of the central executive.[26]

Sheldon Amos, in his works on *The Science of Law* (1874) and *The Science of Politics* (1883), discusses the terms " administration" and " administrative." In the former work he finds that the activity of government is two-fold in character—legislation and administration. Administration consists

in selecting a vast hierarchy of persons to perform definite work; in marking out the work of all and each; in taking such measures as are necessary to secure that the work is really done; and in supplying from day to day such connections or modifications as

[26] F. J. Port, *Administrative Law* (1929), pp. 10-12.

changing circumstances may seem to suggest. This task is of the highest degree of importance, and, in a very primitive condition of society, represents the largest portion of governmental action. In a very complete and advanced condition of society, again, the task of administration is one of inordinate magnitude and difficulty, but it is only a subordinate agency in the whole process of government.[27]

In the *Science of Politics* he considers the distinction between the terms executive and administrative, as follows:

Sometimes the term *Executive*, which strictly means an authority which puts the laws in force, is opposed to the term *Administrative*, which implies the performance of every sort of immediate Governmental act, such as collecting taxes, organizing and directing the army, navy, and police, supervising trade, locomotion, postal communication, and carrying out in detail legislative measures for promoting public health, education, morality, and general contentment; . . . But the term *Administrative* is — especially in scientific and constitutional treaties — less used than *Executive*; and the distinction is not very convenient. . . . On the whole, it is best to use one term, *Executive*, to express the portion of the Supreme Authority which is not legislative in the full and true sense, and only to oppose *Executive* to *Administrative*, when, for a special purpose, it is necessary to consider apart from all other functions the function of ensuring obedience, in detail, to the Law as it is.[28]

Salmond, in his work on *Jurisprudence,* also recognizes administrative law in the following brief statement:

The two divisions of public law are Constitutional and Administrative Law. It is impossible, however, to draw any rigid line between these two, for they differ merely in the degree of importance pertaining to their subject matters. Constitutional Law

[27] Ch. 14, p. 297.
[28] Ch. 2, pp. 99-100.

deals with the structure, powers, and functions of the supreme power in the state together with those of all the more important of the subordinate departments of government. Administrative Law, on the other hand, is concerned with the multitudinous forms and instruments in and through which the lower ranges of governmental activity manifest themselves.[29]

In his lectures on the *Constitutional History of England* (delivered in 1887-8, but not published until 1908) Sir Frederick Maitland examined and criticized Austin's and Holland's definitions of administrative law. He noted that " We shall look in vain for any such term as administrative law in our orthodox English textbooks." He emphasized the interdependence of all parts of the law and the difficulties of sharp distinctions of classification, but noted that about half of the cases in modern reports of the Queen's Bench Division " have to do with the rules of administrative law."

In marked contrast with these English writers in recognizing administrative law, was the attitude of Professor A. V. Dicey in his well known work on *The Law of the Constitution* (1885). In a chapter on *Droit Administratif*, he states:

*Droit Administratif* is a term known under one form or another to the law of most continental states, but it is one for which English legal phraseology supplies no proper equivalent. The words " administrative law," which are the most natural rendering of *droit administratif*, are unknown to English judges and counsel, and are in themselves hardly intelligible without further explanation.

This absence from our language of any satisfactory equivalent for the term *droit administratif* is significant; the want of a name arises at bottom from our non-recognition of the thing itself.

[29] J. W. Salmond, *Jurisprudence* (1902, 4th ed., App. IV, 8th ed., 1930).

In England, and in countries which, like the United States, derive their civilization from English sources, the system of administrative law and the very principles upon which it rests are in truth unknown.

After quoting statements by French writers, Dicey continues that *droit administratif* may " be best described as that portion of French law which determines (i) the position and liabilities of all state officials, and (ii) the civil rights and liabilities of private individuals in there dealings with officials as representatives of the state, and (iii) the procedure by which these rights and liabilities are enforced."

This system, Dicey held, rests on two leading ideas alien to the conception of modern Englishmen, though similar to views held in England during the times of the Tudors and Stuarts: special privileges of government servants and the separation of powers. The leading characteristics of French administrative law, in his opinion, are: the relations of government officials and private citizens are determined by special rules; ordinary tribunals have no concern with administrative law; and it is administered by special official courts, with a special tribunal to determine conflicts of jurisdiction. In conclusion, he stated that " The authority of the courts of law, as understood in England, can therefore hardly co-exist with the system of *droit administratif* as it prevails in France. We may perhaps even go so far as to say that English legalism is hardly consistent with the existence of an official body which bears any true resemblance to what foreigners call ' the administration.' " [30]

[30] *Law of the Constitution* (1885), pp. 180-203, 398. Cf. Francis Lieber, *On Civil Liberty and Self-government* (1853), chs. 10 and 18, pp. 109, 220 on the supremacy of the law and the absence in the United States of " administrative judgments."

A careful study of Dicey's discussion will show that his main criticisms are directed to his conception of certain characteristics of the French and continental methods by which administrative law was applied. From his own statement of the content of administrative law, it seems clear that English law necessarily dealt with the same problems, though by different methods. Later writers, beginning with Professor Goodnow, have criticized Dicey's views as to the operation of the continental systems, and also his assumption that English law made no distinction between rules of law applicable to public officials and to private citizens; while later developments, both in England and the United States, have emphasized the need for a separate treatment of the law of public administration and an increased recognition of its importance.[31]

[31] In later editions of his *Law of the Constitution*, Dicey greatly revised and added to his chapter on *Droit Administratif*, tracing its development, and noting that it " has in recent years been more or less ' judicialised.' " " *Droit administratif*, though administered by bodies which are perhaps not in strictness courts and though containing provisions not reconcilable with the modern English conception of the rule of law, comes very near to law, and is utterly different from the capricious prerogatives of despotic power." At the same time he maintained that it is not to be identified with any part of the law of England, and " rests upon ideas absolutely foreign to English law." 17 *Law Quarterly Review* (1901), 302; Notes to sixth edition; seventh edition (1908), pp. 364, 383.

In a later article, discussing the case of *Local Government Board v. Arlidge*, he made a further concession in these words: " Modern legislation has conferred . . . upon servants of the Crown a considerable amount of judicial or quasi-judicial authority. This is a considerable step towards the introduction . . . of something like the *droit administratif* of France, but the fact that the ordinary law courts can deal with any actual and provable breach of the law committed by any servant of the Crown, still preserves the rule of law which is fatal to the existence of the true *droit administratif*. 31 *Law Quarterly Review* (1915), p. 148. Cf. " Law and Opinion in England," Introd. to 2nd ed. (1914), p. xliii; *Law of the Constitution* (8th ed., 1915), p. 385, Appendix, Note 12, on Proceedings against the Crown.

### The United States

In the United States, the term administration received statutory and judicial recognition in New York state by 1874. In a case arising under " An act to secure better administration in the Police Courts of the city of New York," one of the judges of the court of appeals defined administration as " the act of administering—of conducting the office, or in this case is the execution of the powers and duties of the courts named; the administering the laws by these courts in their application to particular persons or cases." [32]

The word administration also came to be used with reference to the periods of the presidential terms. Lamphere's *The United States Government* (1880) gave some attention to the executive departments and administrative services. Lalor's *Cyclopedia of the Political and Social Sciences* (1882) had a brief article on " Civil Administration," by Dorman B. Eaton. A pamphlet on *Administrative Organization of the United States Government* was published in 1884. In the first volume of the *Political Science Quarterly* (1886-7), Professor Goodnow (then beginning his work at Columbia University) published an article on " Judicial remedies against administrative actions."

The second volume of this journal contains an article by Woodrow Wilson on " The Study of Administration," in which administration is described as " government in action; it is the executive, the operative, the most visible side of government, and is, of course, as old as govern-

---

[32] *Wenzler* v. *People*, 58 N. Y. 516 (1874); dissenting opinion by J. Allen. Cf. A. de Tocqueville, *Democracy in America* (1838), pp. 51-64, on administration in New England and general remarks on the administration of the United States.

ment itself." " Public administration is the detailed and systematic execution of public law. Every particular application of general law is an act of administration." " It is the object of administrative study to discover, first, what government can properly and successfully do, and secondly, how it can do these proper things with the utmost possible efficiency, and at the least possible cost either of money or energy."

Black's *Dictionary of Law* (1891) gave the following definition of administration: " The administration of government means the practical management and direction of the executive department, or, of the public machinery or functions. The term 'administration' is also conventionally applied to the whole class of public functionaries, or those in charge of the management of the executive department." [33]

The publication of Goodnow's *Comparative Administrative Law,* in 1893, marked the beginning of fuller recognition and more extended study of public administration in the United States, and it is important to understand his conception of the subject. Recognizing its wider senses, he defined administration, as a function of government, as " the entire activity of the government, exclusive of that of the legislature and the purely judicial work of the courts, in the five-fold direction of foreign, military, judicial, financial affairs." Administrative law he defined as " that part of the public law which fixes the organization and determines the competence of the administrative authorities, and indicates to the individual remedies for the violation of his rights." [34]

In a later work on *Politics and Administration* (1900),

---

[33] Quoted in *People* v. *Salisbury*, 96 N. W. (Mich., 1903), pp. 936, 941.
[34] Frank J. Goodnow, *Comparative Administrative Law*, I, pp. 4, 8.

Goodnow analyzed the basic functions of government as (1) the expression of the political will (politics) and (2) the execution of that will (administration). But the administration of justice may be differentiated from the administration of government; and in his *Principles of the Administrative Law of the United States* (1905), he considers the function of administration only in the latter sense—" the execution, in non-judicial matters, of the law or will of the state as expressed by the competent authority." [35]

While Goodnow introduced the term administrative law into American law, he noted that some important branches of this law had already been considered, in such works as Dillon's *Law of Municipal Corporations* (1872), Cooley's *Law of Taxation* (1876), and Mechem's *Law of Officers* (1890). These titles serve to indicate some of the topics he included in the term administrative law and the existence of a body of legal rules dealing with these topics.

In his two works on administrative law, Goodnow did not attempt to cover the whole field as treated by continental European writers. In both works, he followed the same general plan, with " books " on the separation of powers, central administration, local administration, the official relation, methods and forms of administrative action, and control over the administration. There is no detailed consideration of " the directions of administrative action " in the various administrative services. This would have widely expanded the scope of his works, which were intended for the beginner in the study of administrative law.

Some phases of this more detailed analysis were, how-

[35] Frank J. Goodnow, *Administrative Law of the United States* (1905), p. 14.

ever, carried out, under his supervision, by his students and published in the series of Columbia University Studies in History, Economics, and Public Law. These included studies on English local government, the separation of powers, and state administration in a number of the American states. Goodnow also made further contributions by his works on *Municipal Home Rule, Municipal Problems, Municipal Government,* and collections of cases on government and administration, the law of public officers, and the law of taxation.

Since the appearance of Goodnow's pioneer work, there has been an enormous expansion of interest in public administration and administrative law, as shown by university courses; the publication of books and articles; intensive studies by official and unofficial agencies, such as bureaus of governmental research; and special national and state commissions on efficiency and economy. Some of these are of a general character, but most of them deal with more specialized phases. Thus there are books and courses on national, state, municipal, rural, colonial, and international administration. Other books and courses deal with particular fields of public service: the foreign service, immigration, judicial administration, military administration, police, ports, the postal service, public health, prohibition, public lands, public libraries, public works, school administration, social welfare, trade and public utility regulation, and workmen's compensation. Still others deal with administrative problems common to different fields, such as administrative organization, finance administration, and personnel administration. A further group deals with distinctly legal problems.[36]

[36] Attention may also be called to the development of university courses and books on business administration in general, and to specialized treatment of such subjects as banking, corporation management, farm organiza-

The extent of this development may be indicated by reference to bibliographical publications, such as R. C. Books, *Bibliography of Municipal Problems and City Conditions* (1897, 2d ed. 1901); W. B. Munro, *Bibliography of Municipal Government* (1915); Sarah Greer, *Bibliography of Public Administration* (1926, new ed. 1933); and bibliographical references in W. F. Willoughby, *Principles of Public Administration* (1926); Fairlie and Kneier, *County Government and Administration* (1930); and Frankfurter and Davison, *Cases and other Materials on Administrative Law,* 1932).

In 1903 another American work appeared on the *Principles of the Administrative Law Governing the Relations of Public Officers,* by Bruce Wyman. In this, administrative law was defined as " the body of rules which defines the authority and the responsibility of that department of government which is charged with the enforcement of the law." Fifteen chapters dealt in turn with: the law of the administration, its position, independence, power, duties, membership, organization, theory, authority, execution, legislation, regulation, adjudication, processes, and jurisdiction. In comparison with Goodnow, this gave less attention to the organization of public administration and none to legislative and judicial control of the administration; nor did it consider the various administrative services, but went more fully into the various forms and types of administrative action.

Some years later Professor Ernst Freund, of the University of Chicago, published a collection of cases on administrative law. This dealt with the subject from the point of

tion and management, household management, institutional management, labor administration, mine administration, newspaper administration, public utilities management, and railway administration; and to finance and personnel administration in business.

view of private rights, as the law controlling the administration and not as law produced by the administration. It thus covered only part of the field included by the continental writers and Goodnow and concentrated on the part not covered by Wyman. Part I included cases illustrating administrative power and action, and Part II (the larger part) with relief against administrative action.[37]

In a more recent work, on *Administrative Powers Over Persons and Property* (1928), Professor Freund deals with a different branch of the subject. In this he analyzes statutory provisions conferring powers on administrative agencies, which he classifies as enabling and directing powers, and more specifically as licensing and permit requirements, administrative orders, examining powers and summary powers. He still limits his study, however, to powers directly affecting private rights and clearly states that he does not attempt to deal with administrative powers in the management and operation of public services.

Later, in the *Encyclopedia of the Social Sciences,* Freund defines administrative law as the law of official powers and of its subjection to judicial control. The main problems of administrative law relate to the nature and operation of official powers, formal and procedural conditions for the exercise of powers, official and communal liability, specific remedies for the judicial control of administrative action, and the question of administrative finality. Constitutional problems relate to the delegability of legislative power and to due process in administrative power and as involving subjection to judicial control.

Another writer, in an article in the *Harvard Law Review* (1918), defined administrative law as " the law applicable

[37] Ernst Freund, *Cases On Administrative Law* (1911, 2nd ed., 1928).

to the transmission of the will of state from its source to the point of its application." [38]

Professor M. E. Dimock defines American administrative law

as that body of law which relates to the organization of the administration; its relation to other departments of government; the rights and duties of holding office; and the nature and extent of the powers, regulations and methods by which the objectives of government are carried out administratively. The second part of the subject deals with the liability of the officer and of the government for illegal acts which injure the citizen; and the remedies, judicial and administrative, which the government provides in order to assure relief.[39]

The development of new administrative agencies in the United States with so-called quasi-legislative and quasi-judicial powers has led to a different emphasis on the content and character of administrative law in this country. This is illustrated by a course of lectures on *The Growth of American Administrative Law* given under the auspices of the Bar Association of St. Louis in 1923. In the original announcement of this course, administrative law is defined as " a convenient term to indicate that branch of

[38] A. A. Berle, " The Expansion of American Administrative Law," 30 *Harvard Law Review* (1917), p. 430. Cf. also articles by J. Y. Brinton in 61 *University of Pennsylvania Law Review* (1913), p. 135; by Roscoe Pound in 9 *American Bar Association Journal* (1923), p. 409, and 2 *Wisconsin Law Review* (1924), p. 321; by Felix Frankfurter in 75 *University of Pennsylvania Law Review* (1927), p. 614; by Justice Rosenberg in 23 *American Political Science Review* (1929), p. 32; and by Charles G. Haines in 26 *American Political Science Review* (1932), p. 875.

[39] 15 *Journal of Comparative Legislation* (3rd series, 1933), p. 33. Cf. also other articles by Professor Dimock in 9 *Public Administration* (1931), p. 417; 26 *American Political Science Review* (1932), p. 894; *Annuaire de l'Institut Internationale de droit public* (1932), p. 542; 20 *California Law Review* (1932), p. 162.

modern law relating to the executive department when acting in a quasi-legislative or quasi-judicial capacity."

In one of these lectures, on the constitutional aspects of administrative law, Judge Cuthbert W. Pound, of the New York Court of Appeals, gave a more extended definition of administrative law as follows:

> In its widest sense it includes the entire system of laws under which the machinery of the state works, and by which the state performs all governmental acts. . . . In a narrower sense, and as commonly used today, administrative law implies that branch of modern law under which the executive department of government, acting in a quasi-legislative or quasi-judicial capacity, interferes with the conduct of the individual for the purpose of promoting the well-being of the community . . .

This view of the subject is reflected in the topics of the lectures, which included three of a general nature, presenting a historical survey, the constitutional aspects, and federal departmental practice; and three on the more recent specialized agencies—the Interstate Commerce Commission, the Federal Trade Commission, and state public service commissions.

Further illustrations of this view are to be seen in such works as Hart's *Ordinance Making Power of the President* (1925); J. P. Comer's *Legislative Functions of National Administrative Authorities* (1927); John Dickinson's *Administrative Justice and the Supremacy of the Law* (1927); E. W. Patterson's *The Insurance Commissioner* (1927); G. C. Henderson's *Federal Trade Commission* (1927); W. C. Van Vleck's *The Administrative Control of Aliens* (1932); Scharfman's *Interstate Commerce Commission* (1931); Frankfurter and Davison's *Cases and Materials on Administrative Law* (1932); and numerous articles in legal and other periodicals.[40]

[40] Cf. articles in 10 *American Political Science Review* (1917), pp.

4

The last named of these works states the concern of administrative law to be the systematic exploration of the problems of these newer agencies. " Government regulation of banking, insurance, public utilities, industry, finance, immigration, the professions, health and morals, in short the inevitable response of government to the needs of modern society, is building up a body of enactments not written by the legislatures, and of adjudications not made by the courts, and only to a limited degree subject to their revision." Following this conception, this collection (after cases dealing with the separation of powers and the delegation of powers) gives about half of its space to cases on judicial control of administrative action with reference to specific topics, such as utility regulation, taxation, control of aliens, federal trade regulation, postal regulation, control of the public domain, police regulations, and others. From this point of view administrative law is much more comprehensive than the French and continental systems. In contrast with Freund, the regulation and control of public administrative agencies becomes a secondary phase of the subject, and the main emphasis is placed on the law formulated and promulgated through administrative agencies.

There is need for a clearer recognition of the distinction between administrative courts in the continental European sense and the newer American " administrative tribunals." The former are organs of judicial control over public administrative agencies and actions; and examples of such organs in the United States are evident in such bodies as the United States Court of Claims, the Court of Customs, the Court of Customs and Patent Appeals, the Board of Income Tax Appeals, and local boards of re-

235 ff., on administrative tribunals; H. M. Stephens, "Administrative Tribunals and the Rules of Evidence."

view in property tax assessments. The latter are agencies for dealing with problems of conflicting interests of different classes of private citizens.

This distinction is not recognized in the recent report of the American Bar Association committee on administrative law, which considers both classes of agencies as of the same character. The recommendations of this committee for a more systematic organization of administrative tribunals, more careful regulation of their procedure, and more definite provisions for publication of their rules and decisions are commendable. But the further recommendation that after these changes there should be a complete right of appeal, both as to questions of law and of fact to the existing judicial courts, is at least open to question. There is ground for providing for an adequate judicial review on questions of law, which might well be to a central court of appeals on administrative law, with a possible further review on certiorari to the Supreme Court of the United States on constitutional questions.

Attention may also be called to other works dealing with particular phases of administrative law under other titles. These included such subjects as the law of taxation, the law of municipal corporations, and the law of elections. Another important subject, government liability in tort, has been discussed at length by Professor E. M. Borchard and others.[41]

Paralleling these developments in the use and application of the term administrative law in the United States

[41] E. M. Borchard, in 11 *American Bar Association Journal* (1925), p. 494; 34 and 36 *Yale Law Journal* (1924-25, 1926-27); 28 *Columbia Law Review* (1928). Cf. also W. L. Williams, *The Liability of Municipal Corporations for Tort* (1901); R. D. Watkins, *The State as a Party Litigant* (1927); and articles in 75 *University of Pennsylvania Law Review* (1927), p. 555, and 11 *Oregon Law Review* (1932), p. 123.

may be noted an increasing interest in other phases of public administration. The expanding scope of public services was reflected in legislation relating to the civil service, financial methods, and problems of organization; in the development of college and university courses in public administration; in the formation of numerous associations of public officials and private agencies for the improvement of the quality of public services—such as civil service reform associations, municipal leagues, and bureaus of municipal and governmental research; [42] and in intensive studies by official agencies such as President Taft's Commission on Efficiency and Economy (1912) and similar commissions in many states. To a large extent these developments have emphasized particular aspects of administrative problems, but in recent years there has been a definite tendency to consideration of the general problems of public administration as a whole.[43]

A small volume on the *Government of Modern States*

[42] Cf. *Organizations in the Field of Public Administration*, Public Administration Clearing House (1932, 1934). This lists 1901 organizations in the United States and Canada (484 national, 1243 state, 85 regional, and 89 Canadian), not including local organizations. *Twenty years of municipal research* (1927).

[43] Works on the administrative system of the United States national government include: J. C. Guggenheimer, "The Development of the Executive Departments, 1775-1789" (in J. F. Jameson's Essays on the Constitutional History of the United States, 1889); John A. Fairlie, *The National Administration of the United States* (1905); Henry C. Gaus, *The American Government* (1908); H. B. Learned, *The President's Cabinet* (1912); Mary L. Hinsdale, *History of the President's Cabinet* (1912); L. M. Short, *The Development of the National Administrative Organization in the United States* (1923); S. C. Thorpe, *Federal Departmental Organization and Practice* (1923); and the Service Monographs of the United States Government, by the Institute for Government Research (1918). For studies of state and local administration, see: G. A. Weber, *Organized Efforts for the Improvement of Methods of Administration in the United States* (1919); Bibliography in W. F. Willoughby, *Principles of Public Administration* (1927); 27 *American Political Science Review* (1933), p. 317.

(1919), by W. F. Willoughby, criticized the traditional classification of governmental powers into legislative, judicial, and executive and took the position that administration should be considered as a distinct branch and function of government. The administrative function he defined as " the function of actually administering the law as declared by the legislative and interpreted by the judicial branches of governments," while the executive function " is the function of representing the government as a whole, and of seeing that all of its laws are complied with by its several parts."

In his *Principles of Public Administration* (1927), Mr. Willoughby recognized that the term " administration " could be used in two senses. " In its broadest sense, it denotes the work involved in the actual conduct of governmental affairs, regardless of the particular branch of government concerned. . . . In its narrowest sense, it denotes the operations of the administrative branch only." This work employs the term in the latter restricted sense. Using this interpretation, he classified the problems of public administration into five divisions: problems of general administration, organization, personnel, material or supply, and finance. Problems of general administration and organization are grouped together in Part I. Each of the other divisions are treated in a separate part; but problems of material are given only sixty pages, while problems of finance take more than a third of the entire work.

Professor L. D. White, in his *Introduction to the Study of Public Administration* (1926), defines his subject as: " the management of men and materials in the accomplishment of the affairs of the state." He holds that there is an essential unity in the process of administration, whether it be observed in city, state, or federal governments and assumes that administration is a single process, substantially uniform in its essential characteristics wherever observed. He contrasts this with administrative law, where (following Freund) he considers the major objective to be the protection of private rights, while " the objective of public administration is the efficient conduct of public business."

The common problems of all branches of public administration are those of organization, control, personnel, and finance. In comparison with Willoughby, White gives less attention to problems of organization and finance, the latter being considered as a means of integrating the organization. Relatively more attention (nearly half of the book) is given to problems of personnel. While Willoughby's work gives special attention to the national government, White deals more with state and local government. Chapters in White's book on administrative rules and regulations and judicial control deal briefly with topics emphasized in works on administrative law and omitted by Willoughby, but neither of these works considers the development of judicial agencies and procedures within the administration itself.

Professor White's monograph on *Trends in Public Administration* (1933), gives more attention to developments in the various levels of government (national, state, and local) and in the different fields of public service. He deals with developments during the twentieth century under three main captions: trends in the balance of power (centralization and decentralization); the new management (the chief executive and administrative reorganization); and trends in public employment, with a chapter on research in public administration. He does not, however, deal with the more legal phases in the development of the quasi-legislative and quasi-judicial functions of administrative agencies, nor with the relations of the legislative and judicial organs to the administration.

It may be suggested that there is need for a more comprehensive treatment of public administration that will combine a more balanced consideration of the main problems of the business management of public affairs with more attention to the legal problems. It also seems desirable, while recognizing the common problems of all grades and branches of public administration to note some of the special problems of national, state, and local administration and their interrelations, and also special problems in the particular fields of public service.

No periodical in the United States deals execlusively with problems of public administration and administrative law, but several journals give a good deal of attention to these matters, and many others deal with some phases of administrative problems. The most important are: *Municipal Affairs* (1897-1902), *The National Municipal Review* (1912), and *Public Management* (1917). *The American Political Science Review* and the *Annals of the American Academy of Political and Social Science* have frequent articles and notes, and the numerous law journals have frequent articles on problems of administrative law. Nearly a score of state municipal leagues issue regular journals, and there are also many more specialized and technical journals dealing with public engineering, education, finance, social welfare, and other particular aspects.

Recent developments in the increasing recognition and importance of public administration and administrative law in Great Britain may be briefly noted. In the year following the publication of Dicey's *Law of the Constitution* there appeared a small book on the law of executive officers in England, which has been expanded in later editions to a substantial volume of over 700 pages.[44] Critics of Dicey's view called attention to the effect of the non-suability of the Crown in England in limiting the value of the legal right to sue public officials in the ordinary courts and the special procedure of the Petition of Right to secure redress. The Public Authorities Protection Act of 1893 imposed further restrictions on suits against public officials. The importance of these and other factors affecting judicial control of administration officers were reflected in several books and articles.[45]

Official inquiries and reports on various phases of public administration may be noted, from the report of the royal commission on municipal corporations in 1835. A series of royal commissions have reported on the civil service of the central government, from the Playfair Commission of 1874-5 to the Tomlin Commission of 1929-31. The report of the Machinery of Government Committee (1918) proposed a general reorganization of the central administrative system. Since then there have been com-

[44] A. W. Chaster, *Powers of Executive Officers* (1886); *The Law Relating to Public Officers having Executive Authority in the United Kingdom* (1909), p. 706.

[45] Cf. Joseph Chitty, *The Law of the Prerogative of the Crown* (1820); The Petition of Right's Act of 1860, which remodelled procedure; W. B. Clode, *The Law and Practice of the Petition of Right* (London, 1887); W. H. Moore, "Liability for Acts of Public Servants," 23 *Law Quarterly Review* (1907), p. 12; Acts of State in English Law; George S. Robertson, *The Law and Practice of Civil Proceedings against the Crown and departments of government* (1908), p. 933; John S. Chartres, *The Public Authorities Protection Act, 1893* (1912); Ludwig Ehrlich, *Proceedings against the Crown* (1921); H. J. Laski, "The Responsibility of the State in England," 32 *Harvard Law Review* (1919), p. 447; W. S. Holdsworth, "The History of Remedies against the Crown," 38 *Law Quarterly Review* (1922), pp. 141, 280; C. S. Emden, "The Scope of the Public Authorities Protection Act, 1893," 39 *Law Quarterly Review* (1923), p. 341; *The Civil Servant in the Law and the Constitution* (1923); *Report of the Crown Proceedings Committee* (Cmd. 2842, 1927).

mission reports on local government (1925-9), and the report of the committee on ministers' powers (1932).[46]

Recognition of the increasing scope and importance of legislative regulations by executive and administrative authorities was indicated by the Rules Publication Act of 1893, and the annual volumes of Statutory Rules and Orders since 1890. The significance of this development was made more widely known in a brief series of lectures by Robert J. Carr, editor of the Statutory Rules and Orders, published in 1921, under the title of *Delegated Legislation*.[47] About the same time an article in the *Quarterly Review* on the science of public administration discussed some of the general problems: central and local administration, administrative organization, and personnel matters.[48]

Supplementing earlier associations of particular classes of public officials, the organization in 1923 of the Institute of Public Administration (comprising officials of central and local governments) and the publication of a journal on *Public Administration* served to emphasize the common problems in different levels of public service.

[46] This development is also reflected in the greater attention to public administration in later works on British government, and numerous books on particular phases. Cf. the "English Citizen" series (1881†) of 13 volumes, the recent "Whitehall" series on government departments (1925†), Redlich and Hirst's Local Government in England (1903), the series of volumes on English local government in the eighteenth century, by Sidney and Beatrice Webb, and many other works on local government. Note also, *The System of Financial Administration of Great Britain* (1917), and other works on public finance; L. D. White's *The Civil Service in the Modern State* (1930), and *Whitley Councils in the British Civil Service*. A list of official publications on the British civil service is given in Willoughby's *Principles of Public Administration* (p. 693).

[47] Robert J. Carr, *Delegated Legislation* (1921); John A. Fairlie, *British War Administration* (1919); *Administrative Procedure in Connection with Statutory Rules and Orders in Great Britain* (1928).

[48] 225 *Quarterly Review* (April, 1921), p. 413. Cf. B. N. Watson, "The Elements of Public Administration," 10 *Public Administration* (1932).

At the same time, criticism of the growing power of administrative officials appeared, in judicial opinions, in articles by Sir Lyndon Macassey and C. J. Allen, and the drastic attack on the new developments by Chief Justice Hewart, in *The New Despotism* (1929).[49] More balanced discussions of the recent developments appeared in Robinson's *Public Authorities and Legal Liability* (1925), with an introduction by Professor J. H. Morgan of the University of London; Robson's *Justice and Administrative Law* (1928); and F. J. Port's *Administrative Law* (1929), with an introduction by Lord Justice (now Lord High Chancellor) Sankey.

Robson's book aims to examine " the nature and scope of the judicial functions exercised by government departments and other public and private bodies; to analyze the causes which have led to such power being conferred on informal tribunals of this kind; and to evaluate the advantages and disadvantages which result therefrom." No attempt is made to deal with the limitations on the legal liability of the Crown and public authorities. There are chapters on administrative and judicial power, justice in the courts, administrative tribunals, domestic tribunals, the judicial mind, and trial by Whitehall: an evaluation.

Dr. Port begins his work with a discussion of definitions of administrative law, and presents his own definition in these words:

Administrative law then is made up of all those legal rules — either formally expressed by statutes or implied in the prerogative—which have as their ultimate object the fulfillment of public law. It touches first the legislature, in that the formally expressed

---

[49] Sir Lyndon Macassey, " Law Making by Government Departments," 5 *Journal of Comparative Legislation* (3rd series), p. 73; C. J. Allen in 240 *Quarterly Review* (1923), p. 240; *Bureaucracy Triumphant* (1931); Gordon Hewart, *The New Despotism* (1929); Ramsey Muir, *How Britain is Governed* (1930, 3rd ed., 1933), ch. 2.

rules are usually laid down by that body; it touches secondly the judiciary in that (a) there are rules (both statutory and prerogative) which govern the judicial actions that may be brought by or against administrative persons, and (b) administrative bodies are sometimes permitted to exercise judicial powers; thirdly, it is of course essentially concerned with the practical application of the law.

Following the introductory chapter are chapters presenting an historical sketch of administrative powers, and on the three governmental functions and their interrelations, legislation by administrative bodies, administrative bodies in relation to judicial action, administrative law in America, French *droit administratif,* and conclusions.

Another British writer, George W. Keeton of the University of Manchester, in his *Elementary Principles of Jurisprudence* (1929) has clearly set forth the three different senses in which the term administrative law may be used:

1. The rules promulgated by an executive department with the consent and authority of the central legislature.

2. . . . that particular part of public law which describes the nature of the activity of the executive department of the government in action. In this sense it may also be termed the law relating to public administration.

3. Lastly, administrative law may denote that portion of a nation's legal system which determines the legal status and liabilities of all state officials, which defines the rights and liabilities of private individuals in their dealings with public officials, and which specifies the procedure by which those rights and liabilities are enforced.[50]

It may be suggested that the statement placed first by

[50] A recent work on British Constitutional Law (by Wade and Phillips, 1931) contains a chapter on Constitutional Aspects of the Law of Public Administration.

Keeton more properly should come third. It is the second and third statement which represent the older established meaning of the term in France and continental Europe. Some writers in these countries place most emphasis on the third statement and it is this view which has been accepted by Freund. Other American and British writers tend to give more prominence to the first of Keeton's statements. It is certainly important that the different meanings of the term should be carefully distinguished.

The recent report of the committee on ministers' powers considered the development of quasi-judicial and quasi-legislative powers vested in ministers and departments. The need for such powers under modern conditions was recognized, but recommendations were made to safeguard such grants and their exercise, by Parliament and the law courts; however the proposal to establish a definite system of administrative courts was disapproved.[51]

Formal instruction in public administration has been given in British universities only in recent years; but courses and diplomas in this subject are now offered in half a dozen universities—London, Glasgow, Leeds, Liverpool, Manchester, and Sheffield.[52]

Recognition of the importance of public administration and administrative law in other countries is reflected in recent works relating to some of the British dominions, China, India, and Japan.[53]

---

[51] *Report of the Committee on Ministers' Powers*, Cmd. 4060 (1932); *Public Administration* (1932), *Political Quarterly* (1932), 29 *American Political Science Review* (1932), p. 1142; John Willis, *The Parliamentary Powers of English Government Departments* (1933); Chih-Mai Chen, *Parliamentary Opinion of Delegated Legislation* (1933).

[52] A. C. Stewart, "The Approach of British Universities to Public Administration," 11 *Public Administration* (1933), p. 20.

[53] N. Ghose, *Comparative Administrative Law* (1919); G. H. Knibbs, *Local Government in Australia* (1919); *Report of the Commission on Public Service Administration* (Australia, 1920); *Reports of the Pro-*

International administration is also of increasing importance and is discussed in a number of recent works. A list of 39 international agencies established by 1915 has been given, and since this time others have been created, while the League of Nations has developed an extensive system of administrative organs.[54]

Finally, the world wide interest in administrative problems is reflected in international meetings and associations of officials and others interested, such as the International Congresses of the Administrative Sciences (held at Brussels 1910 and 1923, Paris 1927, Madrid 1930, and Vienna 1933), the International Union of Cities, the International City Managers Association and the International Institute of Public Law. Proceedings of these organizations are published,[55] as well as several periodicals, such as the *Revue Internationale des Sciences Administrative* (1928†).

*vincial Administration Commission* (1917) and *Local Government Commission* (South Africa, 1921); "Administrative Law in South Africa," 44 *South African Law Journal* (1927), p. 10; *Report of the Special Committee on the Machinery of Government* (Canada, 1919); R. M. Dawson, *The Civil Service in Canada* (1927); Gnien His, *Le régimé administratif de la Chine* (1923); A. K. Ghose, *Public Administration in India* (1930); B. G. Sapre, *The Growth of Indian Constitution and Administration* (1930); Nakamo Tomio, *The Ordinance Power of the Japanese Emperor* (1923); Y. Oda, *Principes de droit administratif du Japon* (1928); G. M. Harris, *Local Government in Many Lands* (1926, 2nd ed., 1933).

[54] Leon Poinsard, *Les Unions et ententes internationales* (2nd ed., 1901); Karl Neumeyer, *Internationales Verwaltungsrecht* (3 vols., 1910); P. S. Reinsch, *Public International Unions* (1911); F. B. Sayre, *Experiments in International Administration* (1919; P. B. Potter, *International Organization* (1922, 3rd ed., 1928); Norman L. Hill, *International Administration* (1931); League of Nations, *Handbook of International Organizations* (1921); Quarterly Bulletin of Information on the Work of International Organizations.

[55] *Congrès Internationale des Sciences Administratives* (1910†); Union Internationale des villes, *Proceedings* (1913†); L'Institute Internationale de Droit Public, *Annuaire* (1929†).

# PART II

# EXECUTIVE LEADERSHIP IN ADMINISTRATION

# THE PRESIDENT AND FEDERAL ADMINISTRATION

BY

JAMES HART

The purpose of this essay is to sketch a theory of the relation which the President should bear to federal administration in the governmental system of tomorrow. Any prescriptive theory necessarily assumes certain ends. In the present case, the effort is made to avoid purely utopian ends, and to select ends from those which are implicit in some features of the present system in action, as those ends are refined by the comparative study of public administration and the current criticism of liberalism and the democratic dogma.

A prescriptive theory necessarily involves also hypotheses concerning the means of attaining the assumed ends.[1] Since these ends are not purely utopian, it will be possible to seek means which are at least potentially available under existing conditions, and to base the prediction that they will produce the desired ends at least in part upon an interpretation of past experience. At the same time, it must be obvious that such prediction is highly precarious, and that in any event everything depends upon the actualization of the potentially available means. Attention must also be given to the fact that one of the limiting conditions is likely to be the Constitution as it will probably be read by the Supreme Court.

[1] Walter Wheeler Cook, " The Possibilities of Social Study as a Science," in *Essays on Research in the Social Sciences* (The Brookings Institution, 1931), 27-48. In an essay of this sort it is impracticable for the author to acknowledge the oral and printed sources of his ideas.

## I

On paper the range of the President's legal power and
political influence extends to all phases of government
except judicial decisions and the purely mechanical operations of administration. The President is " at once the
choice of the party and of the nation," and " his is the
only national voice in affairs." The country and Congress
alike look to him for a legislative program, and judge
him especially by his legislative leadership. Only at the
height of prosperity could the negative policy of a
Coolidge pass for brilliant success. The President's rôle
as Chief Legislator merges with his rôle as Party Leader
and, during his first term, with his rôle as candidate for
reelection. " The rôle of party leader is forced upon the
President by the method of his selection." " If he lead
the nation, his party can hardly resist him." [2]  Under the
Constitution he has broad powers, including command of
the army and the navy, and especially the conduct of foreign relations. His statutory authority is varied and important. Congress—to give a single example—has delegated to him or to his subordinates discretionary power to
issue ordinances which affect private interests as well as
ordinances which regulate public administration.[3]

[2] Woodrow Wilson, *Constitutional Government in the United States*,
60, 67-69.
[3] James Hart, *The Ordinance Making Powers of the President of the
United States*, chaps. III, IV, and VI.  See also James Hart, " The
Ordinance Making Powers of the President," in *North American Review*,
July, 1923; James Hart, " The Emergency Ordinance: A Note on
Executive Power," in *Columbia Law Review*, June, 1923; James Hart,
" Some Legal Questions Growing Out of the President's Executive Order
for Prohibition Enforcement," in *Virginia Law Review*, December, 1926.
On the continent of Europe the ordinance making power has long been
recognized as a distinct category of executive action. It has traditionally
been regarded as inconsistent with the British rule of law and the American separation of powers. This tradition, however, has not prevented, but

Under the Constitution and the statutes the President bears to federal administration relationships which suggest for him the title of general manager. This rôle has its planning aspect: since 1921 the President has had to present to Congress a financial and work program in the form of his annual budget. Recent Presidents have also concerned themselves with the reform of the administrative set-up.[4] Congress finally delegated to the President

has only obscured its growth. In the last two decades delegated legislation (see Cecil T. Carr, *Delegated Legislation*) has become so extensive in Great Britain as to alarm the traditionalists. Hewart, *The New Despotism*, refers to "administrative lawlessness" (chap. IV). See, however, *Report of Committee on Ministers' Powers* (April, 1932), Cmd. 4060, and William A. Robson, "The Report of the Committee on Ministers' Powers" in *The Political Quarterly*, III, No. 3, 346-364. The method was employed in the United States during the Napoleonic Wars to protect our commerce, and to meet the emergencies of the civil and world wars. The President's rôle as law-giver reached its highest point under Woodrow Wilson in 1917-1918. It has also become important in ordinary times, as notably in connection with legislation which impinges upon our foreign relations. Various tariff acts, for instance, have empowered the President to retaliate against discriminatory commercial policies of other nations. The Fordney-McCumber and Smoot-Hawley tariff acts embodied the principle of the flexible tariff. John Preston Comer, *Legislative Functions of National Administrative Authorities*, 64, 73-112. Concurrently Congress has delegated regulatory powers to the departments. Comer, *op. cit.*, 51, says: "although the President received a major portion of all delegated legislation during the first three periods [1789-1890], a division of labor was appearing in the administrative branch of the government and the basis for practically all legislative powers exercised at the present time by the major departments was being laid."

In the present economic emergency Congress has delegated to President Roosevelt broader power than it has ever before given an Executive in time of peace. This power, indeed, bids fair to become increasingly important as Congress, in common with other representative assemblies, finds itself politically and technically helpless in the face of its twentieth century tasks. In every case to date the Supreme Court has refused to regard the authorizing statutes as unconstitutional delegations of legislative power. See especially *Field v. Clark*, 143 U. S. 649 (1892); *Hampton v. United States*, 276 U. S. 394 (1928).

[4] Mr. Hoover, for example, besides his fruitless efforts in behalf of general administrative reorganization, successfully sponsored the statutory

broad powers for general administrative reorganization and reduction of expenditures by executive order. This illustrates the regulatory or ordinance making aspect of the President's rôle as administrator-in-chief. Special attention must be given to the supervisory aspect of this rôle.

The President has always been on paper administratively stronger than the governor has of late become. He is the only constitutional, the only elective executive officer. No other executive official has a mandate from the people. He shares authority and responsibility with no council, except in treaties and appointments. Even here, the Senate merely passes upon a treaty which he alone negotiates, and it customarily gives him a free hand in the choice of his cabinet and other key men. Except for the period 1867-1887, when the tenure-of-office acts were in force, he has not had to share his power of removal with the Senate.[5] This gives him, at least potentially, the correlative power of direction. Until the rise of government by commission, federal administration was divided between a few single-headed departments. As late as 1902 there were only eight departments. As late as 1913 the only important commissions were the Civil Service and Interstate Commerce Commissions. By comparison with state administrations the federal has been integrated. The President has been on paper the undisputed administrative boss.

The potential administrative control of the President relates, furthermore, to two aspects of administration. To

reorganization of prohibition enforcement, prison control, veterans' administration, and of the Federal Tariff and Power Commissions.

[5] However, for a hang-over provision in the statutes, which was declared unconstitutional only in 1926, see James Hart, *Tenure of Office Under the Constitution*, 230-232.

make this clear it is useful to distinguish two sorts of administrative activity: the functional and the institutional. Functional activities are those which a given service " must perform in order to accomplish the ends for which it has been established and is being maintained." Institutional activities are those which the service " has to perform in order that it may exist and operate as an organization or institution." They " embrace such work as maintenance, care, and operation of plant, the recruitment and management of personnel, the purchase, cus-, tody, and distribution of supplies, the receipt, custody, and disbursement of moneys, the keeping of accounts and the preparation and rendition of reports, the handling of correspondence and files, and other like matters." [6] The functional activities are peculiar to the given service, while the institutional activities are common to all services. The President's functional supervision consists in control over the exercise by his subordinates of the discretion vested in them by law for the carrying out of the purposes of their respective services. His institutional supervision consists in his control over their management of their services as going concerns.

## II

The President's rôle as administrator-in-chief, however, is not realistically portrayed by a paper description of his powers. It must always be borne in mind that he is primarily a political officer [7] who is chiefly concerned with

[6] William Franklin Willoughby, *Principles of Public Administration*, 45-46.

[7] " As the business of the government becomes more and more complex and extended, . . . the President is becoming more and more a political and less and less an executive officer. His executive powers are in commission. . . . Only the larger sort of executive questions are brought to him. Departments which run with easy routine and whose transactions

the interrelations of high policy and high politics. Such questions, moreover, are much more complicated than they were in the last century.[8] They subtract more and more from the time and energy available for administrative planning, regulation, and direction.

The last generation, moreover, has witnessed both an expansion of the President's administrative rôle and revolutionary developments in administration itself. As a result, his supervision of administration, in both its functional and institutional aspects, has become more difficult than it used to be.

bring few questions of general policy to the surface may proceed with their business for months and even years together without demanding his attention; and no department is in any sense under his direct charge. Cabinet meetings do not discuss detail. . . . There are no more hours in the President's day than in another man's. If he is indeed the executive, he must act almost entirely by delegation, and is in the hands of his colleagues. He is likely to be praised if things go well, and blamed if they go wrong; but his only real control is of the persons to whom he deputes the performance of executive duties." Woodrow Wilson, *op. cit.*, 66-67.

[8] Since 1898, and especially since 1914, the President has had to give more and more attention to foreign relations, political and economic. "We can never hide our President again as a mere domestic officer." Woodrow Wilson, *op. cit.*, 78. The expansion of federal functions has also necessitated the President's devoting more and more time and energy to his legislative leadership. He is concerned with favorable publicity to keep popular support (Lindsay Rogers, *The American Senate*, chap. VII), with the use of patronage to win congressional acceptance of his legislative program (Frank R. Kent, *Political Behavior*, chap. V), and with conferences and trial balloons to determine what that program can be. He must prepare messages, consult with his close advisers and with party leaders in and out of Congress, hold press conferences, make occasional addresses, receive delegations with axes to grind, and decide when to threaten or employ a veto.

The President is *chef d'état* as well as the efficient executive, and has social and ceremonial functions as well as political and administrative. He has the literally manual labor of shaking hands with thousands simply because he is the titular head of a democracy (A. N. Whitehead, *Symbolism: Its Meaning and Effect*, 62), and of signing his name to the commissions of all federal officers (William Howard Taft, *Our Chief Magistrate and His Powers*, 40-41).

Thus since 1902 the executive departments have been increased from eight to ten.  With the growth of collectivism and the increasing assumption by the federal government of the governmental burdens of the industrial era, the administrative tasks of the departments have been greatly expanded.  The Interstate Commerce Commission had comparatively little power until 1906.  But since 1914 a long list of federal boards and commissions has been established.[9]  They have nominal or no connection with the executive departments whose heads constitute the President's cabinet.  Many of them were not intended to be presidental agencies.  In any event, it is harder to direct a board than a single officer.  When the number of lines of responsibility increases beyond a very few, continuous and detailed supervision of all of them becomes a practical impossibility.  The activities of each department are various; and the allocation of duties is not made in any thoroughgoing manner along functional lines.  Administrative problems become increasingly technical.  Some of them involve technology, others the complex economic relations of this industrial era.  No one man can personally check the elaborate investigations of complicated facts upon which a long list of subordinates base their conclusions and decisions, nor personally think through all the issues upon which they pass judgment.

The inevitable result is what is commonly called bureaucracy.  Most administrative action involves no new choices.  Much of it is nondiscretionary, and results from the me-

[9] There are *inter alia:*  The Federal Reserve Board (1914), The Federal Trade Commission (1914), The Federal Tariff Commission (1916), The United States Shipping Board (1916), The Federal Power Commission (1920), the Federal Radio Commission (1927), The Federal Farm Board (1929), and the Reconstruction Finance Corporation (1932).  A large number of new administrative agencies has been set up by the New Deal. In the process the Federal Farm Board was abolished.

chanical operation of professional habits. Some of it involves judgment or discretion for the exercise of which there are habitual techniques. Specific routine decisions are made by minor officials, with appeal in some cases to a superior. Even discretionary administrative decisions, moreover, are in a sense impersonal.[10] They are the sole creation of no single official, but the products which emerge from a problem's being passed along the accustomed route within the hierarchy.[11] The signature of a given official does not mean that the order embodies his own creative judgment. His share may have been to carry out the directions of his superior or to ratify the work of his subordinates. It may have involved judgment, but in the former case judgment upon details, in the latter case judgment upon tentatively proposed action.

With habitual routine the President is not normally concerned.[12] Such questions seldom come to his attention, and when they do it is in most cases largely as a matter of form. Even if a decision is by statute delegated in terms to him or falls within his constitutional powers as commander-in-chief or conductor of foreign relations, appropriate departmental action is in contemplation of law his

[10] See *Local Government Board v. Arlidge*, quoted in Ernst Freund, *Cases on Administrative Law* (2d ed.), 159, 279.

[11] Thomas Harrison Reed, *Government and Politics of Belgium*, 92-95, gives an account of how this works in the Belgian bureaucracy. "The typical administrator is a single link in a long chain of delegated work, capped at the top by the responsible Minister as supreme delegator. . . . The right to delegate lies at the very heart of the modern system of public administration." William A. Robson, *Justice and Administrative Law*, 67-68.

[12] " To conceive the President as the general manager of a vast administrative organization with his hand of control resting day by day upon all of its ramifying parts is to imagine a vain thing. The interregnum which was all but complete during President Wilson's long illness offers proof enough if proof were needed." Howard Lee McBain, *The Living Constitution*, 119.

action.[13] For this reason there is no administrative appeal to him from such routine decisions.

The picture of the President as on his own initiative exercising a continuous and detailed direction of all phases of administration is thus a myth. He cannot do all the things which he may do.[14] Most administrative questions never get to the President; they stop, as it were, at some point lower in the hierarchy. For the most part he considers only those which are specifically brought to his attention, and most of these are brought by his subordinates.[15] The sort of consideration he gives, furthermore, varies with the nature of the question.

[13] James Hart, *The Ordinance Making Powers of the President*, 185-188; F. J. Goodnow, *Principles of the Administrative Law of the United States*, 90-91. The exceptions to this rule are there discussed. On the question of delegation and re-delegation of executive power see Fairlie, " Administrative Legislation," in *Michigan Law Review*, January, 1920, pp. 181-200.

[14] " I have throughout my administration," wrote President Wilson to Secretary Redfield when the latter informed him of his intention of retiring to private life, " been able to think of the Department without any concern because I had such perfect confidence in you and was so sure that everything would be looked after as it should be." William C. Redfield, *With Congress and Cabinet*, 292. Cf. *ibid.*, 93-94.

[15] Howard Lee McBain, *op. cit.*, 118-119. Such questions may be forced upon his attention by some grave public crisis, by public charges of departmental corruption or abuse, by press criticism, by congressional inquiries or investigations, or by group demands. Most of them are brought by his subordinates. They have to bring those which involve powers which he cannot delegate, such as his pardoning power and his power to review decisions of courts martial. For the courts may require evidence that such decisions have received the personal attention of the chief executive. James Hart, *Tenure of Office Under the Constitution*, 344-345. Other questions are brought to him by his subordinates merely because the statute refers to presidential action or because it is customary to bring them. Many are brought because they involve choices which are outside the ordinary course of routine and which they regard as of enough importance to submit to the chief. Such choices vary from those which affect in important ways the future course of departmental routine to those which so clearly involve political implications that they are referred to the President as a matter of course.

If the question is one of routine, or if it is one of hundreds like it, the President's part is to ratify proposed action. Two examples from many may be cited. Thus when President Coolidge issued an executive order fixing the speed limit in the Canal Zone,[16] does anybody suppose that he took the initiative, or that he did more than sign his name after reading the order and perhaps an accompanying memorandum explaining the occasion for it? Woodrow Wilson wanted to pass personal and individual judgment upon the candidates for postmasterships, but he ended by asking Postmaster General Burleson: " Where do I sign? " [17]

On the other hand, if the action to be taken is contingent upon a choice of high policy, such, for example,

[16] *Executive Order* No. 4729.

[17] Ray Stannard Baker, *Woodrow Wilson: Life and Letters*, IV, 43-49. The fact that the President must himself grant all pardons does not mean that he makes an independent investigation of each application. It means acceptance or rejection — usually acceptance — of the recommendations of the Department of Justice. " Rules Governing Applications for Pardon " are issued by the Attorney General and approved by the President. These lay down some conditions for consideration of applications. Rule 10 provides: " When none of the persons so consulted advises clemency, the papers shall not be sent to the President except in capital cases or by his special request, or by special order of the Attorney General; but when any one of the officers consulted advises clemency the papers shall be submitted to the President." Rule 6 prescribes officers to be consulted. Application blanks are printed for use by applicants for pardon.

Mr. Roosevelt has been granted the power to reorganize the administrative system. He will doubtless review, with more or less care, the work of his trusted agents before he signs the necessary executive orders. But he will not do the job himself. He has neither the time nor the special knowledge for the spade-work, nor even for the drafting of the orders.

Each year the President must take personal responsibility in his annual budget for a financial and work program. Yet even an independent President reflects only upon the crucial choices of budgetary policy. The Bureau of the Budget was created for the very purpose of preparing the detailed estimates for him so that these choices may be placed before him in a clear-cut and correlated fashion.

as whether to commit the United States to a consultative pact, or to make radical cuts in veterans' compensation, that choice is normally put up to the President, and then routine proceeds upon the basis of his oral instructions or his written orders. Thus in world politics new situations may emerge at any time which cannot be dealt with by the mere application of habitual procedures. Again, each request from a state of the Union for aid in suppressing domestic violence is *sui generis*. Decisions of this character also have important political repercussions. To them the President may have to devote much time and thought in receiving reports, holding conferences, and weighing alternatives.

The significance of the President's political control over his department heads may now be appraised. It is of course important that he has in the power of removal an administrative sanction of the power of direction. It is significant that he may dictate how the discretion of his subordinates shall be exercised, and may get rid of a subordinate who is unsatisfactory to him. The power of removal, however, has its deeper meaning in the fact that it is the badge of the boss. It symbolizes the formal relationship of administrative superior and administrative inferior as between the President and his official family; and this formal relationship doubtless affects the functional relations between a Harding and a Hughes as well as those between a Wilson and a Lansing.

At the same time this formal picture is only one factor in the working relations involved. If the President may control a subordinate's discretion, the latter may also, in the ordinary course of administration, exercise the President's discretion or influence the President in its exercise, as the case may be. Actually the bulk of the total burden is devolved upon the departments concerned. In the non-

political services the process of devolution is all but complete. Routine is involved, moreover, in the day-by-day
conduct of foreign affairs as well as in the ordinary work
of the Department of Agriculture. The sole difference lies
in the fact that in the Department of State's task there
have in the past been more political choices to be made.

In the work of all departments, then, the President
merely shares. His share is determined by the fact that
the final responsibility is his, and consists in final choices
with respect to the larger issues which arise. And even
these final choices are made upon the basis of suggestions,
information and detailed preparation from his subordinates and economic advisers and the prediction of political
consequences by his political advisers. The fact that he
has gathered these men around him means that he trusts
them and will listen to them. It depends upon the man
whether he does any independent thinking in the making
of his crucial choices.[18] Yet in any event it becomes highly
significant what manner of men he has appointed or
chosen for unofficial advisers. If they differ, it is also
significant what type he tends to rely upon in the pinches.
For it is clear that in practice each of these is an *alter ego*
of the Chief Magistrate; that much of the so-called power
of direction consists in the choice of advisers. "His only
real control," wrote Woodrow Wilson, "is of the persons to whom he deputes the performance of executive
duties." It follows that a major aspect of his responsibility should be for such choices.

[18] "Self-reliant men will regard their cabinets as executive councils;
men less self-reliant or more prudent will regard them as also political
councils, and will wish to call into them men who have earned the
confidence of their party." Woodrow Wilson, *op. cit.*, 77.

## III

It is with the foregoing picture in mind that the proposals of this essay are made. They are: to accept bureaucracy as an inevitable concomitant of the twentieth century functions of the federal government; [19] to organize it in accordance with the best-thought-out views on public administration; to provide legal checks upon it through an adequate administrative court; and to retain and strengthen the Presidency as the focal-point of all policy-determination.[20]

[19] Cf. Harold J. Laski, review of James M. Beck, *Our Wonderland of Bureaucracy*, in *Columbia Law Review*, XXXII, 1449-1450. "A century and a half of scientific change," says Laski, "more intense than the development of the previous two thousand years could not leave unaltered either the theory of the Constitution or the functions of government. The kind of system applicable to the agrarian age of Jefferson is without meaning for the industrial age of today. The things which Mr. Beck deprecates in principle are the necessary conditions of efficient administration. . . . A little more careful inquiry would have enabled Mr. Beck to know that Lord Hewart's *New Despotism* was recently pronounced by a powerful committee to be in fact a mare's nest. . . . Is Mr. Beck unaware that the attempt of the courts to review facts in problems of administrative law has been abandoned, for the most part, on the initiative of the courts themselves? . . . The truth is that he is a Rip Van Winkle who went to sleep in the era just after the Civil War and has awakened to dismay in a world quite beyond his understanding."

[20] The classical account of presidential leadership is Woodrow Wilson, *op. cit.*, chap. III. See Norman J. Small, *Some Presidential Interpretations of the Presidency*, chap. V. Wilson wrote his *Constitutional Government in the United States* in 1908. He had not appreciated the possibilities of presidential leadership when he wrote his *Congressional Government* in 1883 and 1884. In 1900 he said in the Preface to the fifteenth edition: "The new leadership of the Executive, inasmuch as it is likely to last, . . . may bring about . . . an integration which will substitute statesmanship for government by mass meeting. It may put this whole volume hopelessly out of date" (pp. xii-xiii). Wilson had been anticipated by Henry Jones Ford, *The Rise and Growth of American Politics* (1898). Ford had emphasized Jackson's influence in making the presidency a tribuneship of the people (pp. 212-213, 293). For Wilson's contribution in office see James Hart, "Classical Statesmanship," in *Sewanee Review*, October, 1925, pp. 396-403.

The last-mentioned proposal will be considered first. Policy-determination includes congressional legislation, the presidential budget, presidential ordinances, foreign policy, the other constitutional powers of the Presidency, and the institutional management as well as the functional discretion of all administrative agencies. In all these matters the President should be the focal-point of control and responsibility. To call him the focal-point means, negatively, recognition of the fact that he cannot attend personally to the details of this wide range of discretionary action, or even in most cases initiate it. Positively, it means that his should be the final choices and his the final responsibility. The thesis is advanced that this is the best available means of securing a balanced combination of wholesome leadership in national purposes,[21] intelligent experimentation, coordinated planning based upon a concert of interests,[22] and public responsibility.

This objective is meant as a third alternative to the traditional conceptions of liberalism [23] and democracy [24] on the one hand and irresponsible dictatorship on the other. Many thinkers who have come to appreciate the inadequacy of the democratic dogma tend to favor the dictatorship of a Mussolini or of a Stalin. Both sorts are

[21] " True leadership calls for the setting forth of the objectives and the rallying of public opinion in support of these objectives.

" When the nation becomes substantially united in favor of planning the broad objectives of civilization, then true leadership must unite thought behind definite methods." Franklin D. Roosevelt, *Looking Forward*, 50-51.

[22] George Soule, *A Planned Society*, passim. " I have described the entire compass of my policy as a ' concert of interests ' — north and south, east and west — agriculture, industry, commerce and finance." Franklin D. Roosevelt, *op. cit.*, 241.

[23] Cf. George Soule, *op. cit.*, chap. III.

[24] " The old constants of our thinking have become variables. It is no longer possible, for example, to believe in the original dogma of democracy." Walter Lippmann, *Public Opinion*, 248-249. See also his *Phantom Public*.

too sharply in conflict with American habits of thought to come within the range of probability unless our system collapses utterly into chaos and revolution.

On the other hand, the public responsibility which is sought is not that which is envisioned in orthodox democratic dogma. However useful the idea of giving the people what they want may have been when first opposed to the claims of autocracy or class government, however applicable it may have been to a small agricultural community which furnished an approximate equality of opportunity, in relation to a large and economically unequal industrial society, it is both unreal and indefensible. It is unreal because it assumes that the mechanism of an election can give an equal distribution of political power in an economically unequal society. It is unreal because it ignores the inequality of political pressure as between unorganized individuals and organized groups. It is unreal because it assumes the existence of a *volonté générale* or public opinion apart from a common factor of habitual preconceptions, specific attitudes accepted at the suggestion of an active few, and the reactions of separate interest-groups added together.

The democratic dogma is indefensible because it suppresses the application of creative intelligence to governmental problems. This indictment is more applicable in this era than ever before. The common factor of habitual preconceptions includes the rugged individualism of Hoover and the states' rights of Ritchie. The second industrial revolution has made *laissez-faire* a shibboleth which protects plutocracy from regulation at the expense of the individual. Hence a revolution in ideology is the first requisite of the new era.[25] This requires the slow

[25] James Hart, review of Franklin D. Roosevelt, *Looking Forward*, in *American Political Science Review*, June, 1933, pp. 472-473; William

process of education, but it also requires leadership. The President is the national spokesman to undertake the latter task.[26] Yet the democratic dogma stands in his way. In particular, it forestalls presidential competition with pressure-propaganda groups in the shaping of specific attitudes toward current policies.

The representative system has been a symbol of democracy. But Congress is all too concerned with the securing of local favors, and succumbs all too readily to the demands of organized minorities.[27] A multiple assembly debates one measure at a time, and can carry through a comprehensive and correlated national program only when subjected to a strong leadership.[28] The inadequacy of the

Bennett Munro, *The Invisible Government*, chap. I (" Fundamentalism in Politics ") ; Charles A. Beard, " The Political Heritage of the Twentieth Century," in *Yale Review*, March, 1929, pp. 457-479.

[26] " His office is a mere vantage ground from which he may be sure that effective words of advice and timely efforts at reform will gain telling momentum. He has the ear of the nation as of course, and a great person may use such an advantage greatly." Woodrow Wilson, *op. cit.*, 77. " To lead is to teach, and the leader occupies a pulpit from which he directs, for good or ill, the opinions and attitude of many thousands. He can raise the whole tone of public thought. . . . Or he can merely try to put himself on the same level as his people, to keep his hand on the public pulse, his ear to the ground, and may shape his own convictions accordingly." William Bennett Munro, *Personality in Politics*, 113.

[27] " The really potent organized minorities of recent years can be listed as follows — the Veterans, the Drys, Labor and the Farmers. . . . In the space of one month Mr. Roosevelt has successfully bucked three of these." Frank R. Kent, " The Great Game of Politics," in *Baltimore Sun*, April 4, 1933. Cf. E. Pendleton Herring, *Group Representation Before Congress*, especially chap. I.

[28] This was the theory on which Cannonism was justified. But that type of " party responsibility " meant oligarchic irresponsibility, with a theoretical responsibility in the next election. Equally unreal was the theory upon which the so-called revolution of 1910-11 was wrought. That revolution made it easier for Woodrow Wilson to assume his legislative leadership. William Bennett Munro, *The Makers of the Unwritten Constitution*, 128-130. Yet the weakness of the present House leadership shows the danger to presidential government which the present system involves. There is no objection which is at all valid to " gag rule " or the supremacy of the

legislative method in the face of the problems of twentieth century government is further attested by the tendency to delegate ordinance making and quasi-judicial functions to administrative organs. This, it is submitted, is the real significance of the enactment in the special session of 1933 of what Lord Herschell has called skeleton legislation.[29] The supplementary policies embodied in presidential executive orders and departmental regulations thus become of supreme importance. They can be correlated with each other and with the authorizing statutes only if there is a focal-point of reference for all the crucial choices involved.

The idea of concentrating power in order to concentrate responsibility is not new. But the last generation laid undue stress upon responsibility as supposed to be enforced in elections.[30] Fear of the next election has a paralyzing effect upon politicians, since it is primarily fear of offending organized groups. The President is less terrified by the pressure of these groups than any other elective officer in the land. This is because he alone is in a

Speakership, provided the Speaker is dominated by the President. Only thus can " party government " be combined with responsibility in a workable and yet wholesome manner.

[29] See Cecil T. Carr, *op. cit.*, 16.

[30] The idea was embodied in the Constitution, and justified in the *Federalist*, No. LXX. It has been a central idea in the short ballot movement in state and local government. But that movement retained many of the assumptions about elections which were part of the democratic dogma, but which the authors of the *Federalist* would have repudiated.

Presidential elections seem actually to turn upon three factors: the extent and intensity of the accumulation of group grievances against the Ins, and the extent to which the Opposition can capitalize them; the extent to which habitual prejudices may by emotional appeals be aroused against the opponent's record or proposals; and especially whether the majority is satisfied with economic conditions. In times of great prosperity, the party in power seems to win, in times of deep depression to lose (Frank R. Kent, *Political Behavior*, chap. XI).

position to mobilize general support behind resistance to group demands. But even the presidential veto cannot always stop raids on the Treasury for the benefit of such groups. His hand needs to be strengthened for normal times in the way indicated below. In its very best light, the presidential election itself is to be regarded as a crude but useful periodic check in which the President is made the focal-point for the majority expression of approval or disapproval of the way things are going in general. The presidential elections of 1920 and 1932 served this purpose in a striking degree.

This blunderbuss check seems necessary if the danger of irresponsibility is to be avoided. The Presidency carries, however, in unique degree responsibility in a more refined sense of the term. This has its subjective as well as its objective aspect. The character of the office tends, it seems, to bring out the best in a man.[31] This heightened sense of responsibility does not operate in the same degree in all cases. Nor does it guarantee good results. Yet it is remarkable that, while some Presidents have been weak or have had mistaken standards, perhaps none has been crudely dishonest in his conduct of office.

[31] Chester A. Arthur had been a New York spoilsman. As President he vetoed a pork-barrel river and harbor bill, signed the Pendleton Act of 1883, carried it out conscientiously, appointing Eaton, one of the trio who had led the fight for the merit system, to the Civil Service Commission, and annoyed General Grant by refusing to make political removals. What caused this apparent psychological revolution in the man? It was probably the peculiar circumstance that he gained the office at the hands of an assassin who said, as he shot Garfield: "I am a Stalwart. Arthur is now President of the United States." For the above facts see James Ford Rhodes, *History of the United States*, VIII, 88, 90, 134, 145-146, 162, 164-166, 198-201, 205-206. No other man has received such a figurative blow on the head at the moment of his coming to the office. The personality and the circumstances of each case make it *sui generis*, and the hypothesis set forth in the text is not susceptible of " proof."

The main reason for this high degree of subjective responsibility is to be found in certain features of the objective responsibility of the office. That is at once more intense and less paralyzing to leadership than that of any other position in American public life. The exaltation and potential power of the office and the very size of the stage make a big difference here. These factors make the Presidency the focal point of the nation's attention, which is sharper than that of the attention of a single state or city. National publicity beats upon the White House with the intensity of a great searchlight. The intelligent support and intelligent criticism of the nation are greater in volume and influence than is the case in smaller communities. The national press is more intelligent than the local. The politics of the nation is less personal than that of the state capital and the city hall. Above all, the President's voice is heard—over the radio literally heard [32]—and his words are heeded as are those of no other person.

No President appears to have taken orders from a boss in the way some mayors and even governors have done.[33] The President is himself restrained by the fact that he is the leader rather than the boss or dictator of his party, and by the fact that the Opposition can always challenge his policies. Congress acts as a sounding-board to indicate how far he can—or must—go in his program. The Senate offers a check in its capacities as forum of national debate, critic of the Executive, and investigator of administrative abuse or corruption.[34] With all its defects, the

[32] President Roosevelt's Sunday evening radio talks have shown the potentialities of the radio as an instrument of presidential leadership as they have not been shown before. Cf. Frank R. Kent, " The Great Game of Politics," in *Baltimore Sun*, March 11, 1933.

[33] William Bennett Munro, *Personality in Politics*, 44-45.

[34] On these rôles of the Senate and their relation to the closure problem, see Lindsay Rogers, *op. cit.*, chaps. V (" Closure "), VI (" Congressional

Senate furnishes a wholesome counterpoise to favorable publicity from the White House and—in the name of the agricultural West and South—to the tendency of most Administrations and of the House to reflect the opinion of the dominant and industrial East.[35]

National administration attracts, by and large, a more intelligent type of men for the Chief Executive to lean upon than does the administration of our commonwealths and municipalities. The presidential office itself has a unique tradition which affects the attitude and expectations of the people. This is partly because the President as *chef d'état* symbolizes the nation and is considered the representative of all classes and hence of the larger public interest. The office stands apart in the public mind. The citizen who is prepared to believe stories of corruption in Congress or cabinet would be shocked to hear the charge that a President had connived at corruption.[36] Such an attitude sobers any man of character. The subjective and objective aspects of presidential responsibility are thus seen to interact. They are sharpened, as the *Federalist*

Investigations "), VII (" Presidential Propaganda and the Senate "), and VIII (" Forum of the Nation and Critic of the Executive ").

[35] " The House of Representatives . . . represents chiefly the East and North. The Senate is its indispensable off-set." " Regions must be represented, irrespective of population, in a country physically as various as ours and therefore certain to exhibit a very great variety of social and economic and even political conditions. It is of the utmost importance that its parts as well as its people should be represented." " The Senate . . . represents the variety of the nation as the House does not." Woodrow Wilson, *Constitutional Government in the United States*, 114, 116, 117. Cf. Arthur N. Holcombe, *Political Parties of Today*, chaps. III and IV. It is to be remembered also that the electoral votes are apportioned on a basis which resembles that of the House rather than that of the Senate.

[36] An interesting subject for investigation would be the editorial and popular reactions to Mr. Harding in relation to the oil scandals. It must be admitted that there is a source of danger in the possible suppression of the truth for fear it will shake public confidence.

predicted,[27] by having a one-man executive who has a fixed term. Because the incumbent is at once the *chef d'état* and the choice of the whole nation as its chief magistrate, the presidential office is potentially a better vantage-point for leadership than even the British cabinet or premiership.[38]

This picture of presidential responsibility is frankly an idealization of factors latent in the political set-up but never perfectly or continuously realized. The chief obstacle to its approximation is that the President normally lacks sufficient political support.[39] He has it only when

[37] " Energy in the Executive is a leading character in the definition of good government. . . . The ingredients which constitute energy in the Executive are, first, unity; secondly, duration; thirdly, an adequate provision for its support; fourthly, competent powers.

" The ingredients which constitute safety in the republican sense are, first, a due dependence on the people; secondly, a due responsibility. . . . But one of the weightiest objections to a plurality in the Executive . . . is that it tends to conceal faults and destroy responsibility. . . . The plurality of the Executive tends to deprive the people of the two greatest securities they can have for the faithful exercise of any delegated power: *first*, the restraints of public opinion."

" Duration in office . . . has relation to two objects: to the personal firmness of the executive magistrate . . . and to the stability of the system of administration which may have been adopted under his auspices." *The Federalist*, Nos. LXX and LXXI.

[38] Emphasis should be placed upon the word *potentially*. For the defects of our system stressed by Bagehot and Wilson handicap presidential leadership in normal times, whereas the British cabinet is " all-but-omnipotent." Ramsay Muir, *How Britain is Governed*, 153. Few students would now propose a change from presidential to cabinet government for the United States. A more desirable and more practicable end is to seek to enable the President to control Congress so long as he can carry the country with him in his program.

[39] " The President's power is after all chiefly the power of publicity. . . . His slightest utterance is headline news. That is his principal whip. . . . The President has also available the flail of the patronage which he may grant to or withhold from members; but the actual utility of this as an instrument of compulsion is probably exaggerated. Certainly it is less efficacious than formerly. . . . But the situation is manifestly precarious. His legal powers are not commensurate with his political responsibilities."

some popular reaction, such as the progressive movement in 1912, or especially some national emergency, such as the world war in 1917-1918 and the bank crisis which immediately preceded President Roosevelt's inauguration in 1933, calls forth the best in the man and enables him to crystallize public opinion in favor of his policy, to subordinate for the moment particular interests to common purposes.[40] In such situations the public is eager to be led, though the stronger the leadership, the greater the reaction.[41] When the emergency passes, the checks and balances of the founding fathers begin to operate again,[42] and continuous planning to prevent future crises is interrupted.

Howard Lee McBain, *op. cit.*, 130-132. Postmaster-General Farley has shown how patronage can be made a powerful weapon, not in its distribution, but in its being withheld until the President's program is enacted.

[40] Cf. Frank R. Kent, " The Great Game of Politics," in *Baltimore Sun*, March 2, 7, 12, 21, and 23, and April 25, 1933. "Under normal conditions," says Mr. Kent (March 12), " the power of a President is greatly overrated. . . . But a crisis changes all that. In a crisis, the popular feeling pushes politics aside, stills the talk about Senatorial prerogatives, causes Congress to concede its incapacity, and produces a willingness to abdicate authority." "The passage of the economy resolution," he continues (March 21), " was a really great and historic achievement. . . . Its passage was undoubtedly due to the bank collapse, which frightened Congress into acquiescence. . . . The bank crisis . . . was a real break for the President, of which he made the most. But . . . there has been no real test of the Roosevelt leadership under normal conditions. In an emergency a President gets a support not possible at any other time."

Woodrow Wilson said of Taft: " If I were to sum up all the criticisms that have been made against the gentleman who is now President of the United States, I could express them all iri this: The American people are disappointed because he has not led them. . . . They clearly long for someone to put the pressure of the opinion of all the people of the United States upon Congress." Ray Stannard Baker, *op. cit.*, III, 181.

[41] This was the case after the war Presidents, Lincoln and Wilson. The writer has seen in the press predictions that it will be the case after Franklin D. Roosevelt. These predictions usually assume that this will be desirable.

[42] " People do not naturally crave leadership," claims William Bennett Munro, " but they clamor for it at times because they want something

On this assumption, the major need is to strengthen the President politically. In the first place, there is required the slow and difficult process [43] of educating the masses in the habit of respecting and insisting upon informed leadership in a continuous program of national planning and national experimentation for the general weal. It is the degradation of the democratic dogma for the man on the street to seek to impose his curbstone judgment about a problem like the war debts. So long as he does so, a President will require unusual courage or the unusual support accorded in a crisis to dare propose a wise solution. Without such education we shall continue to have the paralyzing influence of local and special groups and a policy which tends toward the least common denominator of public understanding—toward the prejudices rather than the intelligence of the nation. These prejudices include

irksome or uncongenial removed, some reform accomplished. When this immediate aim has been achieved there is nothing to keep their zeal for leadership stimulated, and it quickly subsides." If this be so, it seems difficult to expect presidential leadership to be able to combat the economic cycle. Munro claims that "the human being is not by nature capable of a strong, sustained loyalty to any new cause." This does not augur well for popular support of continuous economic planning. "At any given moment, he tends to be an extremist in his political attitudes; and extremes always generate their opposites. That is the psychological fact upon which the law of the pendulum rests." Does this mean an alternation between rugged individualism and planned economy? Munro does not claim that the pendulum swings with any mathematical precision. His thesis seems to have a certain validity. From the standpoint of the position taken in this essay, the outlook is not so pessimistic when it is remembered that the base of the pendulum moves. "During the years from 1850 to the beginning of the World War," says Munro, "the base of the pendulum in all countries kept moving towards the Left, virtually without interruption." "The Pendulum of Politics," in *Harper's Monthly Magazine*, CLIV, 718-725.

[43] In his *Human Nature and Conduct* John Dewey points out the fallacy alike of those who use the instinct psychology to prove that human nature cannot be changed and of those who use habit pscyhology to prove it is very easy to change it.

nationalism in an economically interdependent world and the social ideology of the agricultural era in an industrial age.

Again, if a national planning commission is created,[44] its members should be chosen by and responsible to the President. If his foreign policy is not to be timid, his treaties should require the advice and consent only of a majority of both houses. The terms of Representatives and Senators should be made to coincide with his. Presidential leadership and responsibility with respect to legislative policy are threatened alike by the presence of holdover Senators and by the House election in the middle of his term. He might be given a term of seven years, provided he were also given the power but not the obligation of dissolving a recalcitrant Congress. In the election to follow he would automatically be a candidate for reelection to a full term, but others might be nominated.

These changes would probably strengthen the President's hand in legislative and foreign policy, and incidentally in administrative policy. The potential weakness of the executive under responsible government [45] would be avoided, since the fixed term would be preserved except at the discretion of the President. But the actual weakness of a President who loses the support of Congress or is hamstrung by holdover Senators would also be avoided. At the same time, the leading advantages of the British system would be secured. The President could use the powerful weapon of the threat of dissolution to enforce genuine party discipline in the caucus.[46] Solidarity be-

[44] Cf. George Soule, *op. cit.*, 252.

[45] This weakness is actual in France, but only potential in England, provided the cabinet has a party majority in the Commons. Sidney Low, *Governance of England*, xviii-xx.

[46] Frank R. Kent lists the following advantages of the caucus: (1) " it gives the official leader a coherent and dominating force behind him ";

tween the political departments could be restored by a presidential appeal to the electorate if his program were blocked in Congress.[47] If he had any chance of successful future leadership, he could avoid this appeal or come out the victor, and his hand would then be strengthened. If not, another leader should take his place.

## IV

On the basis of the conclusions already set forth, the relation which the President should bear to the regular departments may be summarized. For reasons already given the functional supervision of the President is practically limited to questions of major policy. This indicates the appropriate limits of his power of appointment and removal. He should have free choice of his department heads and have the power to remove them at pleasure.[48] Each of them—or the President— should have

(2) "Democrats who bolt a party caucus immediately stamp themselves as anti-Administration and, as such, would lose claim to their share of the Federal patronage"; and (3) "the great advantage . . . lies in the protection it gives the individual Senator [or Representative] against the organized minorities which press him from every side. . . . It cannot be discovered whether in caucus he voted with or against the majority, and he cannot be blamed for voting later as the caucus decides." "The Great Game of Politics," in *Baltimore Sun*, March 9, 1933. See also *ibid.*, February 8, 1933.

[47] Cf. Howard Lee McBain, *op. cit.*, 141-144.

[48] Senator Norris has been reported as favoring a ten-year term for the Postmaster-General and several other department heads. *Baltimore Evening Sun*, March 13, 1929, p. 1. He specifically excluded the Secretaries of State, of War, and of the Navy, whose functions relate to the constitutional executive powers of the President which these secretaries often exercise in his name, rather than to statutory executive powers created by Congress and entrusted by it to specific officials whom it sets up for the purpose. Cf. James Hart, *Tenure of Office Under the Constitution*, 276 ff. He said his plan would clear the way for the appointment of all postmasters by the department head, but did not refer specifically to tenure and the President's removal power. Aside from the constitutional and traditional objections which would be raised against restricting the Presi-

the power to appoint and remove at pleasure several assistants corresponding to what the British call parliamentary undersecretaries. Below these assistants should range a permanent staff from a single permanent undersecretary down to the lowest grade of clerks.

The President should be the focal-point of the institutional supervision of all administrative services. He would then be the general manager responsible for the regulation and control of the administrative machine as a machine. For the exercise of this responsibility Congress should create as a direct agency of the President a bureau of general administration.[49] It should vest in the President the functions of budget-making, of centralized purchasing, of allotment of quarters, of prescribing uniform accounting methods, salary classifications, efficiency tests,

dent's power to remove any department heads at pleasure, its wisdom is highly doubtful. The scientific work done in the Departments of the Interior and of Agriculture constitutes functional activities which are carried on by the permanent staff. They are now scarcely affected by the President's control over the broader aspects of departmental policy. Such control he should have, in order that he may be made the focal-point of enlightened public criticism. In the postal system, moreover, the functional and institutional activities are interwoven. Independent department heads would mean *scattered* responsibility, which in matters of policy-choice and administrative efficiency tends to *weaken* responsibility. Particular acts of discretion, as in the exclusion of matter from the mails, require in any event the check whereby an administrative court is given power to annul any order of exclusion for excess or misuse of power. There seems to be no administrative reason why all postmasters should not be included in the classified services. But this would remove from the President a powerful weapon of party discipline in the enactment of his legislative program. Since the chief subordinate of a first-class postmaster does the actual work, this patronage may be a small price for the political control which it gives the Chief Executive over his party colleagues in Congress. Congress, moreover, might be ill-advised to give a ten-year term to any of the patronage-distributors who are now given the Postmaster-Generalship. Rather should each President be liable for his own choice; and his chief patronage man should be one who has his legislative program at heart.

[49] William Franklin Willoughby, *op. cit.*, chaps. III and IV.

personnel regulations, and the like. The President, of course, would only make the crucial choices, while the bureau would attend to details. Its head should be appointed by the President alone, and be removable by him at pleasure. Through this agency the President would bear final responsibility for the inauguration and maintenance of the highest standards in the operation of the bureaucratic machine. For the maintenance of these standards he could, through this bureau, hold his department heads to accountability. Through a continuous reporting system he could exercise an institutional supervision comparable to that exercised by the president of a great railroad.

In such a scheme personnel administration is a crucial institutional problem. The permanent undersecretary should ordinarily be promoted from below. All below him should be recruited, classified, compensated, promoted, demoted, transferred, suspended, removed, and retired in accordance with the approved principles of modern personnel administration. These principles should be embodied in presidential civil service regulations issued under a federal statute and prepared by the bureau of general administration.

The civil servants of each grade in the hierarchy must be subject to the direction of their superiors with respect to their functional duties, and to demotion, transfer, suspension, or removal for unsatisfactory work. It is difficult to draft workable regulations concerning the latter liability which it is not easy to evade. The President could not personally investigate each alleged violation of his regulations. The bureau of general administration might report cases to him for such action as he might see fit. But it can hardly be expected that he would interfere except in flagrant cases. A violation of his personnel regulations should be liable to annulment by an administrative court for excess or misuse of power.

## V

The ideal which has been defended as against an outworn conception of democracy is also threatened in the name of science and judicial impartiality. Thus regulatory commissions were set up as independent establishments with the noble purpose of insulating them against political pressure. But to justify removing them from presidential control it is necessary to assume that " correct" decisions will emerge from expert judgment based upon a scientific investigation of the facts and a judicial hearing of the parties in interest. Such an assumption will not bear analysis.

The use of experts and scientific method in government is one of the hopeful signs of the times. But economic regulation by government is an intensely practical matter. Science is no magic of pulling " correct" answers like rabbits out of a silk hat. It is a method which in economic and social matters is limited by all sorts of difficulties. Governmental officials have to make decisions now. They cannot wait years to see if tentative conclusions can be verified. How indeed can they be verified except by experimentation? Officials are the experimenters rather than those who interpret the results. They should have economic advisers to interpret to them the results of past experience and to suggest lines of experimentation in new situations. They should have at hand technical experts to gather data needed for any given purpose. But discretion and policy cannot be eliminated. " AE summed it all up when he said, ' The expert should be on tap, but not on top.' " [50]

[50] Felix Frankfurter, *The Public and Its Government*, 161.

Legislative criteria involve such variables as " just and reasonable " rates and " unfair methods of competition." Their application depends upon the habitual assumptions and value-judgments of the commissioners. Expert opinion remains opinion. It can never be deduced from however vast an accumulation of data. Facts themselves are not objectively discoverable entities, but variables which are dependent upon the interpretation of complex and only partially available data.[51] It is in the interest of effective responsibility rather than of politics that it is proposed that the crucial choices of regulatory policy be focalized in presidential control.

There is a latent ambiguity in the very purpose for which our regulatory commissions have been set up. This becomes apparent as soon as it is realized that discretionary choice is involved. An administrative tribunal is at once a regulatory and a judicial organ. Its *raison d'être* is to protect a public interest by the control of special groups, but its procedure involves a judicial hearing. If the tribunal regards itself as the representative of the public it becomes at the hearing both judge and advocate, and in its decision primarily the advocate. The hearing becomes merely the presentation of factors which it must consider, and ceases to be a judicial proceeding except in form. On the other hand, if the tribunal regards itself primarily as a court which is bound to base its decision upon an impartial examination of the arguments of counsel,[52] it is apt to lose sight of its main function.[53]

[51] Cf. Frederick Barry, *The Scientific Habit of Thought*, Chap. II (" The Nature of Fact ").

[52] " When I became Governor of the State of New York I found that the Public Service Commission of the State had adopted the unwarranted and unsound view that its sole function was to act as an arbitrator or a court between the public on one side and the utility corporations on the other. . . . I declared that the Public Service Commission is not a mere

Independent courts are more or less well adapted to the protection of particular interests. But judicial procedure is not suited to the development, in fields of dynamic change, of new standards of control in the public interest.[54] A President may appoint to regulatory commissions conservatively minded men who lose sight of the public interest in their perfectly sincere zeal for judicial impartiality. If such appointees constitute a tribunal at once impersonal and independent, the President will not be responsible for the consequences of the exercise of his appointing power. If the number of these independent

judicial body to act solely as umpire between complaining consumer or complaining investor . . . and the great public utility system. . . . I declared that, as the agent of the Legislature, it had delegated authority to act as the agent of the public; that it is not a mere arbitrator . . . but was created for the purpose of seeing that the utilities do two things — give service and charge reasonable rates. I told them that, in performing this function, it must be as agent of the public upon its own initiative as well as upon petition to investigate the acts of public utilities relative to service and rules and to enforce adequate service and reasonable rates.

" The regulation commission must be a tribune of the people. . . . This means positive and active protection of the public against private greed." Franklin D. Roosevelt, op. cit., 143-144.

[53] Cf. also the criticism of private bill procedure in the British Parliament which is made by A. Lawrence Lowell, The Government of England, I, 387 ff.

It matters not that the most important party in interest — the public — may be represented by counsel. A " People's Counsel " functions before the Maryland public service commission. Henry G. Burke, The Public Service Commission of Maryland. But this involves the assumption that the commission is a court rather than a regulatory agent of the public. The writer finds a growing realization of this inconsistency on the part of students of government.

[54] The inadequacy of the ordinary courts for this purpose is well set forth in William A. Robson, op. cit., 250-254, 259-262, 275, 315-317. That the same applies to administrative tribunals which combine regulatory and judicial functions he indicates in the following passage: " The greatest danger . . . is the likelihood that . . . an attempt may be made to cut through our economic difficulties by handing over the disposal of economic controversies to official tribunals armed with plenary power of decision and enforcement . . . But such an idea is based on a fallacy. . . .

tribunals is multiplied, numerous areas of public policy will have been turned over to impersonal groups of men who exercise discretion without any sort of responsibility except the control of the regular courts. The very object of this control is to safeguard the private rather than the public interests involved.[55] These areas of public policy, moreover, will be dealt with piecemeal and without correlation by a number of unrelated organs. If each of these organs deals only with situations as they arise, it will not see the woods of its own policy for the trees. The interrelations of public policy, both in a particular field and along the whole economic front, will be obscured, and a general plan will be impossible.[56]

If this analysis is accepted, it follows that a complete overhauling of government by commission is in order. The details of this overhauling it is beyond the scope of this essay to consider. But its general outline seems clear. Government by commission should be incorporated into a reorganized system of federal administrative departments. Its aspect of policy formation should be vested in the appropriate department heads, and should take the form of general regulations. This would bring it in line

There is no such thing known to economic science as a fair price, a fair wage, a fair day's work, or a fair rate of profit. . . .    Professor Ernst Freund . . . says . . .  ' It seems to be believed that by a combination of administrative and judicial action it will be possible to evolve a code of fair trading . . . it is not likely that highly controverted issues will be ultimately settled otherwise than by direct legislative action '."   Pp. 299-301.   The present writer would add: or by ordinance-making or regulatory power delegated by the legislature to agencies integrated by a common responsibility to the President.

[55] " The intense legalism of the English system of law is one of its most notable features, and one which results in a tendency to sacrifice the public welfare to private interests where the latter can lay claim to individual rights."   William A. Robson, op. cit., 251.

[56] Cf. George Soule, op. cit., chap. VI.   " Each of these agencies has been conceived much as if the situation with which it has to deal were an isolated and accidental phenomenon."   P. 155.

with the idea of presidential responsibility, and would furnish in the Presidency a focal-point for general planning of economic control. The accumulation of the data needed for any given purpose and the application of the departmental ordinances to concrete situations should be the functions of an expert departmental bureaucracy acting under the functional control of the political superiors of the department concerned. Such a system of control becomes increasingly needed, but it is of course liable to abuse. An independent administrative court should be created to annul administrative acts for excess or misuse of delegated power, and to give damages against the administration in appropriate cases.[57]

## VI

The multiplication and complexity of the governmental problems of the twentieth century make it necessary for Congress to devolve broad discretion upon federal administrative officers. For the same reasons the expansion of the federal bureaucracy is a practical necessity. He who cries out against these developments resembles the proverbial dog baying at the moon.

This is by no means to say that the present system of ordinance making and bureaucracy cannot be improved, or to deny that dangers of abuse are involved. On the institutional side, moneys may be misspent, the spoils system may creep in, and efficiency and coordination are far

[57] See section VI of this essay. The conclusions of section V with respect to regulatory commissions apply, *mutatis mutandis*, to investigatory organs like the Tariff Commission, to business-operating boards like the United States Shipping Board, to government-owned corporations, and to farm relief agencies like the Federal Farm Board. With respect to the Tariff Commission, for example, read James Hart, *Tenure of Office Under the Constitution*, 98-103, in the light of the conclusions of this essay.

from being attained. On the functional side, administrative acts may be *ultra vires,* administrative power may be used for a purpose other than that for which it was given, discretion may be abused, and damage may be done to persons or property by the improper operation of the public services. To insist that private interests must be controlled in the general interest is not to imply that they should be at the mercy of illegal or arbitrary administrative action.[58]

The most effective political check upon such abuses is presidential control and responsibility. This, however, operates continuously only with respect to crucial choices of general policy. Against the details of regulations and particular administrative acts it operates only intermittently at best, and even then not ordinarily in a way to redress wrongs already done to private interests. For such purposes no political check is adequate, and some sort of judicial remedy obtainable from an organ independent of the administration is needed.

The regular courts, however, as at present constituted, are ill adapted to the purpose. An organ is needed which is accessible at less cost and by a less artificial, less complicated and more expeditious procedure. It should also be left free to develop a new body of case law [59] from which certain rules and attitudes of the regular courts should be expunged. For, paradoxically enough, these rules and attitudes handicap both the operation of the

[58] This is the real point of Lord Hewart's indictment of what he calls " administrative lawlessness " in England as contrasted with " administrative law " in France. See his *New Despotism*, chap. III.

[59] Cf. William A. Robson, *op. cit.*, 262-275, 315-322; Edward McChesney Sait, *Government and Politics of France*, 392-394. It is significant that the *droit administratif* has never been codified, and that, in the hands of the *Conseil d'Etat*, it has had a remarkable development which would have been stifled by the American conception of *stare decisis*.

public services and the securing of adequate private redress.[60]

Thus the judicial assumption of *laissez-faire* and absolute rights is a constant threat to experimental policies [61] and to effective administrative action. The doctrine of personal liability for *ultra vires* action, especially in cases where a jury passes upon a technical jurisdictional fact, is an effective stimulus to nullification.[62] On the other hand, the doctrine of the nonsuability of the state makes it impossible for the individual to get redress for wrongful administrative action unless he can show excess of jurisdiction, or prove negligence or gross abuse, on the part of the officer, or unless he can persuade the legislature to give him relief as a matter of grace. In the former case, there may be a joker in the pack even after the individual secures a judgment: the officer may have nothing

[60] Cf. Leon Duguit, "The French Administrative Courts," in *Political Science Quarterly*, XXIX, 392-393; Edward McChesney Sait, *op. cit.*, 382-384.

[61] This becomes clear in due process cases. But judicial review of *legislation* is beyond the scope of this essay.

[62] It is probably not sufficient that Congress may reimburse him. In *Williams* v. *Rivenburg* (129 N. Y. S. 473) McLennan, P. J., dissenting, said that the conclusion of the court meant that "we may not expect such inspector to take the chances of such a litigation against him, but he will allow the citizens of New York City to continue to eat bob veal." In *Lowe* v. *Conroy*, 120 Wis. 151, 97 N. W. 942 (1904), the Court accepted Mechem's rule: "Inasmuch as the law quite universally protects private property . . . the judgment or discretion of a quasijudicial officer, though exercised honestly and in good faith, does not protect him where, by virtue of it, he undertakes to invade the private property rights of others, to whom no other redress is given than an action against the officer." In *Seaman* v. *Patten*, 2 Caines 312 (N. Y. Sup. Ct., 1805), Livingston, J., asserted that the "general principle" that officers like an inspector general of provisions "act at their peril" is "too well settled to admit of controversy." Yet he referred to the precedents as "revolting" and the rule as a "hard one," and proceeded to distinguish the instant case. These cases are cited from Ernst Freund, *Cases on Administrative Law* (2d ed.), Part 2, chap. VI, sec. 28.

on which the plaintiff can levy. The disinclination of the courts, moreover, to go behind discretion and inquire realistically whether it has been abused or exercised for a purpose other than that intended in the statute, makes it difficult at times for the individual to secure adequate protection against bureaucratic control. At the same time the courts sometimes show reluctance to accept the findings of specialized commissions which are in a better position to judge of economic situations than they are.[63] Finally, is the injunction as satisfactory as the French recourse in annulment? [64]

The existing confusion in the application of the doctrine of jurisdictional facts and the doctrine of no governmental liability in tort can be corrected by legislation. Yet it may be doubted whether the influence of tradition would not cause such legislation to be interpreted with undue strictness. The other defects mentioned need to be corrected by granting some independent tribunal rather free discretion to work out a modernized administrative law. Detailed legislation would defeat this purpose, while the common law tradition would serve as an inhibition if this discretion were left to the ordinary courts. There would also remain the technicalities of judicial proof and procedure and the lack of administrative experience and social science training on the part of judges. For these reasons American students of administrative law tend to favor the establishment of an administrative court modeled after the French *Conseil d'Etat*.[65]

[63] Cf. Frank J. Goodnow, *Principles of the Administrative Law of the United States*, 296, 394-395, 402 ff., 433-437.

[64] See James W. Garner, " French Administrative Law," in *Yale Law Journal*, XXXIII, 597-627.

[65] President Goodnow, in whose honor these essays are written, did pioneer work in introducing American students to comparative administrative law, notably by the publication of his two-volume work which bears that title. Cf. Edward McChesney Sait, *op. cit.*, 396-397.

This should be a single court, divided into appropriate sections.[66] If the needed break is to be made with common law traditions, it should not be manned with common law lawyers. In its development of a new body of administrative case law, it must steer its course between the Scylla of bureaucratic tyranny and the Charybdis of an administration hamstrung by judicial interference. To that end its personnel should consist in part of persons with administrative experience and in part of persons trained in the *droit administratif*. The former may be expected to appreciate the requirements of the effective prosecution of the public services, and the latter the liberal protection which the *Conseil d'Etat* furnishes the individual.[67]

This is no idle dream. There already exist such administrative courts as the Court of Claims, the Customs Court, the Court of Customs Appeals, and the Board of Tax Appeals.[68] These courts hear tax cases and claims against the federal government. Congress will doubtless in time reorganize them and expand their functions. Only the pocket veto of President Coolidge prevented the enactment of a general statute making the federal government liable in tort.[69] There will be a gap in our system of constitutional government so long as there is no such pro-

---

[66] Cf. Senator Norris' proposal in *Congressional Record*, 70th Cong., 2d sess., vol. 70, pt. I, pp. 1030-1033.

[67] Cf. Leon Duguit, *op. cit.*; Maurice Hauriou, *Précis de droit administratif* (1911), 3, 12 ff.

[68] See J. Emmett Sebree, "The United States Board of Tax Appeals," in *Temple Law Quarterly*, VII, 428.

[69] H. R. 9285, 70th Cong., 2d sess. For the Senate report on the House bill see *Sen. Rep.*, 70th Cong., 2d sess., *Report* No. 1699 ("Federal Tort Bill"). For the veto see Arthur W. MacMahon, "Second Session of the Seventieth Congress," in *American Political Science Review*, XXIII, 380. The Senate report refers to statutes which already recognize government liability in tort in limited ways.

vision of law. It does not seem to endanger the sovereignty of the state or to bankrupt the treasury in France for a court which is independent of the executive to pass authoritatively upon damage claims against the government for faults of service. Indeed, the idea of fault might well be eliminated, as it seems to have been minimized in France, and the government made liable, on the principle of insurance,[70] for all damages incidental to the operation of the public services, except those involving purely personal fault. Recourse in annulment might also be taken over from the French system.[71]

The relation of this proposed administrative court to the regular courts will have to be worked out with care. All that can be said here is that, as the goal outlined above is approximated, the administrative court should be further and further released from the control of the ordinary courts. This would be satisfactory, as it is in France, from the standpoints both of administration and of the individual, if this court were given an unequivocally independent status, and made entirely free from administra-

[70] Cf. Thomas Harrison Reed, *Municipal Government in the United States* (1926 ed.), 124-125.

[71] Discussions of the French *droit administratif* may be found in Léon Duguit, "The French Administrative Courts," in *Political Science Quarterly*, XXIX, 385; James W. Garner, "French Administrative Law," in *Yale Law Journal*, XXXIII, 597; Edward McChesney Sait, *op. cit.*, and Frederick John Port, *Administrative Law*. Under this system the public service, the official, and the private individual are protected by the principle that the government rather than the official is liable before the Council of State for damages caused by "fault of service." For clearly "personal fault" the official is liable before the ordinary courts. "Fault of service" may be "an error, an omission, an act of negligence or even a want of judgment on the part of the agent." It includes acts done under an ordinance which has been annuled by the Council of State. It also includes acts which are rather in the nature of unavoidable accidents than of "faults." Furthermore the Council of State will annul administrative acts not only for excess of power, but also for misapplication of power, i. e., for the use of power for purposes other than those for which it was

tive supervision and governmental pressure. It is essential
that this be done at the outset. In legal theory our present
administrative courts are legislative courts whose functions are derived from the statutes, not constitutional
courts set up to exercise the judicial powers enumerated
in Article III of the fundamental law. Their judges, like
those of territorial courts, do not have the constitutional
guarantee of tenure during good behavior. But Congress
should be able to confer such tenure upon them, or at any
rate they should have it by virtue of a practice which is
based upon a recognition of the principle of judicial independence of the executive.

Emphasis has been placed above upon an administrative court as a check upon the functional activities of
administration in the interest of private individuals and
groups. But checks are also needed and appropriate on
the institutional side in connection with personnel administration and the auditing of public accounts. The
administrative court should be given power to annul appointments, transfers, suspensions, and removals when
made contrary to civil service regulations.[72] This will protect at once the governmental employees and the public
service against the spoils system.

It is an accepted principle of public administration that
the auditing of public accounts should be vested in an
organ which is independent of the spending services.[73]
The President stands above these services, and could be
trusted not to abuse his power to remove the chief auditor

granted. An ordinance may be annuled before it has been put into effect.
The Council of State has long been independent in fact if not in law.
Prejudice should not prevent imitation of the French system to the extent
necessary to meet our new needs.

[72] Cf. Walter Rice Sharp, *The French Civil Service*, 68-74.

[73] William Franklin Willoughby, *Principles of Public Administration*,
624-625.

in any crude way. It might appear satisfactory, therefore, to develop a practice whereby the President would not interfere with the particular decisions of this official, but might remove him if on the whole he thought his conduct of the office unwise. But the President would necessarily form his opinion of the matter on the basis of the views of his spending subordinates. Knowledge of this fact might impair the independence of judgment of the chief auditor. It seems preferable to run the risk of having an unwise chief auditor rather than one who is dependent upon the officers whose accounts he audits.

In 1921 Congress attempted to apply this principle in establishing the General Accounting Office headed by a Comptroller General and an Assistant Comptroller General. Both were given fifteen-year terms, and the former was made ineligible for reappointment, in order to prevent his seeking renomination by being amenable. Both were made removable—except on impeachment—only by joint resolution of Congress for specified causes and after notice and a hearing.

## VII

The last point brings the discussion to the final problem with which this essay can deal. Suggestions have been made above the adoption of which would without doubt require constitutional amendments. It is high time that Americans overcame their traditional inhibitions in this respect. A more immediate question, however, is whether the basic proposals made in the foregoing pages are consistent with the Constitution as it is likely to be interpreted by the Supreme Court. It will be impossible to discuss here the relation of administrative and ordinary courts. Nor does the expansion of the ordinance making power bid fair to encounter insuperable constitutional difficulties. There remains for consideration the crucial question whether the proposed relation of the President to the administrative personnel will probably receive the sanction of the highest tribunal.

For present purposes the most useful approach to this question is to adopt as the basis for prediction the views of the late Chief Justice Taft as expressed in the opinion of the Court in *Myers v. United States*.[74] This opinion claimed for the President alone an illimitable power to remove all executive officers whom he appoints by and with the advice and consent of the Senate, and hence to remove all superior executive officers, since they must be so appointed.[75] With this conclusion the position taken in this essay that the President should control all policy-determination is quite consistent.

In no case is it politically expedient for the President to have to share his control and responsibility with the Senate; and this phase of the question of tenure may reasonably be said to have been finally and properly settled by the Myers case.[76] But the opinion in that case made the further claim that Congress may not place any sort of restriction upon the President's power to remove all executive officers whom he appoints with the Senate's consent.[77] Thus Congress may not, in this view, prescribe that the President may remove any such officer only for specified causes and after notice and a hearing.[78]

[74] 272 U. S. 52 (1926).

[75] *Ibid.*, 106, 134-135, 163-164.

[76] *Ibid.*, 121-122. See James Hart, *Tenure of Office Under the Constitution*, 245-246.

[77] *Myers* v. *United States*, 272 U. S. 52, 127-128 (1926).

[78] The present writer has elsewhere maintained that, on a strict application of *stare decisis*, this question was not before the Court in the Myers case. James Hart, *Tenure of Office Under the Constitution*, chap. V, 216-

In his opinion in the Myers case the Chief Justice said: " There may be duties so peculiarly and specifically committed to the discretion of a particular officer as to raise a question whether the President may overrule or revise the officer's interpretation of his statutory duty in a particular instance," and further that " there may be duties of a quasi-judicial character imposed on executive officers and members of administrative tribunals whose decisions after hearing affect interests of individuals, the discharge of which the President can not in a particular case properly influence or control." However, he concluded that " even in such a case he may consider the decision after its rendition as a reason for removing the officer, on the ground that the discretion regularly entrusted to that officer by statute has not been on the whole intelligently or wisely exercised." [79]

This conclusion is unsatisfactory because it assumes that independence of judgment is not dependent upon independence of tenure. It tries to combine judicial independence in the particular instance with presidential control over policy. It illustrates forcefully the contradiction between the regulatory and the judicial aspects of the function of a body like the Interstate Commerce Commission.

217. This contention, however, derives its chief practical importance from the assumption that independence of tenure is desirable for the members of federal regulatory, investigatory and business-operating boards and commissions, or for the heads of some executive departments. *Ibid.*, 25-30, 64-69, 94-116. Such an assumption is repudiated in this essay. The present writer thus comes around to Dr. Langeluttig's position. For the latter's attack upon the position which the present writer formerly held, see Albert Langeluttig, " ' The Bearing of *Myers v. United States* upon the Independence of Federal Administrative Tribunals ' — A Criticism," in *American Political Science Review*, Feb., 1930. For his interpretation of the Myers opinion the present writer owes a purely personal debt both to Dr. Langeluttig and to Professor Cushman, of Cornell.

[79] *Myers* v. *United States*, 272 U. S. 52, 135 (1926).

The inconsistency is basically the same as that involved in the older French conception of the minister-judge.[80] This inconsistency may be resolved by assigning the regulatory aspects of administrative tribunals to presidential agents, their investigatory and enforcement aspects to a bureaucracy under the functional control of such presidential agents, and their judicial aspects to an independent administrative court. If this is done, the constitutional difficulties can probably be avoided.

The important questions which remain are whether Congress may constitutionally prescribe the personnel regulations outlined above for the bureaucracy and independence of tenure for the judges of an administrative court, of territorial courts, and for the Comptroller General of the United States.

The Chief Justice indicated that, whenever Congress sees fit to vest the appointment of an inferior officer in a department head, it then—but only then—may vest in the department head the power to remove him, and regulate the power of removal so vested.[81] By this means it would seem that Congress may provide for a permanent bureaucracy. The Chief Justice further said that Congress, in creating offices, may prescribe qualifications, reasonable classification for promotion, functions and jurisdiction,

[80] Frederick John Port, *op. cit.*, 304.

[81] *Myers* v. *United States*, 272 U. S. 52, 159-162, 173-174 (1926).

The Chief Justice refrained from passing upon the question whether Congress may regulate the tenure of an inferior officer whose appointment it vests in the President alone. *Ibid.*, 161-162. He did express grave doubt as to whether Congress has such power. The legislative branch is not apt, however, to vest in the President alone the appointment of any officer except one whom it intends to be the immediate agent of the President or of his *alter ego*, the department head. Examples are, respectively, the Director of the Budget and members of the so-called little cabinet. For practical purposes, therefore, this constitutional puzzle is unimportant.

terms of office, and compensation—" all except as otherwise provided by the Constitution." He held that the qualifications for office must " not so limit selection and so trench upon executive choice as to be in effect legislative designation." [82] But if Congress may within these limits prescribe reasonable qualifications, even for presidential appointees, it would seem that the door is left open for the statutory requirement that the person receiving the highest grade in a civil service examination must be appointed to any inferior office by the appropriate department head. This is not legislative choice, but the exercise of the power to regulate which Congress secures when it vests the appointment of an inferior officer in a department head.

Under the Myers opinion, then, Congress seems free to regulate the civil service in accordance with the principles of public administration outlined above. It may do so in detail, or leave the details to the President. It is certainly proper and probably necessary for Congress, however, to provide that discretion exercised in the name of the President by others shall be exercised only by officers removable by the President or by his *alter ego*.[83] This is a formal requirement which does not preclude that actual influence upon decisions by the bureaucracy which many writers have noted, and which seems inevitable if not in all respects desirable.[84]

At least one of its undesirable features may be minimized by the control of an independent administrative court. The Chief Justice said: " The questions first, whether a judge appointed by the President with the con-

---

[82] *Ibid.*, 128-129.

[83] James Hart, *Tenure of Office Under the Constitution*, chap. VII, especially pp. 344-358. Cf. *Myers* v. *United States*, 272 U. S. 52, 134 (1926).

[84] See, for example, Ramsay Muir, *op. cit.*, chap. II.

sent of the Senate under an act of Congress, not under authority of Article 3 of the Constitution, can be removed by the President alone without the consent of the Senate, second, whether the legislative decision of 1789 covers such a case, and third, whether Congress may provide for his removal in some way, present considerations different from those which apply in the removal of executive officers, and therefore we do not decide them." [85] It seems reasonably probable that the Supreme Court will rely upon these " different considerations " to uphold a statutory provision that judges of administrative and territorial courts shall hold office during good behavior. It would seem reasonable also for the Court to assimilate the office of Comptroller General to that of a legislative judge. If not, then Congress might vest his appointment in the Supreme Court. As Dr. Albert Langeluttig has pointed out,[86] the Myers opinion seems to say that in such a case the President would no longer have the power of removal. The power would vest, or could be vested by Congress, in the Court; and Congress could possibly regulate its exercise by the Court. This assumes that the Comptroller General is technically an inferior officer [87] whose appointment may be vested elsewhere than in the President with the Senate's consent. Since the existing provision for his removal by joint resolution of Congress seems clearly precluded by the Myers case,[88] one or the other of these devices is necessary under the Myers opinion, if this officer is to be given an independent tenure.

[85] *Myers* v. *United States*, 272 U. S. 52, 157-158 (1926).

[86] See his article on " The Legal Status of the Comptroller-General of the United States," in *Illinois Law Review*, XXIII, 556, 580, 590. For a contrary view see Edward S. Corwin, *The President's Removal Power*, 7.

[87] James Hart, *Tenure of Office Under the Constitution*, 142-145.

[88] *Ibid.*, 137-142.

## VIII

This, then, is the sum of the matter: The President should be strengthened as the focal-point of all policy-determination. His treaties should be subject to the approval of a majority of both houses. On the legislative side, his term of office should coincide with those of Senators and Representatives, except that he alone should be empowered to terminate the terms of all, and appeal to the electorate in a general election. The purpose of this proposal is to make his political power commensurate with his legislative responsibility, and thus to give him a weapon of party control in Congress so long—but only so long—as he can rally the support of public opinion. Only thus can an industrialized democracy organize itself around the concentrated leadership of its highest office for the task of controlling the consequences of the new relationships which the second industrial revolution has thrust into American society.[89]

The legislation thus required should outline the broad objectives around which presidential leadership has rallied popular support and leave to the President or his chosen subordinates the invention, selection and experimental adaptation of means to these objectives. The administrative task thereby imposed will be so great that the President can personally make only the crucial choices. But he should have a free hand in the selection and control of all who compose the inner circle of his advisers and of all who make the minor choices in his name. Under their functional control, the routine of administration should be placed in the hands of a non-partisan and permanent bureaucracy. The institutional control of this bureaucratic machine should be concentrated in the President, and

[89] See John Dewey, *The Public and Its Problems, passim.*

exercised under his general guidance by a bureau of general administration attached to his office and headed by a director appointed and removable by him alone.

The need for increasing governmental control of American economy however, should not blind us to the facts that the President's power is delegated except in the crucial choices of high policy, that the best-meant administrative action may work injustice, and that power will always at some points be abused. There should be established a federal administrative court with judges whose training has not been primarily in the common law and whose tenure is independent of the Executive, and with jurisdiction comparable to that of the Council of State in France. This court should be competent to adjudicate tortious and contractual claims against the federal government and to annul administrative ordinances and individual acts for excess, gross abuse or misapplication of power. Such individual acts should include, of course, postal fraud orders and many other acts which affect private interests. In order to protect the civil service personnel against the spoils system, they should also include appointments and removals which violate civil service statutes or regulations. A section of the court should have the issuance of warrants for all withdrawals of funds from the public treasury. For the progressive development of such safeguards along lines which will neither hamper unduly the public services nor permit administrative tyranny, the proposed administrative court is needed for the reason that the ordinary courts, with their common law traditions, are not suited to the task.

Finally, regulatory and other boards and commissions should be thoroughly overhauled. For they combine in the same hands functions which are inconsistent and which, according to the program as outlined, should be divided up. To presidential agents in the appropriate administrative departments should go their policy-determining functions. To the bureaucratic staffs of those departments should go their technical administrative and investigatory functions, there to be exercised under the functional control of the officers who formulate policies. To the administrative courts should go the judicial aspects of their present duties, there to serve as a protection of the private interests concerned.

In such wise is it proposed that the policy-determining, the policy-executing, and an important phase of the judicial system set up in 1789 be adapted to the needs of 1934. It is fully recognized that these proposals are fraught with their own dangers. But only cowards bear the ills they have and never fly, however conditions change, to others that they know not of. Men of intelligence are men of courage, and remember with Mr. Justice Holmes that all life is an experiment.

# From Political Chief to Administrative Chief [1]

BY

GEORGE W. SPICER

" Political necessity requires that there shall be harmony between the expression and execution of the State will. Lack of such harmony will result in political paralysis."—F. J. GOODNOW.

One of the contributors to this series of essays, writing of the powers of the state governor a little more than two decades ago, observed in conclusion:

From this discussion of the powers of the state governor it should be clear that while his influence in matters of legislation is important and increasing, his authority and control over the state administration is far from complete. His power of appointment and removal are much more restricted than in the case of the President of the United States; and he has little effective power of direction over the administrative officials.[2]

But in a note of subdued prophecy Professor Fairlie adds,

At the same time the growing importance of the governor's position should not be underestimated. Through his political powers he exercises a large influence over the welfare of the state, not only by his constitutional negative on legislatures but also by his positive influence as an exponent of public opinion. And in the field of administration both his express authority and his active influence are increasing, and it may be said should be further increased.[3]

Had Professor Fairlie been less cautious he might have

---

[1] This essay is the by-product of a more elaborate study which is now being pursued under the auspices of the Institute for Research in the Social Sciences of the University of Virginia.

[2] Fairlie, " The State Governor," X, *Michigan Law Review*, p. 474.

[3] *Ibid.*, p. 475.

94

added that the governor " through his political powers " and " as an exponent of public opinion " was destined to become the head of the state administration. At any rate that is what has apparently happened in several of the states since Professor Fairlie wrote. President Goodnow, in whose honor this series of essays is presented, gave the key to this process of development thirty years ago when he wrote that " Popular government requires that the execution of the state will shall be subjected to the control of the organ expressing the state will," [4] but added that " It is also to be noticed that in all concrete governmental systems the highest governmental authorities entrusted with the execution of the law do much towards shaping the law by the influence they exert over the legislative body." [5]

## A Striking Example of this Development in Virginia

It is doubtful if there has been any where in the United States a more far-reaching and dramatic example of the development of the governor's position from political chief to administrative chief than that which has taken place in the oldest American Commonwealth, largely since 1926. Prior to that time the development of the governor's office had not been unlike that of the other older states. The Constitution of 1776 made him completely subservient to the legislature and Council of State.[6] He was required with the advice of the Council of State to " exercise the executive powers of government according

[4] Goodnow, *Principles of the Administrative Law of the United States,* p. 7.

[5] *Ibid.,* p. 14.

[6] This body consisted of eight members chosen by joint ballot of both houses of the Assembly either from their own members or the people at large. (Constitution of 1776, sec. XI.)

to the laws of this commonwealth."[7] His power was perhaps greatest in military affairs, though in this respect the legislature kept a close check upon him. He was elected by the legislature for a term of one year and continued to be so selected until 1852 although his term was increased to three years in 1830.

Under the Constitution of 1830 the governor was required to communicate to the legislature at each session the condition of the Commonwealth and to recommend to their consideration such measures as he deemed expedient and was granted the power to convene the legislature in special session on application of a majority of the House of Delegates, the lower branch of the assembly, or when in his opinion the interest of the Commonwealth required it.[8] Another new power granted to the governor under this Constitution was the power, during the recess of the legislature to fill, pro tempore, all vacancies in those offices which it was the duty of the legislature to fill permanently, the commissions for which were to expire at the end of the next succeeding session of the General Assembly.[9]

These additional powers were merely nominal owing to the governor's complete responsibility to the legislature and his dependence upon the advice of the Council. The Constitution of 1830 reduced the number of the Council to three, any one or more of whom had the authority to act, and required the governor, before exercising any discretionary power conferred on him by the Constitution and laws, to have the advice of the Council of State. This advice was kept in books, signed by the members consenting thereto and laid before the General Assembly when called for by them.[10]

[7] Constitution of 1776, sec. III.
[8] Constitution of 1830, art. III, sec. IV.
[9] Ibid.
[10] Ibid., sec. V.

The Constitution of 1852 effected the first important change in the position of the governor. It abolished the Council of State and provided for his election by the voters of the Commonwealth.[11] Thus the governor was rendered independent of the legislature in his political capacity and was placed in a position to develop a political leadership which was destined to exert a profound effect not only upon legislation but upon administration as well.

A new power granted to the governor in the Constitution of 1852 was the power to require information of executive officers upon any subject relating to the duties of their respective offices. This, however, was ineffective without the power to appoint and remove the officers involved.

The Constitution of 1869 granted the veto power [12] to the governor and thereby made more effective his recommendations to the legislature. From this time on, and to some extent from 1850, the governor's influence over legislation is evidenced by certain acts of the legislature conferring administrative powers upon him. Typical of these acts was one enacted in 1872, empowering the governor to appoint seven physicians from different sections of the state to constitute the State Board of Health and Vital Statistics.[18] These acts, however, affected only a few officers, chiefly members of boards and commissions, and added little to the governor's administrative powers.

The Constitution of 1902 further increased the legislative powers of the governor by granting him the power to veto specific items in appropriation bills and the power

---

[11] Constitution of 1852, sec. I.
[12] Constitution of 1869, sec. V.
[18] Acts of Assembly (1871-72), p. 71.

to suggest amendments to bills.[14] The only other significant addition to the governor's power prior to 1927 came with the Budget Act of 1918,[15] authorizing and requiring the governor to prepare and submit to the General Assembly a biennial budget.

Thus it will be seen that the developments of a century and a half in the office of the Governor of Virginia carried him to a position of legislative leadership and administrative impotence. Through constitutional grants and through his position in the party organization of the state he was now able to play the rôle of leadership if not of actual supremacy, in the conduct of all the political functions of the state government. But in the field of administration he had gained little ground. Such were the restrictions accompanying the grant of administrative powers, and so scattered and disjointed were the various parts of the administrative mechanism that grew up in haphazard fashion in the latter half of the nineteenth century and the first two decades of the present century, that the governor was unable to exercise any effective control even over those officers appointed by him. Thus Professor Fairlie's conclusions of 1912 were, in the main, applicable to the Governor of Virginia in 1926.

In this year there began a transformation in his administrative powers, which it is the primary purpose of this essay to discuss and, in so far as possible, to appraise. It is not intended here to convey the impression that there was no previous agitation for administrative reconstruction. There had been various surveys and recommendations, all of which pointed to the need for increasing the governor's authority over the administration. This year,

[14] Constitution of Virginia, sec. 76.
[15] Acts of Assembly (1918), chap. 64.

however, marked the beginning of the accomplishment of actual results.

By this time the governor had emerged as the representative of the whole people of the state and as such he was expected by the people to assume the leadership in formulating and carrying into effect a constructive program of legislation. The separation of powers to the contrary notwithstanding, they had come to hold him responsible for the enactment of legislation as well as for its proper execution.

### Effectiveness of Governor's Legislative Power

How well a governor can succeed in the accomplishment of these legislative results is well illustrated by the record of Governor Harry F. Byrd, whose political leadership it was that transformed the governor into administrative chief as well. Of more than thirty-five specific recommendations made to the legislature of 1926, only five, it appears, failed to receive approval from the General Assembly. This record continued throughout his administration.

In connection with the veto power the Governor of Virginia is granted the power to recommend amendments to bills presented to him by the General Assembly, if he approves of the general purpose of the bill, but disapproves of any part or parts thereof. In this case he returns the bill to the house in which it originated, and if the two houses, after reconsideration, agree to the governor's recommendations by a majority of those present in each, the bill is again sent to the governor and he may act upon it as if it were then before him for the first time.[16] The

---

[16] Constitution of Virginia, sec. 76.

existence of this unusual power [17] sometimes makes it unnecessary for the governor to veto a single bill during the session of the legislature. Thus Governor Byrd in two regular sessions and one extra session of the legislature returned a total of forty-two bills with recommendations for amendment, and all suggested amendments were concurred in.[18]

Most of these bills were returned because of some technical defect or because they were inconsistent with or duplicates of other bills. The pocket veto exercised in the ten day period following the final adjournment of the legislature usually is confined to this same type of bills. So closely does the governor follow his legislative program through the legislature and so effective is his influence over that body that it is rarely necessary for him to exercise his veto on grounds of constitutionality or public policy while the legislature is in actual session. In the sessions of 1926 and 1927 no bills were vetoed and in 1928 only three were vetoed, and these met with overwhelming approval when returned to the legislature.

While a detailed discussion of the legislative powers of the governor is beyond the scope of this essay, what has been said will, it is hoped, indicate the extent and effectiveness of this power. It should not be forgotten that the governor's influence over legislation is due not only to constitutional grant but even more to his position as the leader or one of the leaders of his party and as the exponent of public opinion. It was this power that was

[17] Only two other states grant this power to the governor, namely, Alabama and Massachusetts.

[18] See House Journal (1926), p. 1135, and Senate Journal (1926), p. 973; House Journal (1927), p. 339 and Senate Journal (1927), p. 327; House Journal (1928), p. 1028 and Senate Journal (1928), pp. 889-890.

used by a recent governor to effect a dramatic reconstruction of the administrative organization of the state.

## The Byrd Reorganization

Although it is not the purpose of this essay to deal with personalities, it would be difficult to avoid reference at this point to the outstanding accomplishments of former Governor Harry Flood Byrd. It was his character, capacity, and tactful leadership, applied to the political powers of his office, that made him and his successors the actual heads of the state administration. He had inherited and acquired an extraordinary measure of political influence which he used to give administration its proper place in the government of the Commonwealth.

## The Governor's Relation to Administration [19] in 1926

At the beginning of the Byrd Administration in 1926 the administrative system of Virginia was in an extreme state of confusion. The administrative activities of the state government were distributed, or scattered, among ninety-five separate agencies. Of these, twenty-seven were constitutional and sixty-eight statutory. Twenty-nine were single officials, and the rest were boards and commissions. Of the single officials, eight were elected by the people. Many of the boards and commissions were composed in whole or in part of ex officio members. Several administrative agencies were appointed by the General Assembly.[20] The governor was permitted to select the members of

[19] The term " administration " as used in this essay means the execution, in non-judicial matters, of the law or will of the state as expressed by the legislative authority. Goodnow, *op. cit.*, p. 14.

[20] New York Bureau of Municipal Research, *Organization and Management of the State Government of Virginia* (Richmond, 1927).

only twenty of the so-called administrative bureaus and commissions. Many of the most important administrative officers owed him no direct responsibility for the conduct of their departments. As the New York Bureau of Municipal Research pointed out in the report previously cited, administrative authority and responsibility were " scattered, diffused, and dissipated."

Despite the executive budget the governor had no effective control of the financial affairs of the state. Sixteen uncoordinated agencies were concerned with carrying on the fiscal functions of the state. With all of these agencies it was difficult, if not impossible, for the governor to know the status of financial matters in the different offices, departments and institutions.

This, in brief, was the status of administration in Virginia at the beginning of the reorganization of 1927-1928. This system had developed in haphazard fashion without any definite plan and was to some extent the result of political jockeying.

### How the Reorganization was Effected

A striking example of the dependence of administration upon politics is found in the methods by which the reorganization of this administrative system was effected.

In his campaign for the governorship in 1925, Mr. Byrd ran on a general reform platform, the major plank of which called for the reorganization of the state administration in such manner as to make the governor the responsible head thereof. Coming into office on February 1, 1926, with his election majority still fresh in his memory, he reminded the General Assembly and his fellow citizens of his campaign pledges; that after his nomination these pledges became the platform of the Democratic party;

that it was, therefore, the duty of the whole party to redeem these pledges; that, however, the opportunities of Virginia " are broader than any party, and I appeal to all Virginians to help those in authority to realize them." [21]

Two days later in a notable message to the General Assembly on " Simplification of Government in Virginia," he laid before the legislators his plans for reconstruction of the state administration. In vigorous and courageous language he left no doubt in the minds of his legislative co-workers as to his plans and purposes. He said in part:

Energy and efficiency of administration of the business of a great corporation requires concentration of authority as well as responsibility in the executive head. . . . The cumbersome machinery with which we worried along a decade ago will not operate with modern efficiency.

Recognizing that there is a condition to be remedied, what can be done in a practical way?

he asked, and his emphatic answer was:

The first fundamental change must be to make the Governor the real executive head of the state. In order to do this the essential agencies of the state government and their heads must be responsible to the Governor. The number of officers elected directly by the people must be reduced, activities of the hundred bureaus and departments must be consolidated into a few departments, and the state's activities must be headed up to the Governor as the activities of a great private business corporation are headed up to its president.[22]

It is doubtful if such " heresy " had ever before been uttered by any governor of the Commonwealth.

Specific recommendations designed to carry out these principles were:

[21] Inaugural Address of Harry F. Byrd, Governor, February 1, 1926 (Richmond).
[22] See Sen. Doc. No. 8 (Sen. J. 1926).

1. That the General Assembly propose constitutional amendments to the people providing the short ballot, leaving to direct popular vote only the governor, the lieutenant governor and the attorney general.

2. That the heads of administrative departments be appointed by the governor who is directly responsible to the people for administrative efficiency.

3. That the various bureaus, boards and commissions be grouped into eight or ten departments, that many be abolished and that a business survey be conducted to make clear the way to economize.[23]

The legislature promptly and generously responded to these proposals by (1) authorizing the governor to employ a group of outside experts to make a survey of the state administration, and appropriating $25,000 for this purpose,[24] and (2) by passing a joint resolution proposing short ballot amendments to the Constitution.[25] In accordance with a previous recommendation of the governor, a commission of seven outstanding jurists, headed by the President of the Supreme Court of Appeals, was created to recommend changes in the Constitution looking towards a general revision of that instrument. This latter step was deemed necessary in order to effect a complete and effective reorganization. The pending short ballot proposals were accepted by the commission.

The Governor had said in reference to the need for an expert survey of the state's administrative agencies that if authority were given him, he would select an outside firm " so that this work may be done free of political or

---

[23] Ibid.
[24] Acts of Assembly (1926), p. 136.
[25] Ibid., p. 472.

personal considerations." [26] For this task the Governor employed the New York Bureau of Municipal Research.

However, in order to " adopt and adapt the recommendations suitable to our conditions " and to combine the " ability of disinterested business specialists and the common sense and local knowledge of Virginia citizens of practical affairs," [27] the Governor requested and received the authority to associate with him for this purpose " a Commission composed of outstanding business men of Virginia." One is inclined to suspect that a more important motive in the mind of the Governor was to win popular support for his program.

A large Citizens' Committee on Consolidation and Simplification in State and Local Governments, headed by Mr. William T. Reed, Richmond tobacconist, was accordingly appointed by the Governor to study and to adopt such recommendations of the New York Bureau as were deemed suitable to the needs and conditions of Virginia.

Each of the above bodies presented its report to the Governor early in 1927, the report of the Reed Committee following that of the New York Bureau by only six weeks. The Governor in turn called a special session of the General Assembly to convene on March 16, 1927, and laid before that body these reports. He urged favorable action on the report of the Commission to Suggest Amendments to the Constitution at this extra session in order to expedite the submission of proposed amendments to popular vote. With minor exceptions he endorsed the recommendations of the Citizens' Committee which modi-

---

[26] Governor's Message on Simplification of Government in Virginia, Feb. 3, 1926 (Richmond), p. 5.

[27] Governor's Message on Reorganization of the Government of Virginia, March 16, 1927 (Richmond).

fied considerably the recommendations of the New York Bureau as regards the set-up of individual departments. For example, single heads for all departments were not proposed by the committee, as were by the New York Bureau and by implication in the Governor's message on simplification of government. However, there was substantial agreement on the fundamental principle of making the governor the actual head of the state administration. It was proposed by the Committee that many useless agencies be abolished and that the remainder be consolidated, " with certain minor exceptions," [28] into eleven administrative departments and the governor's office.

A skillful use of political power to effect administrative reform is revealed in one of the concluding paragraphs of the Governor's message to the 1927 extra session of the General Assembly. Again reminding the legislative body of his campaign pledges to the people, he said:

My recommendations to the General Assembly of 1926 and the reports of the Reed and Prentis Commissions and the call to you to consider now these reports, is an earnest of my efforts to redeem the pledges I made the people. *Nothing less than the adoption of the essential recommendations as made will enable the fulfillment of these pledges.*[29]

The answer to this appeal was the passage by unanimous vote in both houses of the General Assembly of the reorganization bill formulated by the Citizens' Committee in close cooperation with the Governor, and the passage of a resolution proposing the constitutional amendments recommended by the Prentis Commission to the people. These constitutional amendments, providing for the ap-

[28] *Report of Citizens' Committee on Consolidation and Simplification in State and Local Governments* (Richmond), p. 6.

[29] *Reorganization of the Government of Virginia* (Richmond), p. 12.

pointment by the governor of several important administrative officials, subject to alteration by the General Assembly, and other changes in the administrative structure necessary to complete the reorganization, received favorable action from the 1928 session of the General Assembly and were submitted to popular vote and approved on June 19, 1928. By this legislation the governor became the administrative chief of Virginia.

## The Reorganized Government and Its Relation to the Governor [30]

It is beyond the scope of this essay to undertake any detailed description of the various departments under the reorganization act. It does seem appropriate at this point, however, to show in general how this act and the constitutional amendments adopted soon thereafter affected the governor's control over administration.

The reorganization resulted in the abolition of more than thirty minor and useless administrative agencies and in the consolidation or regrouping of the remainder into twelve departments and the governor's office. In the governor's office there are four divisions; namely, the Budget, Records, Military Affairs, and Grounds and Buildings. The head of each of these divisions is appointed by the governor without restriction to serve at his pleasure.

The twelve departments are: Taxation, Finance, Highways, Education, Corporations, Labor and Industry, Agriculture and Immigration, Conservation and Development, Health, Public Welfare, Law, and Workmen's Compensation. The organization of some of these departments is quite anomalous from the standpoint of coordination of

[30] See chap. 33, Acts of Assembly (1927).

functions and fixation of responsibility within the individual department. In some cases they consist of several so-called divisions loosely hung together with no departmental head, but the heads of these divisions are appointed by and responsible to the governor. An example of this type of departmental organization is found in the Department of Conservation and Development. It is provided that this department shall consist of the " State Commission on Conservation and Development, the Commission of Game and Inland Fisheries, the Commission of Fisheries and the Commissioner of Fisheries." [31] There has been no change in the law affecting these agencies except that the Commission of Game and Inland Fisheries was formerly known as the Department of Game and Inland Fisheries. In order that cooperation among the said commissions may be promoted and duplication of work avoided and in order further that each may be informed of the plans and work of the others, they are directed to hold joint meetings at least semi-annually.[32]

The governor's control over this so-called department is complete but somewhat dissipated. He appoints the seven members of the Commission on Conservation and Development, subject to confirmation by the Senate, and designates one of them as chairman. He may remove any member at any time.[33] He exercises identical powers with reference to the seven members of the Commission of Game and Inland Fisheries. The Commissioner of Fisheries and the other four members of the Commission of Fisheries are appointed by the governor without restriction to hold office at his pleasure. Several other departments are organized in a similarly cumbersome

[31] *Ibid.*, sec. 19.
[32] *Ibid.*
[33] See Va. Code (1930), sec. 585 (34).

fashion but in all except two departments, namely Corporations and Law, the governor's control is well nigh complete through the power to appoint, direct and remove.

The Department of Corporations is "headed" by the State Corporation Commission composed of three members elected by the General Assembly. This commission is a constitutional agency and is probably one of the most powerful of its kind in the United States, having important judicial powers as well as those of a legislative and administrative character.[34] Governor Byrd preferred this method of choosing the Commission because "judges of the Supreme Court and circuit courts are elected" by the legislature.[35] The Constitution provides that at least one of the commissioners shall have the qualifications prescribed for judges of the Supreme Court of Appeals.

The governor likewise has no direct control over the Department of Law inasmuch as the head of this department, the attorney general, is elected by popular vote at the same time and for the same term as the governor. One is inclined to regard this as one of the serious omissions of the short ballot. In the first place the governor would select a better attorney general, and in the second place it is inconsistent with the principle that the governor's authority should be commensurate with his responsibility. Under the Constitution the governor is made responsible for the faithful execution of the laws of the Commonwealth but is given no control over one of the most important officials upon whom he must depend for the performance of this task. It was argued by Governor Byrd and other advocates of the short ballot for Virginia

[34] James E. Pate. *State Government in Virginia* (Richmond, 1932), p. 153.
[35] Inaugural Address, *op. cit.*, p. 13.

that because the attorney general renders certain legal opinions which have the force and effect of law until altered by court decision, and because these opinions may, and sometimes do, concern the duties and powers of the governor, he should be elected by the people and not appointed by the governor.[36]

These restrictions upon gubernatorial control are subject to the modification that the governor has the power to fill vacancies in the Corporation Commission and in the office of attorney general. Under section 155 of the Constitution the governor has the power and the duty, whenever a vacancy occurs in the State Corporation Commission, forthwith to appoint " a qualified person to fill the same for the unexpired term, subject to confirmation by the General Assembly or until his successor be chosen as provided by law." Also when a vacancy occurs during the recess of the General Assembly in the office of attorney general the governor shall fill, pro tempore, the vacancy by commission to expire with the expiration of such unexpired term or at the end of thirty days after the commencement of the next session of the General Assembly, whichever shall happen first.[37] This power is more effective than appears at first glance. Since the General Assembly is ordinarily in session only sixty days in two years, most vacancies naturally occur when this body is not in session. The administrative officers selected by the governor in these circumstances are almost invariably superior to those selected originally either by the General Assembly or the people. If such an appointee has the time to establish a record, the chances are very great that

[36] Spicer, "The Short Ballot Safe in Virginia," *National Municipal Review*, Vol. XXI, No. 9, p. 552.

[37] See Virginia Code, sec. 122.

he will be continued in office by the legislative body or the people as the case may be.

The heads of all other departments or of important divisions, in case there is no single head, and the members of important boards connected with some of the departments are appointed by the governor. Some of these appointments are unrestricted, some are subject to the approval of the Senate and some to the approval of both houses of the General Assembly. The governor may remove some of these officials at his pleasure; others he may remove for cause; and a few he apparently may not remove at all. These latter include those officers named in the Constitution, namely, the State Treasurer, head of the Division of the Treasury in the Department of Finance; the State Superintendent of Public Instruction, executive officer of the Department of Education; the Commissioner of Agriculture and Immigration, head of the department by that name; the members of the State Board of Education; and of the Board of Agriculture and Immigration. In the case of the Treasurer it seems certain that the governor may, during the recess of the General Assembly, suspend him from office " for misbehavior, incapacity, neglect of official duty, or acts performed without due authority of law." [38] This power extends to all executive officers at the seat of government and would certainly include at least those officers named in Article V of the Constitution, headed " Executive Department," among whom is the Treasurer.

In addition to the foregoing the governor has the " power to appoint and remove without restriction " in most cases the members of numerous fact finding, examining, and regulatory boards and commissions. Furthermore, he now has the power to fill all vacancies in all

[38] See Constitution of Virginia, sec. 73.

state offices for the filling of which no other provision is made by law, whether the officer be originally elected by the people or the General Assembly, or appointed by the governor. In case of an office originally filled by the people the appointee shall hold office until the next general election.[39]

The restrictions imposed upon his power to appoint and, in a few cases, his power to remove are not as great a handicap as would appear from a reading of the law. In fact recent governors of Virginia have rarely, if at all, been embarrassed by the fact that certain of their appointees were subject to confirmation by the General Assembly or the Senate. For example, during the recent term of Governor John Garland Pollard every appointment was unanimously confirmed. However, if the governor is to be held to a strict accountability to the people who elect him for all of his public acts, sound principle as well as fair practice demands that he have unrestricted legal power to appoint and remove his subordinates.

Appointment and removal are not the only methods of administrative control available to the Virginia governor. All heads of departments and institutions are required to make annual reports to the governor, and to make under oath, any other time that the governor may require, reports upon any subject relating to their respective offices and institutions to be made in such form and with such particulars as the governor may require.[40] Furthermore,

whenever the Governor deems it necessary and proper he may require any such officer, superintendent or board to appear before him, and he may also require the production of any official books, accounts, vouchers, and other papers relating to their office and

[39] Acts of Assembly (1932), p. 135.
[40] Code of Virginia, sec. 320.

duties. For the proper inspection of such records, vouchers and papers he may employ accountants.[41]

## The Governor's Financial Control

The most effective means of continuous control available to the governor is that over the finances of the state effected through the Department of Finance and the office of Auditor of Public Accounts. Inasmuch as one of the chief purposes of the reorganization was the establishment of an effective administrative control over the finances of the state, a brief account of these agencies is justifiable.

The Department of Finance is organized in four divisions as follows: Division of Accounts and Control, headed by the Comptroller; the Division of the Treasury, headed by the State Treasurer; the Division of Purchase and Printing, headed by the director thereof; and the Division of Motor Vehicles, headed by a director. The most important of these divisions is that of Accounts and Control under the direction of the Comptroller. The head of each division is appointed by the governor, subject to confirmation by the General Assembly; and each, with the exception of the Treasurer, holds his office at the pleasure of the governor for a term coincident with that of the governor making the appointment. Thus the governor's control of the personnel of these divisions is well nigh complete. The department as such has no head except the governor.

In connection with the establishment of the division of accounts and control under the reorganization act, a new uniform system of accounting was installed and put into effect on March 1, 1928. Prior to the reorganization there

---

[41] *Ibid.*, sec. 321.

were forty-eight different collecting and disbursing agencies, with forty-eight different bank accounts. A large percentage of State and institutional revenue was not deposited directly to the credit of the State Treasurer and several millions of dollars never passed through the office of the Treasurer. It required an exhaustive and time consuming audit to determine the state's financial condition. Under the new system the Treasurer receives and disburses on proper warrant of the Comptroller all revenues whether received from taxation or the income of any institutions of the state. Each afternoon a balance sheet is laid on the desk of the governor showing the state's assets and liabilities and available cash surplus for that day.

All settlements made with the Treasurer by departments, institutions and other state agencies are accounted for. Every expenditure of State monies is audited before payment on the basis of complete information. Over-expenditure of quarterly allotments, without the consent of the governor, is prevented by a central control over purchase orders.

The Auditor of Public Accounts is theoretically a check on the governor as the head of the chief spending department of the government. Actually he is also a distinct aid to the governor in maintaining an effective control over the finances of the state. He is elected by the General Assembly but is required to report to the governor as well as to that body. Moreover, if the office becomes vacant during the recess of the General Assembly, the governor may make an appointment to fill the vacancy by a commission to expire at the end of thirty days after the commencement of the next session of the General Assembly.[42] Both the present Auditor and his immediate

[42] Code of Virginia, sec. 331.

predecessor were originally selected in this manner, and both were subsequently elected by the General Assembly. The Auditor may also be suspended from office by the Governor " during a recess of the General Assembly for misbehavior, incapacity, neglect of official duty, or acts performed without due authority of law," the General Assembly determining at its next session whether he shall be restored or finally removed.[43]

This officer is required to audit all accounts kept in the Department of Finance and all accounts of every other state department, officer, board, commission, institution or other agency in any manner handling state funds. It is further required that if he " should at any time discover any unauthorized, illegal, irregular or unsafe handling or expenditure of state funds," or if at any time it should come to his knowledge that any such practices are " contemplated, but not consummated, in either case he shall lay the fact before the governor, the members of the Auditing Committee of the General Assembly,[44] and the Comptroller." [45] The Auditor also audits the accounts of local officials handling state funds.

The governor's financial powers received two significant additions in 1932. Under the appropriation act of that session of the General Assembly, the governor was authorized and directed so to administer this act as to prevent any over-draft or deficit in maintenance appropriations made payable out of the general fund of the State Treasury. To this end it was provided that " the

[43] *Ibid.*, sec. 330.
[44] A standing committee of five members appointed from the two houses of the General Assembly, whose duty it is to examine annually or oftener the books and accounts of the State Treasurer and other executive officers handling or accounting for state funds.
[45] Code of Virginia, sec. 585 (69).

governor may reduce all of said appropriations pro rata
when necessary to prevent an overdraft or deficit for the
fiscal period for which such appropriations are made." [46]
To aid in the execution of this authority the governor
was given full power to examine and survey the progress
of the collection of the revenue out of which such appropriations were to be payable, and to declare and determine
the amounts that could, during each quarter of each of
the fiscal years of the biennium, be properly allocated to
each appropriation of the general fund. " In making such
examination and survey he may require estimates of the
prospective collection of revenues" from the revenue
assessing and collecting agencies of the state having information pertinent to such inquiry.

In the biennium ending June 30, 1934, the governor
reduced the appropriations of the general fund step by
step until in the second year of the biennium the reductions reached thirty per centum, thus cutting more than
$5,000,000 from the general fund appropriations for the
biennium. The appropriation act for the present biennium
confers this same power upon the governor with the
limitation that appropriations may not be reduced in
excess of five per centum,[47] which was ordered at the
opening of the fiscal year. This is one of the most extraordinary powers ever conferred on any state executive and
it has been freely exercised.

It should be noted at this point that the governor's
control over the financial affairs of the state is to some
extent limited by the existence of certain special funds,
such as highway revenue, which are not included in the
general fund, but are budgeted separately.

A further extension of the governor's financial control

[46] Acts of Assembly (1932), chap. 147, sec. 30.
[47] Acts of Assembly (1934), chap. 358, sec. 39.

by the 1932 Assembly authorizes the executive to cause an ouster proceeding to be instituted against the treasurer of any county or city of the state, or any other officer charged with the collection of the public revenues, whenever he has reason to believe that such officer has failed to perform the duties required of him by the laws of the state with reference to the collection and disposition of and accounting for the revenue. Upon the institution of such proceeding the governor may suspend the officer from his office and the performance of the duties thereof and appoint another to act in his place until the determination of the ouster proceeding.

### The Governor and Criminal Law Enforcement

If the governor's administrative control is strongest in the realm of finance, it is weakest in the realm of criminal law enforcement. Although the Constitution vests in him the chief executive power of the state and imposes upon him the duty of seeing that the laws are faithfully executed, it is well settled by the practice of strict and narrow judicial interpretation that these general grants confer no specific powers upon the governor. Such powers must be sought in the express terms of the Constitution or statutes in pursuance thereof and neither has been generous with the governor in the field of criminal law enforcement in Virginia.

In the enforcement of criminal law the governor is dependent in part upon the attorney general over whom, as previously shown, he has no control; but primarily he is dependent upon locally selected sheriffs and prosecuting officers, and chiefs of city police whom he has no power to remove for corruption or neglect of duty. The Ouster law as applied to these officers is ineffective because it vests the power of removal in the courts and the officer may demand a trial by a jury composed of his neighbors. In these circumstances governors will rarely undertake the initiation of ouster proceedings, especially if the local officer is very popular or the law which he refuses or neglects to enforce is very unpopular with his neighbors.

It is true, of course, that in cases of great emergency the governor may call out the militia, but this organization can not be used for ordinary law enforcement. It is cumbersome and impractical even for emergency use and sometimes leads to bitter popular resentment.

This weakness in the governor's armor was recognized and, to a small extent, remedied by the 1932 session of the General Assembly. The governor is given the power to appoint, whenever he deems necessary, and to remove at will, temporary special police, who shall be directly responsible to him. These officers are conservators of the peace and have the same jurisdiction throughout the state in the enforcement of the criminal laws that sheriffs of counties and the police of cities and towns have within their respective localities.[48]

## Some General Conclusions

It should be clear from these too numerous and tedious facts that the Governor of Virginia is now not only the legislative leader of the state but also the undisputed head of the administration, except in the field of criminal law enforcement. It should also be clear that this position of administrative supremacy issued from his position of political supremacy. Without his political power he could not have attained his administrative power, nor effected

[48] Code of Virginia (1932 Supp.), sec. 332 (c).

this vast transformation in the administrative organization of his state. This being so, it follows that administration is continuously subject to political control in this state. This, of course, was true before the reorganization but the control of that day was obscure and dissipated; the control of today is vested in the legally constituted head of the administration and is, therefore, simple and direct.

In short, the plan of administrative organization which has been in operation in Virginia since the Byrd administration is based upon the theory that administrative power should be concentrated in the governor. A number of other states have proceeded on this theory and have set up similar plans of administrative organization. The theory applied, in whole or in part, in these states is that held by a majority of students of political science and so-called public efficiency experts. This, of course, does not guarantee its perfection, or even its superiority over other theories of administrative organization. This majority view is by no means without minority opposition. One of the most thoughtful and constructive of these minority critics in academic circles is Professor Harvey Walker [49] of Ohio State University. Says Professor Walker in the article cited, " The hypothesis that the governor should be the head of the administration seems to me to need revision in view of experience, as well as in view of sound theory." [50] In support of this view he points out that experience in Ohio has demonstrated that the governor cannot assume the rôle of responsible head of the administration. Here he finds a situation which to him seems inevitable, " namely that the chief of the

[49] See his " Theory and Practice in State Administrative Organization," *National Municipal Review*, Vol. XIX, No. 4, pp. 249-254, April, 1930.
[50] *Ibid.*, p. 252.

governor's staff agency [the director of the Department of Finance] shall be the real chief administrator." [51] This situation is due according to Professor Walker, to the fact that the governor's time must be spent largely on non-administrative tasks and to his lack of knowledge of administrative structure and its functions, and of the principles of sound administrative practice.

Another point at which experience seems to belie theory " is in connection with the hypothesis that adequate control over the governor will automactically result from the adoption of the principle of integration." [52] If such an hypothesis has ever been advanced there is no doubt that experience will show it to be a pure fantasy. If, however, the theory is that, through the concentration of administrative authority and responsibility in the governor popular control of the administration is rendered simpler and more effective, then there is much doubt as to whether experience belies theory.

Professor Walker thinks that the grant of such sweeping powers to the governor should be accomplished by correspondingly effective controls and that no such controls have been offered. He contends that the only means for enforcing the responsibility of the governor are available before reorganization. The ballot is the most effective of these means and it is true that it is available regardless of reorganization. What Professor Walker does not consider, however, is the relative effectiveness of the ballot under a complex and simple method of popular control, and the possibility of the operation of public opinion between elections under a simple method of control.

Since the foregoing criticisms are based largely upon

[51] *Ibid.*
[52] *Ibid.*, p. 253.

observation and experience in a single state, it seems fair to consider the experience of the Virginia reorganization in relation to the two points raised. In the first place, it can be stated with little reservation that in Virginia the governor not only can be, but has been since the reorganization, the responsible head of the administration. No one who has had any connection with the state government in recent years can be unmindful of this fact. Moreover, this type of administrative leadership has been, in the main, highly satisfactory. Three governors to date have served under the reorganized government, and at no time has there been any appreciable popular dissatisfaction with its operations. It has resulted in substantial economies in overhead administration and in more efficient service to the public.

With few exceptions the governor has used his power of appointment wisely to secure a competent and relatively permanent personnel. Probably nothing has done more to win popular favor for the reorganization than the character of the governor's appointments. No one in the administration, whether department head or subordinate appointed by the former, stands in fear of dismissal so long as he renders efficient service. It has been customary for an incoming governor to reappoint the department heads of his predecessor. While this is obviously not the occasion for detailed statistical data, it can be conservatively stated that the Virginia reorganization has been successful in reducing the cost of operating the administrative machinery of the state, in bringing about a more efficient conduct of administrative functions, and in making the government more responsible to the people.

Regarding the second point raised, it may be asserted that there is no evidence that any leader of the Virginia reorganization movement ever assumed or pretended to assume that adequate control over the governor would automatically result from its adoption. It was contended that the concentration of administrative authority in the governor would simplify and make more effective popular control of the administration.

It must be admitted, however, that the problem of exercising an effective control over the administration is one of great importance and no little difficulty. If control is to be effective the means of control must be simple. The more complex the control mechanism, the less effective is the control. No motorist would be able to operate a motor car equipped with a dozen steering wheels, but with only one he has little difficulty so long as his mental and physical powers remain unimpaired. Concretely then, it would seem that such control should be exercised through a single head of the administration. But this leaves unanswered the question whether more effective control can be exercised through the governor or through some specially created leader of the administration.

This leads to the consideration of Professor Walker's proposal for the office of chief administrator. Concluding that experience has shown that the governor cannot assume the rôle of responsible head of the administration, he suggests the adoption of " the hypothesis that the chief administrator should be chosen for an indefinite term by the legislative body from nominations by the governor, and that he should be subject to suspension by the governor and discharge by the legislature at any time. Such a scheme," he opines, " would retain the political leadership of the governor, establish a continuous control over the administration and make it far more possible to secure a competent expert as leader of the administration." [53]

This interesting proposal suggests a number of ques-

[53] *Ibid.,* p. 254.

tions that leave doubt in one's mind about the possibility of its accomplishing the purposes for which it is designed. In the first place, if the governor is to remain the legislative leader, will he not determine the choice of the chief administrator? If he is really the leader of the legislature his nomination of the administrator will be confirmed as a matter of course. If he is temporarily not the leader, but is of the opposite party or faction, then there is the danger if not the inevitability of an impasse between the governor and the legislature over the choice of the chief administrator. What would be the result in this event? It would seem then that if the scheme retains the political leadership of the governor it could not establish any continuous control over the administration except through the governor. As President Goodnow pointed out in the passage previously quoted, "Popular government requires that the execution of the state will shall be subjected to the control of the organ expressing the state will." [54] Now if the governor is the leader of the legislature and shapes the course of legislative policy, the administration will in the final analysis be subject to his control. Indeed such control is necessary in order to maintain the necessary "harmony between the expression and execution of the state will." [55]

At best then the only purpose accomplished would be to establish an assistant to the governor. The scheme does not alter the political control of the administration except to make it more complicated. If the governor needs an assistant, and in some states he may, one is inclined to suggest that he be permitted to appoint him and thus avoid complication of the control mechanism.

[54] See *supra*, p. 95.
[55] Goodnow, *op. cit.*, p. 7.

There is need for a more continuous control over the administration, but there seems little hope that it can be achieved in the manner suggested. As long as the present type of legislature exists and the present relations between the governor and the legislature remain as they are, the most effective method of administrative control seems to lie in making the governor the head of the administration. In the circumstances there is no other simple method of effecting popular control of the administration. Such control to be effective presupposes the existence of a reasonably intelligent and industrious electorate, without which no popular government can succeed.

# PART III

# GOVERNMENT IN RELATION TO INDUSTRY

# JUDICIAL REVIEW OF THE FINDINGS AND AWARDS OF INDUSTRIAL ACCIDENT COMMISSIONS

BY

## CHARLES GROVE HAINES

### I

One of the foremost problems in the development of the practice and procedure of administrative boards and commissions is the extent to which the findings of fact and orders of the boards are subject to judicial surveillance and reversal and the effect of such review upon the growth of administrative law. To one phase of this problem relating to the review of the decisions of industrial accident or workmen's compensation boards, consideration will be given in this essay.[1]

Industrial accident legislation changed some of the underlying ideas in the relations between employers and employees. Under the former common law and statutory procedure in the states when an employee was injured the employer could plead in opposing a suit for damages that the employee had assumed in his contract of employment the consequent risks involved, or that the laborer contributed to the injury by his own negligence, or that the negligence of another employee was the proximate cause of the injury. Many employees could not afford to bring suit and if redress was sought it was necessary to turn cases over to lawyers on a contingent fee basis and

[1] This study is based upon an examination of the cases decided by the courts as included in the National Reporter System from September, 1931 to September, 1934, and upon other relevant data concerning the administration of the workmen's compensation acts. The study is limited to the appeal of industrial accident cases arising under state laws and to the review of such cases by state courts. In the gathering of the data and the preliminary analysis of cases, I have had the aid of research assistants in political science Saul Rittenberg, Norman Hinton, and Edward Walther.

to bear most of the loss incurred. In the trial of cases in the courts employers usually had superior advantages and opportunities and the employee seldom secured damages in any sense adequate to compensate for the loss incurred.

One of the first steps to remedy the prevailing evils of damage suits arising from industrial accidents was to take from the employer the common law defenses of assumption of risk, contributory negligence, and the " fellow-servant " doctrine. Strenuous opposition was raised to such changes in trial procedure, but legislatures and courts gradually approved the removal of these defenses. At the same time an effort was made to substitute a system of voluntary insurance for industrial accidents administered either by a special state board or by the ordinary courts. These preliminary steps were followed by compulsory industrial accident laws either setting up a state insurance system or requiring employers to provide insurance either in private companies or by self-insurance. The first American industrial accident laws were enacted by Montana in 1909, New York in 1910, with Wisconsin and nine other states following in 1911.[2] The movement spread quickly and a majority of the states soon had some type of an industrial accident law.

Because of the constitutional obstacles the laws are usually of the voluntary or elective type. What coercion there is generally takes the form of the abrogation of the common law defenses. Wisconsin in 1931 enacted a compulsory compensation act with a proviso that if the act was held void the former act should become effective. The fact that a compulsory act was approved by the federal supreme court[3] has not appeared satisfactory to the

---

[2] Foreign countries led the way by providing compensation systems — Germany in 1884; Austria, 1887; and Great Britain, 1897.

[3] *Mountain Timber Co.* v. *Washington*, 243 U. S. 219 (1916). The

opponents of the compulsory features of the acts in most of the states.

In accordance with industrial accident legislation, the theory of fault is eliminated and the employer is no longer deemed guilty of a breach of duty toward the employee. The basic principle is adopted that compensation for injuries arising out of employment is to be borne by the industry as a part of the cost of production. Through insurance the business and the ultimate consumer of its products, rather than the injured employee, bear the burden of accidents incident to the business. About fifty per cent of industrial accidents have been estimated to be due neither to the fault of the employer nor the employee, and it was possible to prove negligence by the employer in only about twenty per cent of cases in the courts. Thus the most reasonable and fair application of the law possible under the old system left much the larger part of the accidents of industry uncompensated.[4]

The primary objectives in the enactment of industrial accident laws were:

uncertainty as to the constitutional issues involved is indicated by a 5 to 4 vote of the justices. The minority did not state the reasons for their dissent.

[4] The modern doctrine of responsibility for industrial accidents was stated by Chief Justice Nichols of the supreme court of Ohio as follows: " The theory upon which the compensation law is based . . . is that each time an employee is killed or injured, there is an economic loss which must be made up or compensated in some way, that most accidents are attributable to the inherent risk of the employment—that is, no one is directly at fault—that the burden of this economic loss should be borne by the industry rather than by society as a whole, that a fund should be provided by the industry from which a fixed sum should be set apart as every accident occurs to compensate the person injured, or his dependents, for his or their loss." *State* v. *Ind. Comm.*, 92 Ohio St. 434, 450, 111 N. E. 299 (1915). For the general principles of compensation legislation see "A History of the Legislative Control of Workmen's Compensation in Wisconsin," 27 *Ill. Law Rev.* (June, 1932) 137.

1. To assure certain, prompt, and reasonable compensation to an injured employee.

2. To utilize for injured employees a large part of the money wasted under judicial procedure in suits for damages.

3. To provide a tribunal in which disputes between employers and employees in relation to compensation might be settled promptly and inexpensively.[5]

The essential conditions for the award of compensation are that the employer and employee are both subject to the act, that the injury resulted from services growing out of and incidental to the employment, and that the injury was proximately caused by an accident.

To sustain an award for compensation to a claimant, the industrial accident board or workmen's compensation commission is normally expected to make findings on five essential points:

1. Whether the claimant was an employee;
2. Whether he was injured as the result of an accident;
3. Did the accident arise out of and in the course of his employment?
4. What were the nature and extent of the injury?
5. What was the claimant's average weekly wage?

The nature of claims under workmen's compensation laws makes them difficult of proof. And it is not always realized that the ordinary civil suit presents to a certain extent different considerations from an industrial accident case.

[5] Cf. R. A. Brown, " 'Arising Out Of and In the Course of the Employment,' in Workmen's Compensation Acts," 7 *Wis. Law Rev.* (Dec., 1931) 16 and *The Administration of Workmen's Compensation* (Univ. of Wisconsin, 1933).

## II

In most of the states hearings in industrial accident cases are to be held in accordance with the rules adopted by the commission and need not be limited by the common law or statutory rules of evidence and procedure. The commission is expected to follow the methods best calculated to ascertain the substantial rights of the parties and carry out justly the spirit and provisions of the act.

Though by these provisions the commissions are not deemed bound by technical and formal rules of procedure obtained in courts, and the processes and procedure before them are usually directed to be " as summary and simple as may be," it is insisted nevertheless that they are bound by the fundamental principles of justice and substantive law. One of these principles, it is maintained, is " that every person against whom a judgment may be rendered should at all reasonable times and manners be entitled to have access to and knowledge of any evidence which has been offered to be used against him." [6] In this respect state courts applying the customary requirements and criteria of due process of law follow a different rule from that adopted by the English courts.[7]

Courts adopting a strict interpretation of industrial accident laws hold that, except as otherwise provided by the compensation act, hearings before the commission are treated as though they were trials in the superior court, and to such hearings the fundamental rules governing proceedings in such courts have been applied. Hence, the

[6] *Fox West Coast Theatres* v. *Ind. Comm.*, 7 P. (2d) 582, 584 (Ariz., 1932).

[7] *Local Government Board* v. *Arlidge*, [1915] A. C. 120. In this case the compulsory production of papers was not deemed necessary to assure substantial justice where an administrative order had been made interfering with property rights.

commission in making its awards is bound by the same principles of law and justice as are the courts.[8] A more liberal attitude is sometimes apparent in the dictum that only departures from rules which hamper petitioners in presenting their case will be seriously considered by the courts.

Statutes frequently exempt commissions from the limitations of courts in the consideration of hearsay evidence. And though the judges admit that hearsay evidence may properly be received and considered,[9] the rule against such evidence is asserted to be not technical, but vitally substantial and may not properly be disregarded without grave danger of collusion, imposition, and injustice.[10] The rule against hearsay evidence cannot be lightly brushed aside for it is founded upon " the experience, common knowledge, and conduct of mankind." [11] Some courts follow a purported rule to the effect that an award may in part at least be based upon circumstantial evidence, but this relaxation of the rules of evidence it is held must not permit awards to be made as a result of mere guess or conjecture. Thus an attempt is made to draw a shadowy line which many cases have failed to clarify. Despite statements to the contrary the courts still do not go much beyond the common law in permitting a claimant to prove his case by circumstantial evidence.

Judicial review of the orders and awards of industrial accident boards has been limited by statutory restrictions

[8] *King* v. *Alabam's Freight Co.*, 12 P. (2d) 294, 295 (Ariz., 1932).

[9] *Waddell George's Creek Coal Co.* v. *Chisholm*, 161 A. 276 (Md., 1932).

[10] *Lallier Construction and Eng. Co.* v. *Ind. Comm.*, 17 P. (2d) 532, 534 (Colo., 1932).

[11] *Walker* v. *Speeder Machinery Corporation*, 240 N. W. 725 (Ia., 1932). Cf. also *Englebretson* v. *Ind. Accident Comm.*, 151 P. 421 (Calif., 1915).

to which the courts have reluctantly given approval. The supreme court of Arizona notes that in the review of the awards of the industrial commission the statute expressly limits its jurisdiction to either affirming the award *in toto* or setting it aside in the same manner and " we have no power to make findings of fact, to modify the awards, to enter such award as it appears to us the commission should have made, or to send it back to the commission with specific instructions, to make any particular kind of award." [12]

The usual grounds for review provided in statutes are whether —

1. The board acted without or in excess of its powers;
2. The order or award was procured by fraud;
3. The order or award is in conformity with provisions of the act;
4. The findings of fact support the order or award.

As a result of the *Ben Avon Case* [13] there was apprehension that the Illinois compensation act would be held unconstitutional and hence the legislature passed a law authorizing the court to review all questions of fact as well as of law, with the provisos that the findings of fact made by the commission shall not be set aside unless con-

[12] *King v. Alabam's Freight Co.* 12 P. (2d) 294, 296 (1932). In this case it was held that a reversal of an award of the commission requires a trial *de novo* by the commission.

[13] *Ohio Valley Water Co.* v. *Ben Avon Borough,* 253 U. S. 287 (1920). According to the *Ben Avon Case,* in valuation proceedings for the fixing of rates by a public utilities commission the courts must form their own independent judgment on the law and the facts. For the majority of the court in this case the issue as to valuation for rate-making purposes is a question of law; for the minority it is one of fact to be conclusively determined by the public utilities commission in accordance with the intent of the legislature.

trary to the manifest weight of the evidence and that no additional evidence shall be heard by the court.[14] Applying the federal dictum to compensation cases the Illinois courts require that proof for an award by the industrial commission must be by direct and positive evidence from which inferences may be fairly and reasonably drawn; liability can arise from facts established by the preponderance of the evidence only; and an award cannot rest upon a choice of two views equally compatible with the evidence.[15]

In Oklahoma, as in many other states, the findings of fact of the industrial commission are held to be conclusive where the findings are supported by competent evidence, but "where a cause is presented to the supreme court and the findings of the commission upon questions of fact are assailed, it becomes the duty of the court to determine, as a matter of law, whether there is any evidence to support the findings" and for this purpose the supreme court goes fully into the facts of compensation cases and makes its own findings.[16] Such review is deemed necessary to sustain the constitutionality of the act, be-

[14] Smith-Hurd Rev. St., 1927, C. 48, secs. 138 ff.

[15] *Nelson* v. *Ind. Com.*, 178 N. E. 346 (1931); *Allith-Prouty Co.* v. *Ind. Comm.*, 185 N. E. 267 (1933); and *Rittler* v. *Ind. Comm.*, 184 N. E. 654, 660 (1933). In a period extending approximately over two years 58 cases were considered by the Supreme Court of Illinois with reversals of the award of the commission in 27 cases.

[16] See *Parson-Gibson Buick Corporation* v. *Fox,* 4 P. (2d) 38, 42 (1931); *Long Bell Lumber Co.* v. *Patterson,* 5 P. (2d) 130 (1931).

J. Kornegay in an opinion reversing an award of the Oklahoma Industrial Commission said: "We are fully aware of our decisions holding that under the workmen's compensation law the findings of fact of the commission in industrial cases should be followed, but the qualifier is that there must be evidence reasonably tending to support the award." *Continental Oil Co.* v. *Pitts,* 13 P. (2d) 180, 183 (Okla., 1932). And in the *Long Bell Lumber Co. Case,* above, he said: "The great fundamental principles that are guaranteed by the constitution, of a trial without prejudice, are applicable to hearings before the industrial commission," p. 135.

cause of article 7, section 2, of the constitution which provides that "the original jurisdiction of the supreme court shall extend to a general superintending control over all inferior courts and all commissions and boards created by law." Due process of law provisions in federal and state constitutions are considered rather generally as making it mandatory for the courts to review both the facts and the law in compensation cases.

## III

Strange inconsistencies and circumlocutions occur in the opinions of courts on the nature and weight of the evidence in industrial accident cases. The weight of the evidence is usually held to be a matter exclusively for the industrial commission. Where there is no competent evidence to support the findings of the commission, however, the courts insist that it is their duty to interfere with awards.[17] Since the courts may set aside an award if the findings of the fact of the commission do not support the award, the commission must make " sufficiently detailed findings of fact so that courts can determine whether the order or award is supported by facts." [18] Though it is customary to observe that courts will not pass on the weight of the evidence, the qualifications are likely to be more significant than the rule. For since the law puts the burden on the applicant of establishing each fact necessary to a legal award of compensation, courts usually insist that " the proof by which such burden is discharged must be based on something more than mere guess, conjecture, surmise or possibility." And in arriving at rea-

[17] *Public Service Co. of Colorado* v. *Ind. Comm.,* 3 P. (2d) 799 (Colo., 1931).

[18] *Hayden Bros. Coal Corporation* v. *Ind. Comm.,* 10 P. (2d) 325 (Colo., 1932).

sonable inferences from the facts " judgment must be exercised in so doing in accordance with correct and common modes of reasoning." [19] Liability can arise only out of facts established by " a preponderance of the evidence." [20]

The discrepancy between profession and practice is recognized by the supreme court of Connecticut. It is well settled, said Judge Hinman, though not always recognized in the taking of appeals as to corrections of the findings of compensation commissioners, that " the finding as to subordinate facts cannot be changed by the supreme court unless the record discloses matters found to be facts without evidence or fails to include material facts which are admitted or undisputed." [21] But when are findings without evidence and what material facts are admitted or undisputed? The field is wide open for the examination of the evidence by the reviewing court and the reports are filled with detailed statements of facts and the judgments of the courts as to the correctness of the commission's findings of fact.[22]

Apparently courts like to speak in riddles. Thus, the supreme court of Massachusetts referred to the rule of our law " that the superior court has no authority to overturn a decision of fact made by the industrial accident board if there is any evidence which will support the findings on which the decision rests, unless as a matter of

[19] *Milholland Sales and Engineering Co.* v. *Griffiths,* 178 N. E. 458, 460 (Ind., 1931) and *Frazer* v. *McMillin & Carson,* 179 N. E. 564, 566 (Ind., 1932).

[20] *Nelson* v. *Ind. Comm.,* 178 N. E. 346, 348 (Ill., 1931).

[21] *Bailey* v. *Mitchell,* 156 A. 856, 857 (1931).

[22] In a case of conflicting testimony the supreme court of Utah reversed the finding of the commission denying compensation and placed its own interpretation upon the evidence. The dissenting judges objected on the ground that " it is not the function of this court to weigh conflicting evidence and to decide where the preponderance lies." *Henderson* v. *Ind. Comm.,* 15 P. (2d) 302, 307 (1932).

law a different finding is required on the evidence." [23] Or again "the findings of fact by the industrial accident board must stand if there is any evidence to support them. . . . The only function of the superior court is to determine as a matter of law what kind of decree ought to be entered upon the decision made by the board." [24] In reviewing findings of fact, said Judge Drew of the superior court of Pennsylvania, "we are limited to such consideration of the record as will enable us to determine whether there is sufficient competent evidence to support the findings, and if the law has been properly applied." [25]

We are told over and over again that only questions of law are reviewable by the courts on appeal from industrial accident boards. It is not the scheme of the act to make the court reviewer of facts. But it is declared to be the duty of the court "to relieve against fraud, to keep the commission within jurisdictional bounds, and to correct an award not supported by the facts found." [26] There can be no review of an award, said the supreme court of Oklahoma, unless "it clearly appears that there was an abuse by such tribunal of its discretion in rendering the judgment or making the award complained of." [27] Review of abuses of discretion by industrial commissioners and examiners predicates a basis for rather frequent reversals of the awards of industrial accident boards.

[23] *Perangelo's Case,* 177 N. E. 892, 893 (1931).
[24] *Walsh's Case,* 183 N. E. 421, 422 (1932). The statute provides that when the record of the industrial accident board is presented to the superior court the court is to "render a decree in accordance therewith," G. L. (Ter. Ed.) C. 152, sec. 11. Though the findings of fact of the commission are conclusive, "when, as here all the evidence is reported, it becomes a question of law whether there was any evidence upon which the findings could have been made."
[25] *Lewis* v. *S. M. Byers Motor Car Co.,* 156 A. 899 (Pa., 1931.).
[26] *City of Milwaukee* v. *Ind. Comm.,* 151 N. W. 247, 248 (1915).
[27] *Stephenson* v. *State Ind. Comm.,* 192 P. 580, 583 (Okla., 1920).

If a review of the findings of fact is supposed to be precluded by the statute there always remains the commonly asserted necessity of a review on matters of law. Thus, Chief Justice Moschzisker of Pennsylvania referred to cases where " the court is convinced that the findings of fact are not sustained by legally competent evidence, and therefore such findings must fall as a matter of law, which, of course, requires a reversal of the award." [28] And by a kind of magic wand what are considered by ordinary canons of interpretation as findings of fact become conclusions of law.

A striking instance of the evasion of a predetermined legislative policy to limit judicial review of administrative action is found in the attitude of the judges in Utah. It is the plain policy of the workmen's compensation act, said Chief Justice Cherry, to vest in the industrial commission exclusive power and responsibility of deciding questions of fact, the language of the act being as follows: " The findings and conclusions of the commission on questions of fact shall be conclusive and final and shall not be subject to review." This language was interpreted, when a case was appealed to the supreme court, as follows: " We are committed to the rule that the review is limited to the question of whether the commission in denying compensation has arbitrarily or capriciously disregarded uncontradicted evidence. . . . We therefore, upon this review, examine the evidence, not to ascertain what weight or credibility we should give it, not to determine whether in our opinion a different result should have been reached, but whether or not the commission has arbitrarily or

[28] *Driscoll* v. *McAlister Bros.*, 144 A. 89, 91 (1928). It is pointed out in this case that before such judgment of reversal is made final, the compensation board is given an opportunity to furnish legally competent evidence.

capriciously disregarded and refused to follow and give effect to uncontradicted testimony." [29] The Utah supreme court in another case held that though the commission by statute is not bound by the common law or technical rules of evidence, " yet when it makes its findings every finding of fact must be based on some substantial legal and competent evidence "; [30] and at another time it was held that " the commission was in duty bound to fairly and impartially consider all the evidence relating to a material issue . . . and may not arbitrarily or capriciously disregard evidence or disbelieve testimony." [31] Neither by the statute nor by judicial decisions, observes Justice Straup in this case, " was it intended that the commission in reviewing and considering evidence was at liberty to disregard the common law or statutory rules of evidence and adopt those of Latin countries." The courts of Nebraska seem inclined to examine the evidence in compensation cases and where questions of fact are in doubt to decide against claimants.[32] New Jersey courts follow a similar policy but assert that conclusions on questions of fact will not be " lightly disturbed." [33]

Commissions and lower courts have generally adopted a broad view of the question as to the admissibility and the weight of the evidence. Appellate courts, on the other hand, have adhered more closely to the conventional standards of proof. The reports are indeed " full of reversals of board decisions on the ground that there is no evidence supporting the finding of the board, or that no

[29] *Kelly* v. *Ind. Comm.,* 12 P. (2d) 1112 (1932).

[30] *Garfield Smelting Co.* v. *Ind. Comm.,* 178 P. 57 (1918).

[31] *Diaz* v. *Ind. Comm.,* 13 P. (2d) 307, 310 (1932).

[32] Cf. *Babcock* v. *School Dist.* No. 107, 243 N. W. 831 (1932) and *Pensick* v. *Boehm,* 244 N. W. 923 (1932).

[33] *Granowitz* v. *Hay Foundry and Iron Works,* 157 A. 130 (1931) and *Newell* v. *Workman's Comp. Bureau,* 157 A. 244 (1931).

reasonable man could find as the board found on the evidence given." [34]

Differing from the practice in certain states in which the judges require the commission to be guided by the preponderance of the evidence with the court reserving the right to say which way the preponderance lies, and to decide against the claimant in doubtful cases, the courts of Minnesota have adopted another method of approach. When on review of an order of the commission the court discovered that the commission might well have found for the relator, but having found for the respondent upon competent evidence, it was held that on a disputed question the court could not interfere.[35] On another occasion the Minnesota rule was stated to be that "unless a consideration of the evidence and inferences permissible therefrom clearly require reasonable minds to adopt a conclusion contrary to the one at which the commission arrived, a finding by the commission upon a question of fact cannot be disturbed." [36] To the same effect the supreme court of Michigan maintains that it is the province of the commission rather than the courts to draw legitimate inferences and weigh probabilities on questions of fact.[37] In Missouri it has been held that the appellate courts have no power or jurisdiction to make findings of fact in a case arising under the workmen's compensation act. That power, it has been stated repeatedly, lies with the commission, and its finding of facts, when made

[34] Frank A. Ross, "The Applicability of Common Law Rules of Evidence in Proceedings before Workmen's Compensation Commissions," 36 *Harv. Law Rev.* (Jan., 1923) 266.

[35] *Hoeflin* v. *Riverside Press*, 238 N. W. 676 (1931).

[36] *Zitzman* v. *Macht*, 245 N. W. 29 (1932).

[37] *Beer* v. *Brunswick Lumber Co.*, 241 N. W. 800 (1932). The above statement does not preclude a rather high percentage of reversal of awards in Michigan. See table *infra*.

within its powers, is conclusive.[38] To set aside an award the facts must be inconsistent with the award, for in cases where the competent evidence is conflicting the commission's finding of facts is conclusive.[39]

A considerable amount of rather fruitless litigation would have been obviated and industrial commissions would have been strengthened if the observation of the judges in a New York case had been applied in compensation controversies. " It is not well for this court," said Judge Howard, " to fall into the habit of discussing the facts, even for the purpose of showing that the findings of fact are reasonable and meet with our approbation. We cannot, except by usurpation, invade the realm of facts, for it was the clear intent of the legislature that ' the decision of the commission shall be final as to all questions of facts.' " [40] Following the principle thus announced in the early years of industrial accident legislation, the supreme court of Wisconsin maintained that " if there is evidence which supports the findings of the commission, even though it be against the great weight or clear preponderance of the evidence, the finding may not be disturbed by the court on review." And in cases where

[38] *Jones* v. *Century Coal Co.,* 46 S. W. (2d) 196 (St. Louis Court of Appeals, 1932).

[39] *State v. Haid,* 51 S. W. (2d) 1008 (1932). According to Judge Becker, " we are required to consider the case just as if it was a case where the facts had been determined by a jury without considering the weight of the evidence or the credibility of the witnesses." *Travellers' Ins. Co.* v. *Davis,* 42 S. W. (2d) 946 (St. Louis Court of Appeals, 1931).

Speaking of the interpretation and application of the Wisconsin compensation act, Mr. Barry notes that the courts with a clear understanding of the human element involved have construed the acts with great liberality, keeping uppermost at all times that labor should be reasonably compensated for the losses incident to industry. John S. Barry, " Judicial Construction of Certain Provisions of the Workmen's Compensation Act," 17 *Marquette Law Rev.* (April, 1933) 175.

[40] *Rhymer* v. *Heuber Bldg. Co.,* 156 N. Y. Supp. 903, 904 (1916).

the evidence is evenly balanced and an inference may be drawn one way as easily as another, the scale should be turned in favor of the claimant.[41] Recognizing the finality of fact finding by the industrial commission the supreme court of North Dakota observed that " the statute contemplates no review of its determination as to the facts. On the contrary, it jealously guards against such review by the courts. We think the legislature acted wholly within its power when it thus provided." [42]

Despite statutory injunctions to the contrary, courts frequently review the findings of fact in compensation cases. And the extent to which the facts in detail are repeated, and reexamined with new and different findings, can scarcely be realized until the grist of cases which the appellate courts are grinding each year is surveyed.

If there is any competent evidence to support the findings of fact of the industrial commission, the North Carolina courts hold an award will not be disturbed, although the courts may disagree with the findings of fact as made by the commission.[43] But the door for judicial surveillance of the commission's decisions is left rather wide open by the observation that the superior court on appeal from an award of the commission has jurisdiction to review all the evidence for the purpose of determining whether as a matter of law there was any evidence to

[41] *Tesch* v. *Ind. Comm.*, 200 Wis. 616, 619 (1930). In this case, it was held, however, that " the attempt to support a finding by taking bits of testimony out of their context and considering them alone apart from other undisputed circumstances in the case, and then claiming that a finding supported in that manner is beyond review because supported by testimony, is wholly inconsistent with the fundamental principles embodied in the legal concept of a hearing as that term is used in American law." At p. 623.

[42] *State* v. *Workmen's Comp. Bureau*, 207 N. W. 555, 557 (1926).

[43] *Kenan v. Duplin Motor Co.*, 164 S. E. 729 (1932).

support the award.[44] Thus by insisting upon the practice of defining the really significant phrases of the compensation acts and by requiring an examination of the facts to assure the judges that an award was not made without evidence the courts have found ample warrant to review any industrial accident case which they desire to consider.

Many fruitless actions commenced in the district courts of Colorado for a review of findings and awards of the industrial commission of Colorado and writs of error prosecuted in the supreme court to the judgments rendered in such action, according to Mr. Lester " testifies to a general misapprehension among the members of the bar of the conclusiveness of such findings and awards upon the review thereof by the courts." [45] The Colorado courts have insisted from the beginning that in the review of workmen's compensation cases they will review questions of law only and that it is no part of the duty of the courts nor do they have the right to retry the facts. This rule was relaxed somewhat by the holding in the case of *Industrial Commission* vs. *Elkas*,[46] wherein the court held that in matters of this kind we are " permitted to consider only questions of law, but it is familiar that the question whether the verdict is supported by evidence is a question of law, and the same must be true of an award. We must conclude, therefore, that the district court has power to do what it did and that we have power to consider the matter." The courts have not, as some feared might be the result of the *Elkas Case*, weighed the evidence presented by the commission's findings in all cases submitted to

[44] *Poole's Dependents* v. *Sigmon*, 162 S. E. 198 (1932), holding that there was no evidence that claimant was an employee.

[45] William E. Lester, " Finality of Findings and Awards of the State Industrial Commission," 5 *Rocky Mountain Law Rev.* (Dec., 1932), 17.

[46] 216 P. 521 (1923).

the court, and set the award aside because they differed
from the commission as to the weight and credibility of
the evidence. But the professed finality of fact-finding by
the commission is an empty form in which the reasoning
is cast, and it is consistently ignored when judges regard
it necessary to preserve common law dogmas of judicial
control.

Speaking of the rule prescribed by the statute that the
commission's findings of fact shall be conclusive and shall
not be disturbed by the courts unless there is an entire
lack of evidence to support the commission's conclusions,
an industrial accident commissioner observes: " It would
seem that this law would tend to keep to a minimum the
number of cases which are appealed from the commission
to the courts. The fact is, however, that a considerable
number of cases are appealed even though the findings
of fact made by the commission are well substantiated by
testimony." Theoretically the courts are bound by the
commissioners' findings of facts; but practically, this is not
so, since the courts take the position they will consider
whether there was " sufficient competent evidence " to
sustain the finding of fact.

But most important of all judicial review of the facts
or evidence in accident cases has tended to involve the
application of criteria which it was the obvious purpose
of the new legislation to eliminate. A few illustrations
may suffice to show how overrefinements of legal reasoning may result in the reversal of apparently reasonable
awards of commissions.

An Indiana court reversed the board's finding that a
watchman's death was the result of an accident " arising
out of and in the course of employment," when the evidence disclosed that the watchman was fatally shot by an
unknown assailant while on duty at the employer's fac-

tory.[47] A maid employed to clean rooms was denied compensation because of an injury which resulted while attempting to clean a light well.[48] Where an act included under hazardous employments the business of transfer and storage it was held that a party engaged only in a truck transfer business did not come within the terms of the act.[49]

Commissions inclined to take a more humane view of claims for compensation were reversed on appeal when an award was given for death from injuries sustained when a foreman as a practical joke turned air from a high compression hose on an employee engaged in his regular work, and the employer contested the case; [50] when a salesman employed to demonstrate and sell used automobiles, was injured while cranking a car, was held not engaged in a " hazardous employment "; [51] and when the misuse of the words " and/or " in the findings and judgment of the industrial commission was held to render them too uncertain and indefinite to support an award.[52]

Courts at times object to the efforts of employers or insurance carriers to secure unjustifiable delays to force an employee to take less than the law allows.[53] When a case came to the court of appeals of Georgia a second time, Judge Guerry remarked: " This case is like Banquo's ghost, it continues to reappear." It had appeared and reappeared from the commission to the courts and back

[47] *Alexandria Metal Products Co.* v. *Newsome,* 185 N. E. 520 (1933).

[48] *Williamson* v. *Ind. Acc. Comm.,* 171 P. 797 (1918).

[49] *Followill* v. *Marshall,* 5 P. (2d) 149 (Okla., 1931).

[50] *Barden* v. *Archer Daniels Midland Co.,* 246 N. W. 254 (Minn., 1933).

[51] *Northway* v. *Tryon,* 21 P. (2d) 501 (Okla., 1933).

[52] *Putnam* v. *Ind. Comm.,* 14 P. (2d) 973 (Utah, 1932).

[53] See criticism of J. Clarkson on what he considered an unjustifiable delay extending over two and a half years, *Cabe* v. *Parker-Graham-Sexton, Inc.,* 202 N. C. 176, 186 (1932).

again for twelve years.[54] Though not extending over such a long period the appellate court of Indiana noted in a similar cause that for the second time these parties have been before this court on matters arising out of the same accident.[55]

It would be a mistake to give the impression that administrative boards are always more liberal in considering claimants applications than the courts. In more than a hundred cases included in the groups examined the courts reversed orders of the commission denying compensation, and in an appreciable number of cases commission awards were increased. Courts are likely to differ with commissions on the issue as to whether an accident arose in the course of employment,[56] or on the findings as to a question of dependency,[57] and may disagree with the findings of fact as warranting a basis for an award under the terms of the statute.[58] But the number of such rever-

[54] *United States Casualty Co.* v. *Smith,* 167 S. E. 771 (1933).

[55] *Bickel* v. *Ralph Sollit and Sons Const. Co.,* 184 N. E. 196 (1933).

[56] Representative cases of reversals on this ground are: *Adams* v. *Colonial Colliery Co.,* 158 A. 183 (Pa., 1932); *Munson* v. *State Ind. Acc. Comm.,* 20 P. (2d) 229 (Ore., 1933); *Younger* v. *Motor Cab Transp. Co.,* 183 N. E. 863 (N. Y., 1933); *Kasari* v. *Ind. Comm.,* 181 N. E. 809 (Ohio, 1932); *Burchfield* v. *Dept. of Labor and Industries,* 4 P. (2d) 858 (Wash., 1931); *Reinoehl* v. *Hamacher Pole and Lumber Co.,* 6 P. (2d) 860 (Ida., 1931); *Frazer* v. *McMillan and Carson,* 179 N. E. 564 (Ind., 1932); *Arquin* v. *Ind. Comm.,* 181 N. E. 613 (Ill., 1932); *Manley's Case,* 182 N. E. 486 (Mass., 1932); *George* v. *Waldron, Inc.,* 166 A. 102 (N. J., 1933).

[57] *Barker* v. *Reynolds,* 179 N. E. 396 (Ind., 1932); *Community Baking Co.* v. *Reissig,* 164 A. 176 (Md., 1933); *Nordmark* v. *Indian Queen Hotel Co.,* 159 A. 200 (Pa., 1932); *Caldwell* v. *Kreis and Sons,* 50 S. W. (2d) 725 (Mo., 1932); *Harness* v. *Ind. Comm.,* 17 P. (2d) 277 (Utah, 1932).

[58] *Henderson* v. *Ind. Comm.,* 15 P. (2d) 302 (Utah, 1932); *Cole* v. *State Comp. Com'r.,* 169 S. E. 165 (W. Va., 1933); *Nielsen* v. *State Ind. Acc. Comm.,* 13 P. (2d) 517 (Calif., 1932); *Ind. Comm. of Colorado* v. *Swanson,* 26 P. (2d) 107 (1933); *Banister* v. *State Ind. Acc. Comm.,* 19

sals is so small as to be of relatively slight significance in the administration of the acts with the exception of a few states such as West Virginia, Ohio, Missouri, and Washington.

## IV

The review of administrative action had its origin in part at least in the common law doctrine of *ultra vires* with the result that review centered around the issue of jurisdiction instead of a proceeding to correct an error or abuse by an inferior tribunal. Finding it necessary to extend the older doctrine of review on jurisdictional grounds in passing upon the orders or awards of administrative commissions a formula was adopted that the tribunal acted without jurisdiction if it disregarded a principle of law or issued an order without evidence.[59] The basis for this broad review of the quasi-judicial determinations of administrative officers is frequently called the doctrine of " jurisdictional facts." By this doctrine after the findings of fact of the administrative board there must be another trial or hearing to determine whether the board has not exceeded its authority.

The real obstacle in the way of the recognition of the principle that the findings of fact of industrial accident boards are final and conclusive, is, therefore, the common law doctrine that it is the duty of the courts to inquire and determine whether public authorities keep within their jurisdictional limits. In one of the first cases under workmen's compensation laws it was held that the question of jurisdiction is one always open to the courts for review, since no officer or board can endow itself with

P. (2d) 403 (Ore., 1933); *Murphy* v. *Ind. Acc. Board,* 16 P. (2d) 705 (Mont., 1932).

[59] Cf. John Dickinson, *Administrative Justice and the Supremacy of Law* (Cambridge, 1927), p. 307.

authority.[60] When the New York courts maintained that it was their duty to regard the industrial accident board's findings of fact as final, review on jurisdictional grounds was deemed inescapable for, said Judge Howard, " if there are no facts, and the decision is arbitrary, unfair, and unreasonable, a question of law arises and we may right the wrong." [61]

The doctrine of " jurisdictional fact," which applies to most administrative agencies, has been defined by Professor Dickinson as follows:

Where a statute purports to confer on an administrative agency a power to make decisions, but is construed as conferring that power only over, or with reference to certain kinds of objects, situations or acts, then the fact-question of whether or not in any given case of such a decision the object, situation or act was, *in fact,* of the kind specified in the statute goes to the jurisdiction of the administrative agency to make the decision at all. . . . The practical result of the doctrine of " jurisdictional fact " is to throw open for complete reexamination in courts facts which, if they were not held to be " jurisdictional " would be concluded, either by the decision of the administrative body, or at least by evidence at its disposal.[62]

And in *Crowell* v. *Benson,* Chief Justice Hughes, speaking for the court, has given the doctrine of jurisdictional fact a place of primary significance in the review of compensation cases.[63]

[60] *Borgnis* v. *Falk,* 147 Wis. 327, 359, 133 N. W. 209, 218 (1911).

[61] *Rhyner* v. *Hueber Bldg. Co.,* 156 N. Y. Supp. 903, 904 (1916).

[62] John Dickinson, " Crowell v. Benson: Judicial Review of Administrative Determinations of Questions of ' Constitutional Fact,' " 80 *Univ. of Penna. Law Rev.* (June, 1932), 1059, 1060.

[63] See *Crowell* v. *Benson,* 285 U. S. 22 (1932). In relations to " basic," " pivotal," or " jurisdictional " facts, Chief Justice Hughes said: " It is the question whether Congress may substitute for the constitutional courts, in which the judicial power of the United States is vested, an administrative agency—in this instance, a single deputy commissioner—for the final

The customary attitude of the courts toward the review of a finding on a jurisdictional fact has been well stated by the California courts. An award of the industrial commission was held to be " subject to review and annullment in this court where the finding on any jurisdictional fact is without the support of substantial evidence, and this notwithstanding the provision of the act that the findings of the commission on questions of fact shall be conclusive and final "; [64] and " the court may, under a writ of certiorari, inquire into the sufficiency of the evidence to sustain findings of the jurisdictional facts underlying the power of the commission to award compensation." [65]   In Ohio, as in California, review is declared to be mainly on jurisdictional grounds, the prime questions being the relatively simple ones whether the claimant is an employee and whether he was injured in the course of employment.[66]

There is a tendency to consider a number of matters within the jurisdictional scope, such, for example, as the claim that a proper petition is jurisdictional and

determination of the existence of the facts upon which the enforcement of the constitutional rights of the citizen depend. The recognition of the utility and convenience of administrative agencies for the investigation and finding of facts within their proper province, and the support of their authorized action, does not require the conclusion that there is no limitation of their use, and that Congress should completely oust the courts of all determinations of fact by vesting the authority to make them with finality in its instrumentalities or in the executive department. That would be to sap the judicial power as it exists under the federal Constitution, and to establish a government of bureaucratic character alien to our system, wherever fundamental rights depend, as not infrequently they do depend, upon the facts, and finality as to facts becomes in effect finality in law." *Ibid.*, 56, 57.

[64] *Employers' Assurance Corporation* v. *Ind. Acc. Comm.*, 170 Cal. 800, 801, 151 Pac. 423 (1926).

[65] *Western Indemnity Co.* v. *Pillsbury*, 170 Cal. 686, 704, 151 Pac. 398 (1926).

[66] *State* v. *Ind. Comm.*, 180 N. E. 61 (1932) and *County of San Bernardino* v. *State Ind. Acc. Comm.*, 13 P. (2d) 829 (1932).

where there is no proper petition, no award can be upheld.[67] " It is of course the settled rule everywhere that these acts are to be liberally construed in favor of the workman," noted Chief Justice Wilson, " but this does not mean, as counsel seem to argue, that the rule as to the measure of proof, or the sufficiency of evidence, is different from the rule in ordinary cases. The burden is on the plaintiff to reasonably satisfy the trial court that the accident arose out of and in the course of the workman's employment." [68] Otherwise the industrial accident board does not have jurisdiction of the case. The *sine qua non* of the basis for a claim must be that the accident is in some manner related to the work or services of the employer, for the federal Supreme Court has intimated that without such an established relationship " an attempt to make the employer liable would be so clearly unreasonable and arbitrary as to subject it to the ban of the Constitution." [69] Where there is a disposition to sustain rather than to reverse the findings of fact of commissions, this result is arrived at by the statement that the commission's finding on a jurisdictional fact will be sustained if it could have been reached by reasonable men on the evidence presented.

That the matter of review on jurisdictional grounds in last analysis resolves itself into a point of view or method of approach by judges toward administrative tribunals is shown in the different results arrived at in the review of orders of the Interstate Commerce Commission and the Federal Trade Commission.[70] And it has been frequently

[67] *Deadwyler* v. *Consolidated Paper Co.,* 244 N. W. 484 (1932).

[68] *Sivald* v. *Ford Motor Co.,* 247 N. W. 687 (Minn., 1933), citing *State* v. *District Court,* 168 N. W. 555 (Minn., 1918).

[69] *Cudahy Packing Co.* v. *Parramore,* 263 U. S. 418, 423 (1923).

[70] " On a comparatively broad interpretation of legislative policy, the

pointed out that the duty to provide a trial *de novo* or a complete review of facts, which the jurisdictional fact doctrine considers an essential requirement of justice according to the common law, places an undue burden upon the judiciary and undermines the effectiveness of administrative action.

The way by which the courts arrived at the basis for judicial interference with the administrative application of rules or standards was the commonly asserted doctrine that an order or award will be set aside if there is no evidence to support it, or that the administrative determination could not rationally have been reached by fair-minded men from the evidence considered. This rule was obviously borrowed from the law governing court control of juries.[71] And it is based upon the commonly accepted assumption that in controversies before courts the law and the facts may be separated, the law being reserved for interpretation and application by the court and the facts being passed upon by the jury. So much significance is given to this practice by attorneys and judges in trials in compensation cases that some of the misconceptions related thereto may well be noted.

Analyzing the presumed basis for the separation of law and fact in common law trials, Professor Thayer, in his standard work on evidence,[72] claimed that " to be told that law is for the court and fact for the jury enlightens

Interstate Commerce Commission is sustained in the courts, while the orders of the Federal Trade Commission—subjected to abstract analysis of evidence with the purposes of the statute almost entirely ignored—are easily rejected by the courts." Carl McFarland, *Judicial Control of the Federal Trade Commission and the Interstate Commerce Commission, 1920-1930* (Cambridge, 1933) 17.

[71] Dickinson, *op. cit.,* 320.

[72] *A Preliminary Treatise on Evidence at the Common Law* (Boston, 1898), Ch. V.

us not at all as to the true discrimination between fact
and law." [73] The separation of law and fact is modified
by the practice, he observed, whereby the courts pass upon
many questions of fact that do not get on the record, or
form part of the issue, though this practice is often disguised by calling them questions of law. Defining law
as a rule or standard whose meaning and exact scope, as
well as the definition of terms relating thereto, belong to
the court for determination as questions of law, and considering whether a thing be a fact or not, i. e., whether it
exists or whether it is true, as involving issues to be left
to the jury, Professor Thayer maintained that " the judges
in such a system as ours, are thus forever advancing incidentally, but necessarily and as part of their duty, on the
theoretical province of the legislator and the juryman." [74]
And the most far-reaching basis for judicial control lies
in the contention that it is the duty of the court to see
that the jury keeps within the bounds of reason. In effect
a jury's verdict " must be defensible in point of sense; it
must not be absurd or whimsical." And the test applied
for this purpose is whether a reasonable person could,
upon the evidence, entertain the jury's opinion. Lord Coke
is quoted as insisting that a determination as to reasonableness can only be made in the light of a knowledge
of the law and therefore must be decided by the justices.

   For reasons of policy, Professor Thayer observed,
" courts still continue to retain the determination of a
part of the total issues of fact. If this were confessed,
instead of disguising a question of fact for the court under
the name of a question of law, much confusion would be
avoided." [75] And then the situation regarding the jury's
determination of facts was summarized as follows: " It
seems plain that the doctrine of our common law system

---

[73] *Ibid.*, 183.          [74] Thayer, *op. cit.*, 202.          [75] *Ibid.*, 230.

which allots to the jury the decision of disputed questions of ultimate fact, is to be taken with the gravest qualifications. Much fact which is part of the issue is for the judge; much which is for the jury is likely to be absorbed by the judge, ' whenever a rule about it can be laid down,' as regards all of it, the jury's action may be excluded or encroached upon by the cooperation of the judge with one or both of the parties; and, as regards all, the jury is subject to the supervision of the judge, in order to keep it within the limits of law and reason." [76] There is therefore good ground for the claim that there is no logical distinction between statements which are grouped by the courts under the phrases " statements of fact " and " conclusions of law." [77]

Regardless of the inherent difficulties and uncertainties involved in the supposed distinction between findings of fact and conclusions of law basically the review of the awards or orders of industrial accident boards is predicated upon this distinction. Placing in the courts the review of jurisdictional matters which involve the definition of most of the important phrases in a workmen's compensation act, the determination as to whether there is any evidence to support an award, and the decision whether the inferences arrived at by the board from the facts were such as reasonable men might approve, the judges have drawn a considerable percentage of cases of industrial accidents into the trial vortex, contrary to the obvious intentions in the enactment of workmen's compensation laws. Such a doctrine of review logically applied, noted Professor Dickinson, " would eviscerate the

[76] Thayer, *op. cit.*, 248, 249.

[77] Cf. Walter Wheeler Cook, " Statements of Fact in Pleading under the Codes." 21 *Colum. Law Rev.* (May, 1921) 417 and Nathan Isaacs, " The Law and the Facts," 22 *Colum. Law Rev.* (Jan., 1922) 1.

whole administrative process, and it is not applied logically; but enough of it is left to confuse very badly the utterances of the courts on the question of review of facts." [78]

## V

The professed theory of industrial accident law is that the employers or insurance companies should pay the loss due to accidents and that the cost should ultimately be passed on to the consumer. Actual practice does not conform to this theory. Although the Wisconsin law is rated by insurance companies as standing among the highest in its aggregate benefits, " employers in Wisconsin pay only about 30 per cent of the total loss sustained by injured workmen; and some compensation laws pay less than one-half the Wisconsin benefits." [79] What is actually accomplished by industrial accident legislation is a sharing of the economic loss between employers and employees on a predetermined basis, without reference to fault, and in accordance with a plan designed to insure prompt and certain recovery at a minimum of expense. Despite the fact that the objects to be attained have been only partially realized, the common-law theory of employers' liability has now been supplanted by the principle of workmen's compensation in all of the states of the Union with the exception of Arkansas, Florida, Mississippi and South Carolina.

The method of administration of the acts varies greatly in the different states. As a hold-over of the former common law liability system a few of the states have adopted the plan of court administration of industrial accident laws.

[78] Dickinson, *op. cit.,* 310.
[79] Edwin E. Witte, " The Theory of Workmen's Compensation," 20 *Amer. Lab. Leg. Rev.* (Dec., 1930) 412.

In Louisiana the administration of workmen's compensation is placed in charge of the courts and the law permits settlements of cases by agreement with the approval of the courts. Payments may be either for a lump sum or for the period of disability. The supreme court of Louisiana decided that a lump sum settlement discounted greatly in excess of eight per cent (as provided in the statute) was binding on the parties to a death claim, where there was doubt as to whether the death of the deceased employee was the result of an injury arising in the course of employment. By this decision, it is claimed, " the supreme court opened the door to a practice which undermines the whole intent and purpose of the state's compensation law. The practical effect of this holding is to make it possible for any employer, by raising a controversial issue and threatening litigation, to effect the settlement of any compensation claim against him for an amount greatly under that which the law actually provides for such injury." [80]

As a result of an investigation it was concluded that in all but a few of the cases where lump sum settlements had been agreed upon the amounts were considerably below the allotment due under the statute. The anxiety of attorneys to secure the full amount of their fees at once seems to be one of the principal factors in the encouragement of lump sum settlements.[81]

The law of Tennessee provides that all settlements must be approved by the courts, though less than two per cent are presented to the courts for approval. Settlements are made directly with the claimants, a copy being filed with

[80] See Gladys Nonan, "Administration of Workmen's Compensation Cases in Louisiana," 7 *Tulane Law Rev.* (Feb., 1933) 223 and *Musick* v. *Central Carbon Company*, 166 La. 355, 177 So. 277 (1928).

[81] See Gladys Nonan, *op. cit.*, 229 ff.

the department of labor. With the courts practically exercising no supervision over the agreements made and attorneys expecting a considerable part of the award in serious cases, court administration of the compensation act is declared to be a failure in Tennessee.[82]

The general conclusion is that the courts cannot successfully perform the administrative tasks which are essential to the enforcement of a workmen's compensation act. Four states, New Jersey, Minnesota, Kansas, and Nebraska, originally tried court administration and abandoned it in favor of the commission plan.

A few states combine the method of administrative procedure with provisions for trials in court on the demand of any party to a proceeding and a submission of questions of fact to the jury. In Maryland the procedure on appeal requires that upon motion of either party according to the practice in civil cases the court shall submit to a jury any question of fact involved in a compensation case. In this proceeding the findings and award of the commission are deemed prima facie correct.[83] Whether injuries were received in the course of employment and other issues of fact in Texas are submitted to a jury.[84] The district court in a trial *de novo* is vested with the same power as the industrial accident board to correct a mistake in a compensation claim.[85] So insistent are some of the rigid common law requirements in such trials that

[82] Consult, Tennessee Code, sec. 6877 and *Proceedings* of the International Association of Industrial Accident Boards and Commissions, 1927, p. 228 (cited hereafter as *Proceedings*); Alabama, New Hampshire, New Mexico, and Wyoming also depend primarily upon the courts for the administration of workmen's compensation acts.

[83] *Jewel Tea Co.* v. *Weber*, 103 A. 476 (1918).

[84] *Hartford Accident and Indemnity Co.* v. *Frye*, 55 S. W. (2d) 1092 (1932).

[85] *Fidelity Union Casualty Co.* v. *Dafferman*, 47 S. W. (2d) 408 (1932).

it has been held to be reversible error in the trial courts to prove what action was taken by the industrial accident board.

Most of the states place the authority to administer industrial accident legislation in a board or a commission with a right of appeal to the courts under certain statutory limitations. But the extent to which such boards participate in the process of administration varies considerably. The statutes as well as administrative practice frequently permit the settlement of accident claims by direct agreement between the parties with a visé of the agreements by the board and a right of appeal to the board for a hearing in case of failure to agree on controverted issues.

According to various estimates more than ninety per cent of all compensation claims are settled by direct agreement between the parties without reference to any tribunal. In Michigan an even larger percentage of cases are settled by agreements. For a number of years in New York such agreements when entered into were to be filed with the commission and if found to be in accord with the law were approved. Although the system resulted in a reduction of the period between the accident and the first payment of compensation, due to abuses arising from unwarranted discontinuances in the payment of claims, the system was abolished. It is contended that under the agreement system, as it has been applied in certain states, the injured employee or his dependents do not receive adequate compensation.[86]

The statute under which the Massachusetts board acts provides that in cases where the insurer and the employee are unable to agree, either party may ask for a hearing, which shall be held before a member of the board, who shall make such rulings of law and findings

[86] *Proceedings* (1922), p. 194 and (1925), p. 16.

of fact as the evidence warrants. This requires a proceeding similar to that of the ordinary trial. The board has
adopted an intermediate step, a conference which involves
an informal discussion, to which the parties are summoned
and at which the points of difference are discussed and if
possible a settlement reached. A large percentage of the
disputed cases are disposed of in this manner without
a formal hearing.

Certain states provide that all claims for compensation
must be presented to the industrial accident board. But
in practice a referee or examiner approves a large part of
claims on stipulations of the parties. In New York it is
estimated that ninety-three per cent of the cases determined by the decisions of the referees are disposed of
finally.

Fortunately the informal, arbitral, and non-controver-
sial method of dealing with industrial accident cases is
the prevailing practice in many states for the larger part
of the claims. The matter of the review of the findings
and awards of industrial accident boards can therefore
be readily exaggerated. Though a considerable number
of cases involving industrial accidents find their way into
the courts each year, in the great majority of accident
cases the referees or deputies and the commissions render
what are in effect final judgments. In fact, in certain states
the challenges of the awards of the commission and consequent reversals are almost negligible. According to a
recent summary of the review of the decisions of the
industrial accident board of California it was found
that—

In 10% of the cases a rehearing was requested.

In 3% of the cases a rehearing was granted.

In ½ of 1% of the cases appeals were taken to the
courts.

In $\frac{1}{4}$ of 1% of the cases a writ of review was granted. In $\frac{1}{8}$ of 1% of the cases the commission was reversed on appeal.[87]

Delaware has had seventeen appeals in compensation cases in eighteen years with only six awards of the board reversed, and Maine twenty-three cases appealed in six years with about the same number of reversals. Only 114 cases have been appealed to the Iowa supreme court in twenty years, though appeals on twenty-one cases in 1933 indicates that the litigation of cases is on the increase. In North Dakota employers are not permitted to appeal and only a few cases are appealed by claimants.

The extent of judicial review in some of the states may be indicated by the following summary: In Illinois out of 2,302 cases adjudicated by the commission during the current year there were 765 petitions for review and 143 cases of writs of certiorari to the circuit or superior courts. With 3,743 awards in Kansas from 1927 to 1934 there were 693 cases appealed to the courts and a reversal of the awards in 12% of the cases appealed. In Missouri 1,467 cases were appealed from 1927 to 1933 with reversals of the commission's orders in about 14% of the cases. Forty percent of the commission's awards are reversed in the cases appealed to the courts of Oklahoma. In Texas a large part of the cases considered by the industrial accident board are appealed to the courts. And in states with relatively few cases presented to the courts for consideration there are indications that litigation is increasing. The extent of the review of industrial accident cases by the courts is indicated by the following summary:

---

[87] These percentages are approximate. Another summary gives the percentage of the commissions' decisions annulled as .002 and the percentage of reversals on the cases appealed as 10.9.

SUMMARY OF WORKMEN'S COMPENSATION CASES FROM
SEPTEMBER, 1931 TO APRIL, 1934 *

| State | Cases | Appeals by Em-** ployers and In- surance Carriers | Appeals** by Claimants | Com-*** mission Sustained | Per cent Sustained | Com- mission Reversed | Per cent Reversed |
|---|---|---|---|---|---|---|---|
| Arizona | 24 | 8 | 14 | 14 | 58 | 10 | 42 |
| California [1] | 23 | 13 | 9 | 18 | 78 | 4 | 17 |
| California [2] | 48 | 29 | 19 | 26 | 54 | 21 | 44 |
| Colorado | 33 | 21 | 12 | 22 | 67 | 10 | 30 |
| Connecticut | 22 | 12 | 10 | 14 | 64 | 7 | 32 |
| Georgia | 53 | 33 | 20 | 46 | 87 | 7 | 13 |
| Idaho | 23 | 13 | 10 | 16 | 69 | 7 | 31 |
| Illinois | 58 | 44 | 14 | 31 | 53 | 27 | 47 |
| Indiana | 83 | 40 | 43 | 67 | 81 | 16 | 19 |
| Iowa | 14 | 9 | 5 | 9 | 64 | 5 | 36 |
| Kansas | 29 | 20 | 9 | 20 | 69 | 7 | 28 |
| Kentucky | 48 | 38 | 10 | 34 | 71 | 14 | 29 |
| Maryland | 20 | 12 | 8 | 11 | 55 | 9 | 45 |
| Massachusetts | 43 | 28 | 15 | 31 | 72 | 12 | 28 |
| Michigan | 41 | 31 | 10 | 29 | 71 | 12 | 29 |
| Minnesota | 65 | 45 | 20 | 53 | 82 | 11 | 17 |
| Missouri [3] | 18 | 12 | 6 | 14 | 78 | 4 | 22 |
| Missouri [4] | 121 | 98 | 23 | 91 | 75 | 30 | 25 |
| Montana | 8 | 5 | 3 | 4 | 50 | 4 | 50 |
| Nebraska | 35 | 24 | 11 | 20 | 57 | 14 | 40 |
| New Jersey | 52 | 45 | 7 | 44 | 85 | 8 | 15 |
| New York | 12 | 5 | 2 | 8 | 67 | 4 | 33 |
| North Carolina | 42 | 27 | 15 | 30 | 71 | 12 | 29 |
| North Dakota | 5 | 2 | 1 | 3 | 60 | 2 | 40 |
| Ohio [5] | 46 | 16 | 16 | 29 | 63 | 12 | 37 |
| Ohio [6] | 17 | 2 | 9 | 12 | 71 | 5 | 29 |
| Oklahoma | 437 | 416 | 15 | 270 | 62 | 163 | 37 |
| Oregon | 17 | 1 | 4 | 5 | 29 | 12 | 71 |
| Pennsylvania | 131 | 92 | 39 | 82 | 63 | 49 | 37 |
| Rhode Island | 1 | 1 | 0 | 1 | 100 | 0 | 0 |
| South Dakota | 12 | 11 | 0 | 7 | 58 | 5 | 42 |

* In this table, prepared by Edward Walther, Research Assistant in Political Science, all but a few of the cases reported in the National Reporter System from September, 1931 to April, 1934 were analysed. As a rule only cases appealed to the state supreme court are reported, but in a few states such as California, Missouri, Ohio, and Texas cases decided in the intermediate courts of appeal are included. Since these decisions usually result in a final judgment they are listed in the tabulation.
** To indicate the main source of appeals those for which the employers and insurance carriers and those for which claimants are responsible are listed. A few cases are appealed by the industrial accident commission or by other interested parties. These appeals are not included in this column.
*** Decisions in which awards are modified are not included, but the cases in which the commission is sustained with an increase or decrease in the amount awarded are listed as sustained.
[1] Supreme Court of California.     [4] Courts of Appeal, Missouri.
[2] District Courts of Appeal, California.     [5] Supreme Court, Ohio.
[3] Supreme Court, Missouri.     [6] Courts of Appeal, Ohio.

| State | Cases | Appeals by Em-[**] ployers and In- surance Carriers | Appeals[**] by Claimants | Com-[***] mission Sustained | Per cent Sustained | Com- mission Reversed | Per cent Reversed |
|---|---|---|---|---|---|---|---|
| Texas [7] | 10 | 6 | 4 | 5 | 50 | 5 | 50 |
| Texas [8] | 69 | 51 | 15 | 35 | 51 | 34 | 49 |
| Utah | 33 | 16 | 17 | 17 | 52 | 16 | 48 |
| Virginia | 14 | 11 | 3 | 8 | 59 | 6 | 41 |
| Washington | 41 | 0 | 16 | 23 | 56 | 18 | 44 |
| West Virginia | 41 | 4 | 37 | 16 | 39 | 25 | 61 |
| Wisconsin | 45 | 36 | 5 | 30 | 67 | 15 | 33 |
| | 1834 | 1277 70—% | 476 26—% | 1195 65+% | | 622 34+% | |

[7] Commission of Appeals, Texas.          [8] Courts of Civil Appeals, Texas.

Contrary to the main purposes and objectives of industrial accident law an examination of the cases reviewed
by the courts shows an increase in the amount of compensation litigation.  Instead of the gradual development of
standards for the disposal of cases there is a disposition
to resolve each case upon its own peculiar circumstances
and facts.[88]  Provisions of existing compensation laws are
not infrequently based upon common law theories or statutory phrases strictly interpreted to the serious impairment
of an effective carrying out of the object of such laws.
Courts have in many instances failed to deal with the
compensation acts as providing a new juristic scheme and
hence have tended to restrict rather than to develop the
body of compensation law.  And the matter of the gravest
importance in most jurisdictions is the constant efforts of

[88] Charles M. Kahn, " The Workmen's Compensation Law," 1 *Idaho
Law Journ.* (Feb., 1931), 56, 72.  Recognizing the uncertainty prevailing
in the decisions of the courts on the question whether a claimant was an
employee or an independent contractor, the supreme court of Nebraska
reversed the compensation commissioner and the district court and insisted that it is for the court to determine the question from the circumstances of each particular case. *Showers* v. *Lund,* 242 N. W. 258 (1932).

some insurance companies to escape their moral and legal obligations by resorting to minor technicalities.[89]

Unless there is a strong and independent state board to administer the workmen's compensation laws there are some marked inequities in the handling of claims. The insurers have separate departments for such claims with lawyers doing compensation work only and with trained experts and investigators. Many competent and well known lawyers will not represent workers in industrial accident cases. Few claimants are able to employ counsel except upon a contingent fee basis. Compensation boards and bar associations have only begun to eradicate the evils connected with the contingent fee system. Legal aid societies render aid in such cases but they can give assistance in comparatively few cases. The situation is one in which the state through its organized agencies should obviously participate to a greater extent than has yet been undertaken to establish somewhat nearer parity in the interests of the parties concerned.[90]

## VI

In an attempt to evaluate the prevalence of court review of the findings and awards of industrial accident boards and the effects of such review upon the development of this branch of the law, one is impressed with the observation of Sir Maurice Sheldon Amos that " in the English-

---

[89] See comment of Commissioner Walter O. Stark, *Proceedings* (1931), p. 3.

[90] " In spite of the efforts of legislature and commission to equalize the position of the claimant and the respondent," notes Professor Brown, " it is indubitable that the ideal of perfect parity is not attained. Unfortunately justice has not yet attained to the position where the employee usually impecunious and often uninformed does not suffer some disadvantage when competing against the experienced, intelligent, and financially superior employer and insurer." *The Administration of Workmen's Compensation*, 57, 58.

speaking world the profession and administration of the law suffers and has long suffered from the overweening and unbalanced emphasis placed upon litigation." [91]   A field in which simplicity, expeditious settlements, and a minimum of expense should be the prevailing practice in the disposal of cases, attorneys, insurance specialists, and so-called " adjusters " have been permitted to prey upon the weak and defenseless often with the apparent sanction of the agencies for the administration of justice. Though the claimants themselves aided and abetted by lay " advisers " or attorneys who specialize in this type of litigation frequently insist upon litigation rather than the acceptance of a compromise settlement, too many cases are brought to the courts by employers or by insurance carriers who expect to gain advantages through delay and expensive litigation.[92]

Commenting on the English practice about a score of years ago Lord Wrenbury said: " No recent act has provoked a larger amount of litigation than the workmen's compensation act. The few and seemingly simple words ' arising out of and in the course of the employment ' have been the fruitful (or fruitless) source of a mass of decisions turning upon nice distinctions and supported by refinements so subtle as to leave the mind of the reader in a maze of confusion. From their number counsel can, in most cases, cite what seems to be an authority for resolving in his favor, on whichever side he may be, the question in dispute." [93]   That lapse of time and a multiplicity of suits have not clarified the meaning of these

[91] From the lecture on " Roscoe Pound " in *Modern Theories of the Law* (London, 1933), 87.

[92] More than two-thirds of industrial accident cases are appealed to the courts by employers or insurance carriers. Cf. table, *supra*.

[93] *Herbert* v. *Samuel Fox & Co., Ltd.* [1916] 1 A. C. 405, 419.

words is the claim of Justice Offut of the court of appeals of Maryland, who quoted an earlier case in that state to the effect that after the examination of many cases defining these words, the precedents furnish little aid or assistance in determining their meaning and effect. Practically their meaning must be considered in connection with the facts of each particular case.[94] The interpretation of these words by the industrial commission and the courts has, indeed, been no easy task, and in the judgment of Professor Brown the administrative and judicial gloss in a twenty year period have added little to the clarity of the workmen's compensation act.[95]

The avowed purpose of the compensation acts is " to give compensation when the employee is at the time of the injury performing an act reasonably incidental to his employment." But considerable uncertainty and injustice have resulted in certain cases in which the courts have held that employees who, during the regular course of their employment, temporarily and casually have departed from the strict line of duty to administer to the wants of themselves or of third persons, were outside the course of employment.[96] The prevailing uncertainty as to the definition of " casual " employment and as to whether an employment is " hazardous " has been a matter of frequent comment.[97] And the requirement that a real basis

[94] *Schemmel* v. *Gatch & Sons Contracting and Bldg. Co.*, 166 A. 39, 43 (1933).

[95] R. A. Brown, " 'Arising out of and in the Course of the Employment ' in Workmen's Compensation Acts," 7 *Wis. Law Rev.* (Dec., 1931) 16.

[96] Brown, *op. cit.*, 20-22.

[97] See *Gardner* v. *Trustees of Main Street Methodist Episcopal Church*, 244 N. W. 667 (Ia., 1932)—death of employee killed while assisting in excavation of building under construction by a church, held not within ordinary purpose or business of a church; *Covington Motor Co.* v. *Partridge*, 8 P. (2d) 1097 (Okla., 1932)—driving an automobile while collecting bills for employer; *Slick* v. *Voyett*, 16 P. (2d) 237 (Okla.,

for a claim can arise only when there is an accident arising out of the course of employment has been a fruitful source of contentions to deny compensation. So many difficulties arose in determining what is an "accident" that an amendment was added to the Wisconsin law extending the act to include "in addition to accidental injuries, all other injuries including occupational diseases growing out of and incidental to the employment." [98]

Should there not be a more effective and expeditious procedure than a trial in the supreme court of the state to determine whether pain in the feet of an automobile helper or the freezing of a diseased foot,[99] or whether the loss of hearing caused by the noise of escaping gas from a wild oil well,[100] resulted from an "accidental personal injury?" Are the industrial commission and the district court or the supreme court of a state in the better position to determine finally whether an injury was a refracture or merely acute manifestation of neuritis caused by a former injury? [101]

Commissions, courts, and legal writers, it is claimed, have only an intimation as to what should be done, which they are unable to rationalize by the written word. Despite attempts at interpretation of now familiar phrases in many cases by commissions and courts, confusion remains. One conclusion appears obvious from the prevailing con-

1932)—playing baseball under orders and pay of employer; *Hoffman* v. *Broadway Hazelwood*, 10 P. (2d) 349 (Ore., 1932)—employment as a baker, restaurant and confectionery held not a workshop.

[98] Cf. *Wis. Stat.* (1929), sec. 102, 35.

[99] Cf. *Ford Motor Co.* v. *Scruggs*, 7 P. (2d) 479 (Okla., 1932) and *Wright* v. *Keith*, 15 P. (2d) 429 (Kan., 1932), setting aside awards of the Industrial Commission.

[100] *Indian Territory Illuminating Oil Co.* v. *Warren*, 15 P. (2d) 830 (Okla., 1932).

[101] See *Goodwin* v. *Sinclair Pipe Line Co.*, 12 P. (2d) 842 (Kan., 1932).

flicts of opinion and uncertainties, namely, that the facts and problems presented in industrial accident cases are too varied and complex to be resolved by legalistic formulas.[102] Where the legislature has granted to an administrative agency authority to deal with difficult and intricate problems connected with our economic and social life, the courts by insisting upon their prerogative to expound the precise meaning of the language of statutes frequently " do violence to the conception and nature of delegated legislative power." [103]

A representative opinion of the legal fraternity is that of President Hardgrove of the Wisconsin Bar Association. Mr. Hardgrove believes that the trial *de novo* should be made the rule in the judicial review of administrative action; that a finding of an administrative agency on any question of fact should not be made conclusive except in case of technical questions in respect to which a court would be compelled, were the question to arise in ordinary litigation, to resort to expert witnesses. Only by resort to such a trial will the citizen be protected in his private rights.[104] We have here an indication of the supreme regard for private rights of property and contract which is so characteristic of the traditional common law procedure. The fact that a court trial is a luxury which only the rich or well-to-do can afford under conditions that are creditable to lawyers and litigants alike, that the courts are seriously overcrowded because of the rapidly

---

[102] " Legal texts and decisions of courts play but a small part in the commission's deliberations. The dependence seems not to be on the written words of court or commentator, but on an intimate knowledge of Wisconsin statutes and on an intuitive judgment, founded upon years of practical experience in the law's administration." Brown, *The Administration of Workmen's Compensation*, 81.

[103] McFarland, *op. cit.*, 20.

[104] See Bulletin of the State Bar Association of Wisconsin, 1931, p. 134.

increasing controversies arising out of our modern complex industrial civilization, and that court procedure in a number of lines has not been adjusted to take care of the extreme pressure of judicial business, do not deter members of the legal profession from urging a return to the old order wherein the individual rights of person and property are to be adjudicated entirely by the courts.

The special committee on administrative law of the American Bar Association objects to the practice of administrative officers and boards in exercising judicial functions.[105] In their opinion it would be better by the reform of court procedure to have the hearing and trial of all cases in courts of justice. One is not impressed in a study of the legislation and administration in the field of industrial accident law with the readiness or ability of the legal profession to adopt reforms designed to secure substantial justice in industrial accident cases. Nor do the delay, expense, and frequent applications of the technicalities of the law in the review of industrial accident cases augur well for a return to the traditional practice of a judicial trial for the settlement of cases of this kind. Not only in the trial of cases involving awards for accidents but also much too frequently in the proceedings before commissions the rigid and technical rules that grew up in connection with the common law, the lack of confidence in the trial judge and particularly in the jury, and the naturally contentious nature of legal proceedings have been applied to the procedure regardless of their inapplicability or of the evil effects involved.[106]

It is indeed true that " lawyers place emphasis upon a

[105] Cf. Report of Special Committee on Administrative Law, 59 *Amer. Bar Assoc. Proceedings,* pp. 200 ff.

[106] Herbert D. Laube, "Administrative Problems in Wisconsin's Workmen's Compensation," 3 *Wis. Law Rev.* (Jan., 1925), 83.

traditional set of values such as the separation of powers of government, the supremacy of an independent judiciary, proof of every allegation according to time-tried rules of evidence, testing each witness by cross examination, deliberation, jury trial, and the appeal. We know the price we pay is delay, technicality and expense. However, the public is placing its insistence upon a different set of values. It seeks speedy settlement, finality, and freedom from the procedural contentions it pays for, but does not understand." [107]

For those who desire to turn over to the courts again the hearing and trial of all controversies involving the rights of parties, the prospect does not appear promising for an early disposal of the mass of accident cases. During 1930, some three-quarters of a million actions at law were begun in New York City. About one-third of these cases involved accident litigation. The courts are primarily engaged, Professor Oliphant observes, in (a) allocating the risks of accidents arising from modern machine culture and (b) collecting debts as a part of existing credit machinery. Under the present congested conditions it requires from eighteen months to three years for a case to come to trial.[108] How can courts functioning so ineffectively absorb the hundreds of thousands of industrial accident cases and numerous other controversies now disposed of by administrative boards? There may be " urgent reasons for promptly seeking the remedy for the present congested condition of many courts not in some outside

[107] Robert H. Jackson, " The Lawyer; Leader or Mouthpiece," 18 *Amer. Jud. Soc.* (Oct., 1934), 73.

[108] Herman Oliphant, " The Public and the Law—The Three Major Criticisms and Their Validity," 19 *Amer. Bar. Assoc. Jour.* (1933) 46. According to the commission on the administration of justice in New York state 58 per cent of trials take place a year or more after the case is at issue. See *Report*, 1934, p. 12.

agency but in the structures and processes of the courts themselves," but until more substantial progress is made in the direction of relieving the courts in the trial of cases now awaiting determination, those seeking speedy and inexpensive settlement of the controversies resulting from the present complex industrial and social life are likely to continue to favor administrative tribunals with their informal and expeditious procedure.

It may be well for those who wish to carry out the original objects of the workmen's compensation laws to consider the adoption in the American states of a system similar to that in effect in all but a few of the Canadian provinces. The general principle of the Canadian plan with respect to the review of accident cases may be illustrated by the provisions of the Ontario act. Under this statute no action shall lie for the recovery of compensation whether it is payable by the employer individually or out of the accident fund, but all claims for compensation shall be heard and determined by the board. The workmen's compensation board is to have exclusive jurisdiction as to all questions arising under this part of the act and its action or decision is final and conclusive, and not open to question or review by the courts or subject to restraint by injunction or otherwise.[109]

Reporting on this phase of Canadian industrial accident law before the commissioners of the United States and Canada, Mr. Kingston observed: "I think, Mr. Chairman, I may extend my sympathy to the officers of

---

[109] The pertinent language of the act is as follows: "The action or decision of the board thereon shall be final and conclusive and shall not be open to question or review in any court and no proceedings by or before the board shall be restrained by injunction, prohibition or other process or proceeding in any court or be removable by certiorari or otherwise into any court. Sec. 67 (1); also sec. 74 (1) of the British Columbia Act and sec. 64 of the Saskatchewan Act.

the compensation boards on the question of appeals. We are fortunately situated in Ontario; we are supreme courts in ourselves. There is no appeal from our decisions except as to rehearing, and that is taken very informally. I think in the year and three or four months since our act has been in force, action for rehearing has not been taken in more than 1 per cent of the cases, probably not that number. The lawyer has been absolutely read out of our act. The chief justice of Ontario was the instrument in framing our law." [110]

That the system of authorizing an industrial accident board to render final decisions is working satisfactorily in some of the Canadian provinces is indicated by the fact that neither organized labor nor organized employers have requested legislation to secure appeals from the final awards of the board.

The Canadian provinces establish state funds for compensation claims which are compulsory and exclusive. No contributions to the fund are made by the provinces. Instead, the act merely gives to the administering board the taxing power of the province for the purpose of raising by assessment the amount necessary to pay the cost of industrial accidents. Under this system it is claimed that a larger part of every dollar paid by the employer goes to the benefit of the workman or his dependents than under the American practice of providing protection through private agencies or partial state fund systems.

In industrial accident litigation, as in other branches of the law, certain assumptions have stood in the way of the elimination of litigation according to the original intent of most of the acts of the states. One of these assumptions, that only a judge " amid the trappings of the law " can settle controversies involving individual, personal, and

[110] *Proceedings*, 1917, p. 31.

property rights in a reasonable and judicious manner, serves as the foundation for judicial review of administrative action. Imbued with Lord Coke's philosophy, those who support this assumption believe that reasoning in accordance with law by those trained in the law is the only form of reasoning that can have finality when private rights are involved. Though we have gone a long way from the application of the strict and pure form of Coke's doctrine in the development of various branches of the law, there are many who insist that regardless of statutory or constitutional provisions to the contrary, it is the duty of courts to assert the prerogative to review administrative or executive action when individuals insist that their private rights have been violated. No finality can attach to findings of fact or conclusions of law when the judge steps in the breach to preserve the asserted rights of litigants in accordance with common law standards.

The distinction between fact and law is one of the devices which has served the purpose of retaining the desired judicial surveillance. It has a better sound to insist that the court intervenes only to assure the accuracy and certainty of conclusions of law. But only by the examination of the evidence can the appropriate conclusions of the law be extracted. Hence the whole case, at least so far as evidence may be presented or as the record discloses, is before the court. Or if no conclusion of law appears upon the horizon, then " the reasonable man " myth may be called upon, since reasonableness belongs, said Lord Coke, to the knowledge of the law alone, and hence the decision upon the evidence must be scanned to determine whether it is such a decision as a reasonable man could have given under the circumstances. By these devices, as Professor Thayer observed, the judges in our system of jurisprudence continue to advance necessarily, they think, and as part

of their duty, upon the theoretical province of the juryman, the legislator, and the administrator. It is the failure
of the judiciary to accord due respect to 'he findings of
administrative boards that has impaired th e efficiency and
weakened the responsibility of the workmen's compensation commissions.[111]

The interpretation and enforcement of law in the
United States is predicated too largely upon another
assumption, namely, that administration through other
agencies than courts is certain to be arbitrary, inefficient,
and unjust. And to those imbued with conservative legal
principles, the present trend toward the enlargement of
the scope and functions of administrative agencies, particularly in what are regarded as their quasi-judicial functions, is a matter for grave apprehension. The view of
the majority of the legal fraternity, as may be judged from
the expressions of active and assertive leaders throughout
the country, was perhaps best expressed by Chief Justice
Hughes when he said: "The power of administrative
bodies to make findings of fact which may be treated as
conclusive, if there is evidence both ways, is a power of
enormous consequence. An unscrupulous administrator
might be tempted to say, 'Let me find the facts for the
people of my country, and I care little who lays down the
general principles.'"[112]

Supporters of these assumptions seem to forget that a
large part of civil controversies have always been settled
by informal, arbitral methods outside of regularly established courts. The increasing use of arbitration for commercial disputes in many countries is indicative of the
fact that traders, merchants, and those engaged in business

[111] Cf. Ross, *op. cit.,* 269, 270.
[112] C. J. Hughes, New York Times, February 13, 1931 at p. 8. Quoted
in note on *Crowell* v. *Benson,* 46 *Harv. Law Rev.* (Jan., 1933), 490.

transactions prefer the informal procedure of arbitration to the slow and expensive procedure of courts. Industrial accident boards act to a large extent as boards of arbitration and follow in the main the arbitral plan of adjusting the industrial disputes arising out of accidents. There are indeed, as Professor Robson insists, " more judges under the high heaven than those who sit in courts." [118]

No one who examines the procedure of industrial accident boards or considers the awards of such boards can fail to realize that there are some serious defects in the present method of administering workmen's compensation laws. But it is questionable, indeed, whether these defects are being remedied in the system of judicial review which has evolved in accident litigation.

The query may well be raised whether the time has not come to take such administrative tribunals as industrial accident boards for granted, to facilitate their smooth and expeditious functioning, and not to hamper them by insistence upon the formal procedure of court trials and by frequent reversals based largely upon differences of opinion as to matters of fact well within the scope of the industrial commission's authority.

It may be desirable to develop a form of review through special administrative courts and until such courts are established a limited form of review by existing courts on jurisdictional grounds may be insisted upon to conform to the judicially construed requirements of due process of law. But the experience of the Canadian provinces demonstrates that such jurisdictional review is not a necessary requirement to secure substantial justice to the parties concerned.

[118] William A. Robson, *Justice and Administrative Law* (London, 1928) 72.

# Retirement or Refunding of Utility Bonds [*]

BY

MILO R. MALTBIE

The rapid increase in the indebtedness of public service corporations, operating as well as holding companies, and the numerous changes in economic conditions which have taken place in the last four years have caused many to challenge the general practice of utility companies to refund rather than to retire bond issues. Although the universal application of either policy is unsound, there are certain considerations which may assist in charting a course, particularly for operating companies. Holding companies which have no physical property and which have issued bonds to cover the price paid for stocks at the high prices prevailing in 1925-9 will not be considered here. Those who are responsible for such practices have been or will be called to account in due time. The unfortunate part of it is that sound operating companies have been injured by the corrupt and corrupting methods of certain groups which have fleeced thousands of trusting investors.

It should be said at the start that as the financial soundness of a company is not determined by any one factor appearing in a balance sheet or even by an income statement, many elements must be weighed, first separately and then collectively. Possibly the most important is depreciation, for there are many operating companies which have depreciation or retirement reserves of two, four, or six percent, which are refunding every issue of bonds and which are raising funds for every extension and betterment by the issue of new securities—bonds or stocks.

* Mr. Maltbie's article was completed January 1, 1934, and hence does not take into consideration any development which may have occurred since that time.—EDITOR.

Such companies are headed for disaster unless they change their policies either voluntarily or by order of a public authority. But let us define depreciation so that there may be no misunderstanding as to what we are discussing.

## Depreciation

Depreciation is the decline in the value of property from any cause which operates to terminate ultimately its useful life. Decline in value due to changes in price levels is not included here; that will be referred to later. Now a corporation may maintain a sound financial condition in relation thereto either by increasing its assets or by decreasing its liabilities to the extent that its properties depreciate. To illustrate: Let us assume that at the beginning a corporation had assets equal in value to its outstanding obligations and that the plant has depreciated to the extent of $100,000 in a given period. If no attention is paid to such depreciation, the corporation will impair its assets, and the liabilities will exceed by $100,000 the value of the assets at the end of the period. This result may be avoided either by increasing its assets, i. e., purchasing additional property to the extent of $100,000 without incurring any other liabilities, or by retiring liabilities to the extent of $100,000, without disposing of any assets. It is the duty of every corporation to maintain a sound financial condition and never to allow its assets to become impaired.

The principle is thoroughly established and generally accepted that the rates charged by a public utility should be sufficient not only to compensate the owners for the use of their property but also to reimburse them for any portion of their investment which is consumed, destroyed, or otherwise used up or lessened in value during its use for utility purposes. This is accomplished in the case of items of property which are used up quickly, such as coal, repair materials, small tools, gasoline, oil, etc., by including their cost in operating expenses immediately, so that the corporation is reimbursed for them at once. But in the case of an item of property used up gradually, it is not practicable to include the whole cost in operating expenses when the using up process begins. To do so would burden consumers in the early stages of the utility, leaving later consumers to gain a benefit for which they would not pay. It is also unfair to include the whole cost when the using up process ends, since the earlier consumers have a benefit for which they pay nothing.

### Fixed Property Account

Hence, the practice has long been established of charging to a permanent asset account, commonly called " fixed capital " or " fixed property," all property that is to be used for a considerable period of time. In utility accounting, a line is usually drawn at one year, and all classes of property which commonly last longer than one year are included in such account, while those lasting less than one year are charged directly to operating expenses. The term of one year is somewhat arbitrary and is established for convenience in accounting; there is no essential difference between the two classes of property. A tank of gasoline which is consumed entirely in one year is chargeable to operating expenses; the automobile which is consumed (except for salvage value) in three years is also properly chargeable to operating expenses because it is just as truly consumed in the service of the public. The same is true of the building lasting fifty years or the water pipes lasting one hundred. There is no dispute on this point. But differences of opinion arise as to when and how the cost of these items shall be included in operating expenses and as to how their value shall be computed for rate purposes in the intermediate stages of their life.

As already stated, all expenditures for property expected to have a life greater than one year are included in the fixed property account. Once made, these entries remain unchanged under proper accounting as long as the property remains in service. When it is retired from service for any reason—because it has worn out or has become obsolete or inadequate (too small for the amount of service required), or because public improvements require that the utility plant be removed from certain locations, or for any other reason—the amount originally entered for this particular item of property is removed from the fixed property account, so that the account may show at all times the actual amounts expended for property presently in existence and in use for utility service.

The accounting methods just described are universally used and recognized as correct by commissions, courts, and the utilities themselves.

Up to this point, there is no provision for payment by the customers of the cost of the property retired from service (or rather the investment so consumed, i. e., the difference between its cost when installed and its salvage value when retired).

There are four methods of distributing this cost, this consumption of property or capital, which have been used to considerable extent by utilities in this country. There are others, but the discussion of these four will be sufficient to lay a basis for what follows. They fall into two groups.

1. Retirement Accounting:
   (a) The retirement method.
   (b) The equalized retirement method.

2. Depreciation Accounting:
   (a) The straight line method.
   (b) The sinking fund method.

## 1. *Retirement Accounting*

Under strict retirement accounting, when property is retired, its full cost less salvage is included in operating expenses, and rates should be charged high enough to enable these charges to be made and a fair return earned in addition. No reserve is built up in advance to meet these charges. As they occur, they are included in operating expenses, even though they may be very high in one year and very low in another.

Under the equalized retirements method, instead of charging retirement losses occurring in each year to operating expenses in that year, an estimate is made of the average charges over a period of years, a reserve is set up by charging that *estimated amount* to operating expenses each year, whether the actual retirements are greater or less, and a corresponding credit is made to a reserve account. The actual retirement loss in each year is then charged against this reserve, which may have a plus (credit) or a minus (debit) balance at any particular time. Under this system, if large, unexpected retirements are made which would give the retirement reserve a large minus (debit) balance at any one time, this amount is wiped out in later years when the credits to the reserve exceed the retirement charges.

It is claimed by the advocates of this kind of accounting that utility property is neither used up nor lessened in value to any extent until it is actually removed from service, and that as it always has its full original value (cost) until it is retired, each item of property must be retained in the rate base and shown on the balance sheet at its full cost, without deduction for depreciation, up to the time that it is retired.

Of course, these claims are fallacious and contrary to all experience. It is common knowledge that the value of a unit of property does not pass from 100 percent to zero instantaneously at the moment of retirement from service. Even the imaginary " one-hoss shay " did not have a value equal to its cost new the moment before it collapsed. One does not need to be a trained economist to appreciate this fact, and every company that follows retirement accounting has impaired assets except at the very beginning of the property. The assets are gradually decreasing in value, and under retirement accounting no reserve is created, no property is added without increasing obligations, and no obligations are retired. Hence the balance existing at the beginning of the company is gradually destroyed.[1]

## 2. *Depreciation Accounting*

Depreciation accounting is based on the theory that the capital represented by an item of property is not all consumed in the month or the year in which it is actually retired from service but that it has been used up gradually throughout its entire life; that the customers served during its life have benefited from its use, from the consumption of capital that has taken place day by day, just as certainly as they have benefited from the materials physically consumed day by day; and that the proportionate part of the capital consumed should be charged as an operating expense in each accounting period during the service life, and not all at once when final retirement takes place.

---

[1] What may be done with surplus is not here considered. We are discussing only the effect of retirement accounting. The use and functions of other reserves and surplus are another matter.

The straight line method provides for the equal distribution of the capital consumed (the retirement loss, the difference between cost and salvage) over the total service life. In other words, if the item of property lasts ten years, the consumers who are served in the first year pay one-tenth of the cost less salvage, those served in the second year one-tenth, and likewise those served in the tenth year one-tenth.

It is obvious that if the consumers receiving service in the first year pay one-tenth of the cost (less salvage) of property which would last ten years, the owners of the property (the investors) are not entitled to collect a return thereon any longer and that this amount must in equity be deducted from the original investment in determining a rate base thereafter. Under this method accordingly, the rate base is materially below the original cost of the property (except when all new), this reduction appearing in the accounts as a balance in the depreciation reserve on the liability side of the balance sheet, but representing in fact not a liability due to creditors but a deduction from fixed assets. Indeed, on the balance sheets of industrial companies, it is usually shown as a deduction from fixed capital.

The depreciation reserve is not an idle fund or a pure fiction. In first instance, it is represented by cash, coming into the treasury of the company as customers pay their bills. It is a part of the rates for service. Then it is used almost invariably to pay for additions to the system or for improvements, which are charged to fixed capital account. As no stocks, bonds, or other obligations are issued to pay for these additions or improvements, the record of the operation appears in the increase in fixed capital (asset side). The increase in the depreciation reserve (liability side) appeared when the charge was made to operating expenses. As the two exactly equal each other, the financial status of the company has been preserved, the decline in the value of the old property has been offset by the acquisition of other property, and the obligations to investors (stocks, bonds, notes, etc.) remain unchanged. If there is no need for additions or improvements, the cash may be used to pay off liabilities instead.

The sinking fund method is also based upon the fundamental principles of depreciation accounting. It is much more complex than the straight line method, because it provides for the earning of interest by the depreciation reserve (whether invested in outside investments, in the utility's own bonds, or, as is most usual, in additional utility property). On account of this interest earned by the depreciation reserve, the amount that is necessarily charged to operating expense annually is somewhat less in the earlier years than under the straight line method. The difference is not large, except in utilities such as water and hydro-electric generating companies where the average life of the property is very great. There are other variations which it is unnecessary to discuss here.

To sum up, depreciation accounting is consistent with the common experience that the value of a unit of property decreases gradually during its life from its cost new to its salvage value. When depreciation accounting is used, the investment is maintained intact by the acquisition of additional assets or the reduction of liabilities to the extent that the value of the original assets has been impaired.

*Comparison of Retirement and Depreciation Accounting*

The following table illustrates the results from the retirement, straight line, and sinking fund methods. The " equalized retirement " method is too indefinite to express in figures. The example is an item of property having a value of $1,000 and a service life of 10 years, assuming 6 percent, for fair return and interest rate (used only in the sinking fund method). For sake of simplicity, it is also assumed in this table that there will be no salvage at time of retirement and that the value at the beginning of each year is the value upon which the fair return for that year is to be reckoned.

| Retirement Method | Book Cost of Property | Depreciation Reserve | Book Value of Property | Fair Return | Operating Expense Charge | Return Plus Charge |
|---|---|---|---|---|---|---|
| 1 year | $1,000 | ..... | $1,000 | $60 | ..... | $60 |
| 2 years | 1,000 | ..... | 1,000 | 60 | ..... | 60 |
| 3 years | 1,000 | ..... | 1,000 | 60 | ..... | 60 |
| 4 years | 1,000 | ..... | 1,000 | 60 | ..... | 60 |
| 5 years | 1,000 | ..... | 1,000 | 60 | ..... | 60 |
| 6 years | 1,000 | ..... | 1,000 | 60 | ..... | 60 |
| 7 years | 1,000 | ..... | 1,000 | 60 | ..... | 60 |
| 8 years | 1,000 | ..... | 1,000 | 60 | ..... | 60 |
| 9 years | 1,000 | ..... | 1,000 | 60 | ..... | 60 |
| 10 years | 1,000 | ..... | 1,000 | 60 | $1,000 | $1,060 |
| Total | .... | ..... | .... | $600 | $1,000 | $1,600 |

Straight-line Method

| Retirement Method | Book Cost of Property | Depreciation Reserve | Book Value of Property | Fair Return | Operating Expense Charge | Return Plus Charge |
|---|---|---|---|---|---|---|
| 1 year | $1,000 | .... | $1,000 | $60 | $100 | $160 |
| 2 years | 1,000 | $100 | 900 | 54 | 100 | 154 |
| 3 years | 1,000 | 200 | 800 | 48 | 100 | 148 |
| 4 years | 1,000 | 300 | 700 | 42 | 100 | 142 |
| 5 years | 1,000 | 400 | 600 | 36 | 100 | 136 |
| 6 years | 1,000 | 500 | 500 | 30 | 100 | 130 |
| 7 years | 1,000 | 600 | 400 | 24 | 100 | 124 |
| 8 years | 1,000 | 700 | 300 | 18 | 100 | 118 |
| 9 years | 1,000 | 800 | 200 | 12 | 100 | 112 |
| 10 years | 1,000 | 900 | 100 | 6 | 100 | 106 |
| Total | .... | ..... | .... | $330 | $1,000 | $1,330 |

| Sinking-fund Method | Book Cost of Property | Depreciation Reserve | Book Value of Property | Fair Return | Operating Expense Charge | Return Plus Charge |
|---|---|---|---|---|---|---|
| 1 year | $1,000 | . . . . . | $1,000 | $60 | $75.87 | $135.87 |
| 2 years | 1,000 | $75.87 | 924.13 | 60 | 75.87 | 135.87 |
| 3 years | 1,000 | 156.30 | 843.70 | 60 | 75.87 | 135.87 |
| 4 years | 1,000 | 241.55 | 758.45 | 60 | 75.87 | 135.87 |
| 5 years | 1,000 | 331.90 | 668.10 | 60 | 75.87 | 135.87 |
| 6 years | 1,000 | 427.69 | 572.31 | 60 | 75.87 | 135.87 |
| 7 years | 1,000 | 529.22 | 470.78 | 60 | 75.87 | 135.87 |
| 8 years | 1,000 | 636.84 | 363.16 | 60 | 75.87 | 135.87 |
| 9 years | 1,000 | 750.90 | 249.10 | 60 | 75.87 | 135.87 |
| 10 years | 1,000 | 871.82 | 128.18 | 60 | 75.87 | 135.87 |
| Total | . . . . | . . . . . | . . . . . | $600 | $758.70 | $1,358.70 |

It will be noted that the combined charge for return and depreciation is constant under the sinking-fund method, while under the straight-line method it is greater during the first half of the service life and less during the last half. On the other hand, under the retirement method, the charge is less in every year except the last, when it is much greater.

The large excess of total " return plus operating expense charge " under the retirement method and the small excess under the sinking fund method, over the straight line method, is due to the fact that the amounts collected in the early years are smaller under these methods.

In practice, the retirement method does not produce such great fluctuations as are shown in the table, because the property is not all installed in a single year, and because the property installed in a single year is not all retired in the same year. But large fluctuations do in fact exist, as was found by the Interstate Commerce Commission in a recent opinion. For similar reasons, the total depreciation and return under the straight line method do not in practice fluctuate so much as appears in this simplified example.

Under the sinking fund method, the difference between the total depreciation charge of $758.70 and $1,000 necessary to pay the loss on the property at the end of ten years is made up by the compound interest on the depreciation reserve from the time collected until the end of the period at 6 percent. If a lower rate of interest were used, the annual depreciation charge under this method would be increased.

Attention is called to the fact that, under the retirement method, the book value (book cost less depreciation reserve) of the property remains the same as its cost new until it is retired, while under the other two methods, it becomes less each year until it finally disappears. As already stated, the value of property does not remain equal to its cost until it is retired. That is a fact of universal knowledge, *and hence the retirement method does not adequately protect the assets of a corporation or keep it in sound financial condition.* If a company were to refund all of its bonds when they became due and to issue new securities for all additions and betterments under such conditions, it would become overcapitalized and financially unsound.

Whether the other methods do so against all reasonable contingencies is a question discussed later, but it may be pointed out here that the *book* value declines more rapidly under the straight line method than under the sinking fund method (see above tables). In other words, under the former method larger provision is made in the early years for protection against depreciation, and thus there is a greater factor of safety and there is more provision against contingencies under the straight line method than there is under the sinking fund method.

### Debt Amortization

Having shown in brief outline, the workings of the

principal depreciation accounting methods and their effects upon the financial soundness of a utility and its rates for service, let us turn to debt amortization.

If we substitute for an item of property having a value of $1,000, a bond for $1,000 (or rather ten bonds for $100 each) bearing interest at 6 percent, to be paid within ten years; and then provide for payment (a) by the serial bond method or (b) by the sinking-fund method (assuming 6 percent earnings on sinking fund also), the results shown in the following tables will be obtained:

| Serial bond Method | Amount of bonds issued | Amount Retired | Amount Outstanding | Interest | Amortization Charge | Interest plus Amortization |
|---|---|---|---|---|---|---|
| 1 year | $1,000 | .... | $1,000 | $60 | $100 | $160 |
| 2 years | 1,000 | $100 | 900 | 54 | 100 | 154 |
| 3 years | 1,000 | 200 | 800 | 48 | 100 | 148 |
| 4 years | 1,000 | 300 | 700 | 42 | 100 | 142 |
| 5 years | 1,000 | 400 | 600 | 36 | 100 | 136 |
| 6 years | 1,000 | 500 | 500 | 30 | 100 | 130 |
| 7 years | 1,000 | 600 | 400 | 24 | 100 | 124 |
| 8 years | 1,000 | 700 | 300 | 18 | 100 | 118 |
| 9 years | 1,000 | 800 | 200 | 12 | 100 | 112 |
| 10 years | 1,000 | 900 | 100 | 6 | 100 | 106 |
| Total | .... | ... | ... | $330 | $1,000 | $1,330 |

| Sinking-fund Method | Amount of bonds issued and Outstanding | Sinking Fund | Net Liability | Interest | Amortization Charge | Interest plus Amortization |
|---|---|---|---|---|---|---|
| 1 year | $1,000 | .... | $1,000.00 | $60 | $75.87 | $135.87 |
| 2 years | 1,000 | $75.87 | 924.13 | 60 | 75.87 | 135.87 |
| 3 years | 1,000 | 156.30 | 843.70 | 60 | 75.87 | 135.87 |
| 4 years | 1,000 | 241.55 | 758.45 | 60 | 75.87 | 135.87 |
| 5 years | 1,000 | 331.90 | 668.10 | 60 | 75.87 | 135.87 |
| 6 years | 1,000 | 427.69 | 572.31 | 60 | 75.87 | 135.87 |
| 7 years | 1,000 | 529.22 | 470.78 | 60 | 75.87 | 135.87 |
| 8 years | 1,000 | 636.84 | 363.16 | 60 | 75.87 | 135.87 |
| 9 years | 1,000 | 750.90 | 249.10 | 60 | 75.87 | 135.87 |
| 10 years | 1,000 | 871.82 | 128.18 | 60 | 75.87 | 135.87 |
| Total | .... | ..... | ..... | $600 | $758.70 | $1,358.70 |

It will be noted that these tables are identical with the tables showing the results of the straight line and the sinking fund methods of depreciation respectively. This is necessarily so, because the life of the bonds was taken as the same as the life of the property (10 years) and the interest rate on the bonds was taken as the same as the rate of compound interest in sinking fund depreciation (6 percent). In all instances where this relationship is preserved, regardless of the periods or the rates, it will always be found that

(1) The serial bond method produces the same results as the straight line method of depreciation accounting;

(2) The sinking fund method produces identical results whether it is used for depreciation accounting upon the fixed capital or for amortization of bonds.

*The essential fact about each of these methods is that if each is correctly applied, based upon facts correctly weighted and appraised, and if the life of the bonds is made the same as the life of the property and the interest rate (where used) made the same as the return, justice will be done, considering the period as a whole, to consumers and to investors; the financial soundness of the corporation will be preserved; and only reasonable rates will be charged. As previously shown, this is not true of the retirement method of accounting.*

A careful study of the two tables on depreciation accounting and the two on debt amortization will show that if the bonds are retired in a shorter period than the life of the property to which they relate, the financial condition of the company will steadily improve, all of the bonds will be retired before the property is retired, and there will be a steadily increasing excess of assets over liabilities. The converse is also true, viz., that if a longer period than the life of the property is used for the retirement of the bonds, the financial condition of the company will steadily grow worse; that is, there will be outstanding obligations after the property has ceased to be of use, and the excess of obligations over real assets will steadily increase during the period.

## Are Depreciation and Amortization both Necessary?

Are depreciation accounting and amortization of funded debt both necessary or desirable? Excepting two considerations, to which reference will later be made, the answer is in the negative.

To charge operating expenses with adequate depreciation on fixed capital and in addition with amounts sufficient to retire securities issued to acquire such property would be duplication. This would mean either that future users would be supplied with service at a cost which would not include any interest on the investment or on any obligations outstanding, or, if the rates were placed so high as to produce revenues in excess of expenses, that the stockholders would receive a return after their entire investment had been repaid. In other words, either the users or the stockholders of the future would benefit because the users of the past had been required to pay more than the actual cost of the service which they received.[2]

---

[2] An apparent exception exists when the property is not growing, with the result that the cash collected to offset accrued depreciation is not needed for additions and betterments. It may then be used to retire outstanding bonds or even stock without any duplication, since only the actual accruing depreciation is included in the rates charged for service. This, however, is an unusual case.

Of course, stockholders may provide for retirement of bonds by foregoing a portion of the dividends to which they are fairly entitled, in addition to adequate provision in operating expenses for depreciation. But it is not necessary to do this in order to maintain a sound financial position, if depreciation or amortization is properly computed. Whether it is advantageous or not depends upon many factors—such as the relative permanence of the business as a whole, the financial structure of the corporation, and the condition of the money market.

For utilities using retirement accounting (the retirement method or the equalized retirements method so applied as to fall appreciably short of depreciation accounting), the situation is quite different. As already shown, such utilities are not in sound financial condition, and provision for retiring their bonds when due would materially improve their condition. But can the results desired be best accomplished in this way or by requiring such utilities to adopt depreciation accounting?

The following reasons indicate it is better to adopt depreciation accounting:

1. Utility properties are financed by stock as well as by bonds, the ratio between the two varying greatly in different cases. Stock has no date of maturity, hence, it cannot ordinarily be amortized during its life. Depreciation upon the property acquired with the proceeds of such stock must, however, be accounted for during the life of the property. The property acquired through stock issues is not segregated upon the books from that acquired through bond issues. The provision for retirement of bond issues would not, therefore, be sufficient to offset existing depreciation, and additional provision must be

made.[3] Why not make adequate provision for depreciation in the first place?

2. The life of bond issues is affected by financial considerations which often make desirable a life varying greatly from the life of the fixed capital acquired thereby.

In times of easy money, long term bonds are issued at low interest rates, to the advantage of the ratepayers as well as the stockholders. A very small charge to operating expenses would amortize these bonds. The fixed capital which they purchase, however, may be used up and replaced several times during their life. How are sufficient depreciation charges to meet these losses to be provided by a bond amortization plan?

At other times, money must be raised when interest rates are high and short term bonds or notes are advantageous. If charges must be made to operating expenses sufficient to retire these when due, ratepayers during this period are heavily burdened or else the net earnings are reduced and the credit of the utility weakened when it may be most needed.

3. It is extremely doubtful whether amounts collected from the customers for amortization of bond issues could be deducted from the rate base if the utilities concerned claimed that this resulted in confiscation under the federal constitution. The federal courts have not been prone to recognize that customers can obtain any equity in the property of utilities, even when they have contributed amounts for depreciation or other purposes. It seems

[3] It is conceivable that if the period of amortization of bonds were sufficiently shorter than the average life of property paid for by stocks and bonds to make the amortization amounts equal the accruing depreciation in the entire property, proper balance might be maintained; but such a plan would be very difficult of application, particularly with a growing property.

doubtful whether they would recognize an equity obtained by amortizing bonds by means of charges against operating expense even if required by statute. To support any such deductions from the rate base, it might be necessary to establish that the property had actually depreciated in value by an equal amount. In doing this, the *prima facie* advantage attributable to the fact that a reserve has been built up from carefully computed annual operating charges for depreciation, which has been given much weight by the federal courts in recent cases, would probably be lost; certainly it would be weakened.

### Additional Protection against Contingencies

In the preceding discussion, it has been assumed that when depreciation accounting is used, the life of the property has been properly estimated; that is, that by the time an item of property is retired, the depreciation reserve will be sufficient to equal the cost of the property less salvage. Of necessity, the reserve must be accumulated on an estimated basis, and in such estimate every factor which ultimately causes the retirement of the property should be considered—such as wear, tear, decay, inadequacy, obsolescence, and public requirements. This estimate should be based upon the experience of the company with due allowance for present conditions and present trends.

Ordinarily, the estimates of life do not reflect revolutionary changes in the industry or its entire elimination. If provision is to be made to protect a corporation against such contingencies, it should be made separately from the depreciation reserve or from an amortization fund designed to retire the securities when the life of the property represented by such securities shall have ended. It may be that, in the interest of conservative financing and sound business management, a further provision should be made and that a corporation should not presume that the undertaking is to have perpetual life. Whether such provision is wise or necessary depends upon conditions; no general rule can be laid down except that a corporation should err, if it is to err at all, on the conservative side. It should make more provision rather than less to meet unforeseen contingencies and to prepare itself for radical changes in economic and social conditions.

If in the execution of such a policy, securities are to be amortized out of the return to which the security holders are entitled and rates are not fixed to cover such amortization charges, the funds for property acquired or provided thereby should belong to the security holders, and in no way should the existence of such property be used to lower rates or to confer benefits upon the users of the service.

If, on the other hand, any provision for such amortization is made in the rates for service, the consumers have an interest in that fund, and it should not be diverted to benefit security holders. As already indicated, unless some provision is made either by statutory enactment or by judicial interpretation for the recognition of the rights of the consumers in such a fund, injustice will be done and the public will be required to pay for property upon which a return must later be earned.

Upon this point, the promotor and the conservative investor are 180 degrees apart. The former, desiring to reap an immediate advantage regardless of the future, assumes a perpetual life and even denies the existence of depreciation. His lexicon does not contain the word. The latter wants to protect his investment, to see that it is returned to him unimpaired. Consequently, he will aim to protect the undertaking against the unforeseen, the unusual, the unexpected. The promotor aims to get out before any deluge occurs, assuring the investor that it will never happen.

The history of street railway and interurban lines is precisely in point. When cable traction succeeded horse car operation, the cost of the change was generally capitalized, and the non-depreciationists, dominated often by the legal fraternity ignorant of economics and engineering, maintained that no system would ever cease to exist and that any change could properly be financed by future generations. Then came electric traction and the process was repeated with still no provision for depreciation, the lawyers and the legalized engineers still blind to facts of common knowledge. Perhaps they had no regard for investors; or, perhaps they thought they could fool the courts. Then came motor traction, the abandonment of thousands of miles of trolley lines and losses to investors of millions of dollars. It may be that all investors could not have been protected against any loss, but if depreciation accounting had been followed from the beginning and if in the days of huge profits provision had been made for the retirement of bonds even upon a modest basis against contingencies then unforeseen, millions would have been saved to investors by placing the industry in the investment and not in the highly speculative class. Of course, many promotors foresaw the inevitable results of their course and retired from the field, their tin boxes showing no street railway securities upon their owner's demise.

There are many utilities which are following the same policies today. They have made no adequate provision for depreciation. They select lawyers to represent them who say there is no such thing. They produce engineers who testify under oath that the only kind of depreciation that exists is deferred maintenance. Those in control hope

to boost apparent earnings and inflate security prices un-
loading upon the public and escaping before the deluge
comes. If not successful, they plead that the widows and
orphans who have bought securities must be protected.
They think that the public will overlook the fact that the
widows and orphans were persuaded to buy the securities
at inflated prices due to faulty accounting for which the
managers of the properties or the bankers who floated the
issues were responsible. Is it not time that the widows
and orphans collected from those who sold them the
securities and not from consumers through higher rates?
" Let the seller beware " is a slogan that has struck a most
responsive chord. The new era has too long been deferred, but reformation is better late than not at all.

In the preceding discussion, the effect of changing price
levels on property values has been omitted. However, as
long as the courts adhere to the doctrine that prudent
unimpaired investment shall not be the basis for fixing
rates in confiscation cases but that reproduction cost (less
depreciation) shall be an important element, investors
should consider this fact and guard against declining
prices. The fundamental difficulty when one comes to
consider what is the safe and wise course to pursue is that
the court of last resort—the United States Supreme Court
—has not laid down any general rule as to the weight to
be given to the change in price levels represented by reproduction cost; and, in one opinion, the court has even gone
so far as to rule that rate-fixing bodies must attempt to
forecast the future. Yet public utilities, because of their
great importance to the public, should be the industries
where speculation would be the last to enter.

But the law is law, and until the Supreme Court re-
verses itself or differentiates the present era from all that
have preceded, investors in public utilities must consider

changing prices if they wish to protect their investments. As long as prices are rising, there is obviously no need for reserve or surplus accumulations, except that when prices are forced skyward by such abnormal conditions as world wars or speculative markets, it should be remembered that all property expenditures at high prices are likely to be heavily discounted later on, and provision should be made against this probable deflation. And of course when the prices begin to decline after such abnormal conditions, conservative management requires provision be made against the day when reproduction cost will be considerably below the actual cost of the property.

Public utilities differ in two important respects from competitive industries. In the first place, competition is reduced to a minimum, and the need for protection against unfair practices is slight. If they treat the public fairly, there is little likelihood that competition by private or public plants will be permitted. Hence, the fear that in a period of lower prices, plants will be built at less cost per unit of output need ordinarily be given little consideration if the public has been treated fairly.

Secondly, a utility which serves a territory exclusively must provide plant to meet the demand whether prices are low or high. When there are several competitors serving the same area, one may avoid construction at high prices; or a new company may be formed when prices are low, forcing the others with their high-priced plants to meet the new competition. A public utility is often forced against its own judgment to make expenditures because the public must have service. This is another argument why in the case of virtual monopolies prudent unimpaired investment should be the basis of all rate-making and not reproduction cost. But it does not seem to have appealed to the majority of the Supreme Court.

The provision against loss through changed price levels may be made through the accumulation of surplus or retirement of obligations. It may be wise to earmark such surplus and differentiate it from the earnings set aside to equalize dividends, but essentially it has much in common with the latter. It may be provision against something which has not yet occurred, although if no provision has been made for falling prices and a fund or a reserve is built after prices have fallen, it ceases to have this characteristic.

Under present circumstances, little can be said to guide any utility which wishes to protect its investors against the ruling that reproduction cost is an element in determining rates, for the courts have used only vague terms. They have said there are many elements to be considered, and investors are left to guess what will be the principle applied to their company, even if the company has been honestly, efficiently and conservatively managed with the interest of the public fully in mind. But that consideration must be given to changing price levels is indisputable.

It has been stated that provision may be made to offset the effect of falling prices through surplus or retirement of obligations. The net effect is the same, but if a company is growing, and funds are needed in excess of such provision, the better method ordinarily will be through a surplus, as this saves expenses connected with the issue and sale of securities. Of course, it may be wiser to call in bonds issued at a high interest rate and issue a new series at a lower rate, but this introduces another element not here being considered. Assuming an equality of interest rates, the above observations apply.

## Government Utilities

In conclusion, a word may be said regarding the relation of the above discussion to government utilities. These occupy a somewhat different position in that they belong to the public and to a considerable extent customers and taxpayers are the same persons. However, almost invariably the interests of an individual as a taxpayer and as a consumer are not identical. Generally, it may be said that the majority of persons are more directly interested in low rates for service than they are in the reduction of taxes which would come as a result of profits from the conduct of the enterprise. The taxpayer would occupy generally the position of the security holder in the above discussion, but so much depends upon conditions and there are so many varying circumstances that it is difficult to generalize. The application of the conclusions reached in the preceding pages to governmental enterprises is a distinct subject and would require such special treatment that no attempt is here made to do so. I merely wish to point out that there is a field here which I have not attempted to cover.

# The Scope of the Commerce Power

BY

THOMAS REED POWELL

When Mr. Goodnow published his *Social Reform and the Constitution* in 1911, he devoted the major part of his attention to constitutional issues of the scope of national power. He pointed out that other federal systems established in more modern times agree in giving wide powers to the central government and in making the process of constitutional amendment less cumbersome than ours. Our need of far-reaching national power is confirmed not only by the experience of other nations but by the difficulties which we have encountered in our attempts to solve our problems by action on the part of the several states. So it seemed to Mr. Goodnow in 1911 that it has come about that "the federal government is every day assuming to exercise greater powers, and little opposition to this action is manifested except from those whose interest demands freedom from all governmental control, or who still believe, as some do, that what our fathers did in the eighteenth century should not be changed." [1]

With reference to Congressional regulation of transportation, Mr. Goodnow proved his prescience by saying:

Indeed, it is not beyond the bounds of probability that the distinction between interstate and intrastate commerce on land will be abandoned as it has been practically abandoned in the case of navigation. If the distinction between interstate and intrastate commerce is abandoned, a great influence will be available for making our political system conform to existing economic conditions, and necessary political centralization can be secured with-

[1] Goodnow, *Social Reform and the Constitution*, p. 14.

197

out that formal amendment of the constitution which now seems to be so nearly impossible.[2]

This was written three years before the Shreveport Case[3] and eleven years before *Railroad Commission of Wisconsin* v. *Chicago B. & Q. R. Co.*,[4] which sanctioned the provisions of the Transportation Act conferring upon the Interstate Commerce Commission power to regulate intrastate rates wherever necessary to prevent discrimination against interstate rates generally. Without dissent the court recognized the economic interdependence of interstate and intrastate railroad transportation and the power of Congress to deal with the latter so far as is essential effectively to deal with the former.

On the issue of the scope of the national commerce power over trade, there was not much for Mr. Goodnow to say in 1911. He notes that the Knight Case[5] had been substantially abandoned, and that the Swift Case[6] and the Danbury Hatters Case[7] applied the Sherman Law to some local acts that were found to have a sufficiently direct effect on interstate trade. So he concludes that " it may therefore be said that in the case of commerce by land, whether transportation, or not, as well as in the case of navigation, Congress has the right incidentally to regulate intrastate commerce where such regulation is necessary to the effective regulation of interstate commerce."[8] This is a conclusion absolutely required by the necessary-and-proper clause of the Constitution. Congress may deal with matters outside of interstate commerce if they have

[2] *Ibid.*, pp. 98-99.
[3] *Houston, E. & W. T. Ry. Co.* v. *United States*, 234 U. S. 342 (1914).
[4] 257 U. S. 563 (1922).
[5] *United States* v. *E. C. Knight Co.*, 156 U. S. 1 (1895).
[6] *Swift & Co.* v. *United States*, 196 U. S. 375 (1905).
[7] *Loewe* v. *Lawlor*, 208 U. S. 274 (1908).
[8] Goodnow, *op. cit.*, p. 80.

a sufficiently appreciable affect on that commerce. This is safe black-letter law, but like most black-letter law it affords little guide to its application to particular situations. Every new question is an open question until it is answered by the official interpreters of the Constitution.

Many such questions are now on their way toward official answer. The questions may be questions of constitutional law or questions merely of statutory construction. Congress has not been specific in defining the scope of the National Industrial Recovery Act. Its penal provisions are confined to business or transactions " in or affecting interstate and foreign commerce." The power of the federal courts to enjoin violations of codes is not in terms so limited, but it might with fair reason be held that Congress could not have intended acts to be enjoined unless they are acts that could be punished. Since Congress has not been specific, the Supreme Court may develop a " rule of reason " and hold that the phrase " affecting interstate commerce " was not designed to cover all possible effects however remote and minimal. Thus we may have issues of degree settled as issues of statutory construction rather than of constitutional law. Yet the criteria of judgment remain substantially the same in whatever technical guise the issues appear.

These criteria of judgment cannot be derived from the Constitution. The Fathers did not declare themselves on the requisite degree of relationship between intrinsically local matters and interstate commerce to afford the basis of Congressional competence. The issue is not what the Constitution is, but what it should become. The fundamental appeal to the Supreme Court must be an appeal to conceptions of statesmanship and not to the words of a document. The words of the commerce clause and of the necessary-and-proper clause leave the court completely free to decide for itself how far Congress may go. The formulae found in Supreme Court opinions are broad enough to be invoked in approval of every administrative determination that a transaction is one "affecting interstate commerce." No judicial veto of past Congressional action has any close bearing on the issue whether this or that transaction is too remote from interstate commerce to be subject to national power.[9] The Supreme Court can go as far as it likes in allowing Congress and the administration to go as far as they like.

If we thus approach the issue as one of deciding what kind of a Constitution we ought to have, we enter the realm where marked differences of opinion must necessarily obtain. We may all agree that we should have national power adequate to national needs and yet disagree as to what are our national needs and what power is needed to deal with conceded needs. Doubtless all that discussion can do is to clarify issues. We can seek to make our premises and our postulates explicit and thus argue in the open. Yet, however well we succeed in being candid, we must still argue from personal predilections and retain something of the mood of a debater seeking to support a position chosen perhaps we know not why.

---

[9] This is a very different issue from that in *Hammer* v. *Dagenhart*, 247 U. S. 251 (1918), which held that Congress may not forbid the interstate transportation of the products of factories in which children under designated ages are employed. Our concern is with direct, straightforward national regulation of intrinsically local matters, and the issue is one of the relationship between those local matters and interstate commerce. The cases which bear on this issue are those in which activities not themselves interstate commerce or not commerce have been sought to be subjected to national condemnation. Such matters if adequately related to interstate commerce may be dealt with by Congress through direct regulatory statutes though the same desired conduct could not be indirectly coerced by being made a condition of the lawfulness of interstate transportation.

We are not probing into the secrets of nature but choosing between competing values in situations where we may be mistaken about the facts. If we recognize such fallibility in ourselves, it may be less invidious to assume the possibility of fallibility in others even though they sit in the seats of the mighty as executives, legislators, or Justices of the Supreme Court of the United States.

The position of the United States is almost unique in the fact that judges are in a position to pass upon the question as to how far the national legislature may go toward establishing an all-inclusive comprehensive plan of national order. Where in other federal systems judges may do some umpiring between the whole and the parts, the fundamental charter has more explicitly favored national power by enumeration and has thus itself expressed the practical judgment of the interrelation of all commercial and industrial activities instead of making such interrelation the test to be applied by others, as did the framers of our Constitution in 1787. The later dates of other federal charters explain the explicitness which was avoided in eighteenth-century America. Our Constitution left more details for future determination. In the development of our polity the Supreme Court assumed the power to make these determinations and in spite of spasmodic grumblings has established itself as the final arbiter of these issues of practical judgment about what so affects interstate commerce as to be embraced within the national power over that commerce.

The practical limitations on judicial power afford some guide for the spirit in which it should be exercised. Courts can deal with the primarily legislative problem only by saying whether Congress has or has not gone too far in the particular instance and by giving reasons which shed light on what would be the judicial attitude in more or less similar cases. Courts cannot initiate a legislative program and for the most part cannot interfere with a legislative program until considerable progress has been made in its execution. Judicial interference can seldom if ever undo all that has been done. It can sanction the claims of objectors but it cannot secure equality for those who have already acquiesced. With respect to the past, judicial negatives can only make partial what was designed to be general. With respect to the future, judicial negatives can seldom if ever apply to all the parts of what may be designed as a comprehensive plan. Partial excision leaves the rest not the whole that the legislature designed. Until the legislature can act, the court imposes a substitute that may be quite different from what the legislature would deem desirable.

These considerations would have no bearing on judicial duty if the answer as to whether this or that affects interstate commerce could be clearly drawn from the language of the Constitution or from clearly demonstrable conclusions from indisputable facts. They do have a bearing on judicial duty when the answer is conditioned upon judicial views of desirability with all the possibilities of judicial fallibility about facts and their relationship to each other and of judicial susceptibility to influences which derive from personal temperament. The court should be very right in its judgment before denying to Congress a power it has assumed. It need not be so right in deferring to the judgment of Congress. Congress is not compelled to continue the exercise of powers accorded to it as it is constrained to refrain from the exercise of powers denied to it. All the practicalities are in favor of the most scrupulous observance of the judicial canon that all doubts will be resolved in favor of the judgment of Congress.

The considerations are of course not wholly applicable

where Congress has not been specific in its prescriptions. A judicial negative confined to the absence of Congressional intent is subject to Congressional correction. Yet in the case of the Recovery Act, no transaction affecting interstate commerce could be eliminated from the scope of the statute except by the supposition that all comprehensive language must be read subject to some restrictive canon of *de minimis*. There are reasons against the application of such a canon here. When Congress is devoting billions of public money to make loans and gifts to restore the buying power of the nation, it is well-nigh imperative to assume that it would desire its regulations of private enterprise to be as all-inclusive as constitutionally possible to co-operate toward the same broad end. The unlimited scope of the national taxing and spending powers [10] is a persuasive reason in favor of a broad scope of the national regulatory power. Even those who most dislike regulation may well prefer to have Congress armed with broad regulatory powers so that the restoration of private buying power will not be too dependent upon the continuation of public spending.

Doubtless there are those who believe that no government control can increase individual buying power. There must be many more who doubt whether the prescriptions of our numerous codes are wisely adapted to that end. Such doubts are applicable to prescriptions clearly within the commerce power where the only constitutional capsules that could encase them are the restrictions of due process and the canon against delegation of legislative

---

[10] The national taxing power is of course subject to restrictions as to jurisdiction, direct taxation, and regulatory legislation not adequately disguised as taxation. It is unlimited in the sense that it is not restricted to the fields within the scope of other national powers and is not subject to judicial scrutiny on the ground of severity even though some forms of discrimination might be judicially curbed.

power. With such restrictions on Congressional power we are not here concerned, except as they might increase in strength as the matters dealt with got more and more remote from interstate commerce. Conceivably a regulation might be deemed reasonable enough not to deny due process and yet so unreasonable as not to be " necessary and proper " when applied to something not itself interstate commerce. Yet it seems pretty clear that it is a regulation of interstate commerce to regulate what sufficiently affects interstate commerce, and that Congress does not need to invoke the necessary-and-proper clause to bring within its power matters that are intrinsically local. At any rate, our interest at the moment is confined to what Congress may deal with and does not extend to the merits, constitutional or otherwise, of the particular poultice applied.

The question, then, is whether what may be done by some legislative authority may be done by Congress or must be left to the states. The legal form of the question is whether the things outside of interstate commerce so closely affect it that the regulation of them is a regulation of interstate commerce or a regulation that is necessary and proper to the effective regulation of interstate commerce. This, of course, is not one question but many questions. Activities outside of interstate commerce and outside of commerce are legion. Some compete with interstate commerce and thereby affect it directly. Others are followed or preceded by interstate commerce in such a way as to affect it unmistakably. Still other activities outside of interstate commerce affect that commerce only as they affect individual purchasing power. No one can doubt that purchasing power is an absolute essential of commerce. It is the purpose of this essay to argue that it is a legitimate extension of past Supreme Court decisions to sanction the power of Congress to deal broadly with the problem of individual purchasing power because of its inextricable relation to interstate commerce.

The first cases to be considered are those interpreting and applying the Sherman Law. The ones important for our purpose are those in which the Act of Congress has been applied to intrinsically local acts most remote from interstate commerce and which have the least effect on that commerce. These cases are not weakened by the cases in which the Act has been denied application. These latter cases may be pertinent to an issue of Congressional intent or an issue of the delegation of legislative authority but they do not bear on the issue of the scope of national power to make explicit regulations of business conduct, because the Sherman Law is not that type of statute. The Sherman Law gets its meaning from judicial decisions and not from clear-cut administrative commands, and intrinsically local activities are not to be deemed within the range of the Sherman Law unless the offenders have either aimed at interstate commerce or have directly affected it. Notwithstanding a possible intimation to the contrary,[11] it is certain that the judicial delimitations of the scope of the Sherman Law are not safe guides to

[11] Mr. Justice Sutherland in *Atlantic Cleaners & Dyers* v. *United States*, 286 U. S. 427, 435 (1932), says that the history antecedent to the Sherman Act " sanctions the conclusion that Congress meant to deal comprehensively and effectively with the evils resulting from contracts, combinations and conspiracies in restraint of trade, and to that end to exercise all the power it possessed." This remark is made in support of the conclusion that the word " trade " in Section 3 of the Act, which applies to the District of Columbia and the Territories, is not confined to that trade which would be " commerce " within the meaning of the commerce clause. Mr. Justice Sutherland is thinking of the extent of the power intended to be exerted in the District of Columbia, and it would be unsafe to assume that he meant to say that Section 1 was designed to exercise the commerce power to its utmost constitutional possibility.

judicial conceptions of the constitutional scope of Congressional power.

Thus, in *United Leather Workers' International Union v. Herkert & Meisal Trunk Co.*[12] which refused to enjoin under the Sherman law a strike in a factory manufacturing products shipped largely in interstate commerce, Mr. Chief Justice Taft closed his opinion by saying:

> We concur with the dissenting judge in the circuit court of appeals, when in speaking of the conclusion of the majority, he said: " The natural, logical, and inevitable result will be that every strike in any industry, or even in a single factory, will be within the Sherman Act, and subject to Federal jurisdiction, provided any appreciable amount of its product enters into interstate commerce." 284 Fed. 446, 464.
>
> We cannot think that Congress intended any such result in the enactment of the Anti-trust Act, or that the decisions of this court warrant such construction.[13]

Clearly here the Chief Justice did not mean to announce a defect of constitutional power. Moreover, it is significant that the District Judge had granted the injunction, the Circuit Court of Appeals had affirmed it, and Justices McKenna, Van Devanter, and Butler dissented from the reversal ordered by the Supreme Court. Thus, of the thirteen judges passing on the question, six were of opinion that Congress had intended and had constitutional power to deal with unwarranted strikes on the sole ground that they reduced the volume of interstate commerce.

How little more is necessary to bring a strike within the Sherman Law is evident from the unanimous decision in the Second Coronado Case.[14] After the first trial of this case a judgment against a local labor union was re-

[12] 265 U. S. 457 (1924).
[13] *Ibid.*, 471-472.
[14] *Coronado Coal Co. v. United Mine Workers*, 268 U. S. 295 (1925).

versed on the ground that the strike was wholly local and therefore not within the Sherman Law.[15] At the second trial the plaintiff introduced new evidence to show intention on the part of the strikers to affect interstate commerce. The trial court thought the evidence insufficient and directed verdict and judgment for the defendants. The Supreme Court disagreed and held that the case should have gone to the jury. The Chief Justice declared that " there was substantial evidence at the second trial in this case to show that the purpose of the destruction of the mines was to stop the production of nonunion coal and prevent its shipment to markets of other states than Arkansas, where it would by competition tend to reduce the price of the commodity and affect injuriously the maintenance of wages for union labor in competing mines . . ." [16]

When Mr. Chief Justice Taft says that there was substantial evidence to show that " the purpose " of the defendants was to prevent shipment to other states, he must mean " a purpose " or " one of the purposes," for he concedes throughout that there was ample local motive for the action of the defendants. The new evidence consisted of remarks at union meetings which informed the strikers that in fighting their fight they were fighting the fight of others in and out of the state and that the fate of unionism in one mine was bound up with the fate of unionism in other mines whenever the various operators competed with each other for the same market. Undoubtedly this is true, whether strikers are aware of it or not. When they are aware of it and it can be inferred that knowledge becomes motive or intent, then tortious interference with interstate commerce through tortious inter-

[15] *United Mine Workers* v. *Coronado Coal Co.,* 259 U. S. 344 (1922).
[16] 268 U. S. 295, 310.

ference with manufacture gives rise to a cause of action under the Sherman Law.

One could with difficulty have criticised the Supreme Court if it had decided the Second Coronado Case the other way. It was going far to say that Congress meant to bring tortious strikes within the Sherman Law merely because the strikers were aware that unionization of one plant may be affected by presence or absence of unionization of another. One cannot escape the conclusion that the Court reached the result that it did because it desired to reach it. There had been outrageous sabotage and destruction. There had been a verdict for $200,000 and a judgment for treble damages of $600,000. In the First Coronado Case, the Chief Justice remarked that " the circumstances are such as to awaken regret that, in our view of Federal Jurisdiction, we cannot affirm the judgment." [17] The new circumstances adduced at the second trial consisted merely of more definite testimony that the strike leaders in their conventions and conversations made a point of the relation of wage-scales in one plant to wage-scales in another. The strike in question was unconnected with any existing strike in competing mines. There certainly was no evidence at the second trial to coerce the court to change the conclusion it had reached before.

Thus, it is apparent that the conceived wisdom of the result of bringing a strike within the Sherman Law was influential in inducing the Court to reach that result. The economic interrelation of interstate commerce and matters outside of commerce is always merely a matter of degree. Everything that has to do with buying power has always the possibility of some effect on interstate commerce. If all buying power ceased, there would be no interstate commerce. As buying power increases, so will in-

[17] 259 U. S. 344, 413.

terstate commerce increase. Buying power is as essential to interstate commerce as are mining and manufacturing and agriculture. In normal times we assume the continuance of widespread buying power and so do not appreciate so keenly its function as an essential of all commerce. Only when disturbance comes are we required to fix attention on the functional interrelations between different elements in the economic and social order. Functions are best seen as functions when they fail to function.

Diminution of purchasing power affects interstate commerce in substantially the same way as diminution of productive power. The effect of the former is economic; the effect of the latter is physical. The destruction of the mine and the coercion of persons to refrain from work prevents the non-commerce activity that would otherwise take place and be succeeded by interstate commerce. This is a restraint on interstate commerce and does not cease to be such even though it is also a restraint on intrastate commerce and on mining, which is not commerce. If the restraint has the requisite intent, it falls within the Sherman Law, notwithstanding the fact that there is an enterprise that intervenes between the restraint and the commerce. Diminution of buying power may operate on some interstate commerce more immediately than does diminution of manufacture. It lessens direct interstate sales and transportation. It also lessens intrastate sales that would follow interstate purchases. It lessens manufacture for extra-state purchasers as well as for local customers. These restraints on interstate commerce are indirect and are not confined in their effects to interstate commerce, but in these respects they are like the restraints imposed by the strike in a mine.

More indirect but none the less certain are other effects on interstate commerce by the diminution of buying power. Grant the possibility that a person whose buying power is involved would never in any event purchase anything of extra-state origin. He still would buy something if he had something with which to buy. His money would not all remain in a stocking. It would in large part go on to others and from them to others still. Inevitably some of this transferred purchasing power would go for purchases which involve interstate transportation. Buying power is not stored in isolated pools. It flows in a current. Diminish any spring or rivulet and you diminish the whole stream. Diminish the stream of buying power and you inevitably diminish the stream of interstate commerce. As to this there can be no doubt. The practical interrelation between buying power and interstate commerce is incontestable. This does not settle the constitutional issue, for there still remains the question of degree. This question of degree is bound up with the question of the circumstances which invite legislation and the policy of the legislation designed to meet the situation.

The strike in the Coronado Case involved but a single field with a productive capacity estimated at the first trial at 5,000 tons a week and at the second trial at 5,000 tons a day under unrestricted non-union operation. In view of all the coal in the country, cessation of operations in this field would affect a small proportion of interstate commerce. Obviously a strike of a nation-wide union would have a much more serious effect on a larger volume of interstate commerce. In the First Coronado Case there appears the suggestion that " if unlawful means had here been used by the national body to unionize mines whose product was important, actually or potentially, in affecting prices in interstate commerce," [18] the national union

[18] *Ibid.*, 409.

would have been held under the Act. The national body escaped because it was found not to have been a participant. The inference is, however, that national conduct of even an isolated strike would be judged by its necessary effect without the necessity of direct evidence of intention. Concerted action in several states would of course be stronger still, because interstate commerce would inevitably be more seriously involved.

Where the effect of a conspiracy on interstate commerce is sufficiently direct, the conspirators though not themselves engaged in interstate commerce will be held under the Sherman Law even though there is no design to affect interstate commerce other than that design which is to be inferred from the necessary consequence of acts. The directness of the effect seems not to be wholly dependent upon its immediacy in any technical sense. This seems to be the necessary inference from *United States* v. *Patten,*[19] which condemned a corner in cotton obtained by acts confined immediately to the New York Cotton Exchange. Sometimes the court has called this a direct restraint and sometimes it has called it an indirect restraint. In the First Coronado Case Mr. Chief Justice Taft cites it as an illustration of indirect obstructions to interstate commerce that have been rightly condemned by Congress,[20] and a little later in the same opinion he says that the corner was condemned because the control obtained thereby " would directly and materially impede and burden the due course of trade among the states." [21] This is followed by the sentence:

Although running the corner was not interstate commerce, the necessary effect of the control of the available supply would be to

[19] 226 U. S. 525 (1913).
[20] 259 U. S. 344, 408.
[21] *Ibid.,* 410.

obstruct and restrain interstate commerce, and so the conspirators were charged with the intent to restrain.[22]

This sentence would apparently put the case in the class of intended indirect restraints. Yet the intent here was only an intent inferred from necessary consequences. In the Patten Case Mr. Justice Van Devanter puts it as follows:

And that there is no allegation of a specific intent to restrain such trade or commerce does not make against this conclusion, for, as is shown by prior decisions of this court, the conspirators must be held to have intended the necessary and direct consequences of their acts. In other words, by purposely engaging in a conspiracy which necessarily and directly produces the result which the statute is designed to prevent, they are, in legal contemplation, chargeable with intending that result.[23]

While Mr. Justice Van Devanter thus regards the restraint as direct, his only proof of directness is the widespread practical results. He disposes of the issue by saying:

It was a conspiracy to run a corner in the market. The commodity to be cornered was cotton,—a product of the Southern states, largely used and consumed in the Northern states. It was a subject of interstate trade and commerce, and through that channel it was obtained from time to time by the many manufacturers of cotton fabrics in the Northern states. The corner was to be conducted on the Cotton Exchange in New York City, but by means which would enable the conspirators to obtain control of the available supply and to enhance the price to all buyers in every market of the country. This control and the enhancement of the price were features of the conspiracy upon the attainment of which it is conceded its success depended. Upon the corner becoming effective, there could be no trading in the commodity

[22] Ibid.
[23] 226 U. S. 525, 543.

save at the will of the conspirators and at such price as their interests might prompt them to exact. And so, the conspiracy was to reach and to bring within its dominating influence the entire cotton trade of the country.

Bearing in mind that such was the nature, object and scope of the conspiracy, we regard it as altogether plain that, by its necessary operation, it would directly and materially impede, and burden the due course of trade and commerce among the states, and therefore inflict upon the public the injuries which the Anti-trust Act is designed to prevent.[24]

There is here no suggestion that the restraint of the conspirators operated immediately upon transportation from one state to another, or upon the first sale after such transportation. The conspirators did not touch any instrument of interstate commerce except as price is such an instrument. Their acts affected price and price affected interstate commerce by its influence on demand and supply. It was charged and apparently conceded that the volume of trading on the New York Cotton Exchange was such that the price there determined prices throughout the country, or as the trial judge put it, that " prices of cotton are so correlated that it may be said that the direct result of the acts of the conspirators was to be the raising the price of cotton throughout the country." [25] Thus, the conspirators touched a sensitive nerve that inevitably affected the channels of all trade which that nerve touched. The intervening element of the interrelated price system did not keep the conspirators from causing a result which was deemed to be direct.

There were further contentions in the case that the Sherman Law did not apply because the conspirators were not engaged in interstate commerce and that a corner

[24] *Ibid.*, 542-543.
[25] *Ibid.*, 539.

would tend, temporarily at least, to stimulate competition rather than to restrain it. The court below had so held. In reversing these rulings, Mr. Justice Van Devanter said:

> Section 1 of the Act, upon which the counts are founded, is not confined to voluntary restraints, as where persons engaged in interstate trade or commerce agree to suppress competition among themselves, but includes as well involuntary restraints; as where persons not so engaged conspire to compel action by others, or to create artificial conditions, which necessarily impede or burden the due course of such trade or commerce, or restrict the common liberty to engage therein. . .
>
> It well may be that running a corner tends for a time to stimulate competition; but this does not prevent it from being a forbidden restraint, for it also operates to thwart the usual operation of the laws of supply and demand, to withdraw the commodity from the normal current of trade, to enhance the price artificially, to hamper users and consumers in satisfying their needs, and to produce practically the same evils as does the suppression of competition.[26]

Here are a number of phrases which, *mutatis mutandis,* can be applied to the effects of a nation-wide depression. Merely verbal transfers may of course be nothing but puns with all the *non-sequiturs* and fallacies of puns. Analogies are no better than the judgments implicit in them. The analogies here suggested play only the rôle of indices to judgments that have other and broader grounds to rest on.

When we leave the Sherman Law cases, we escape from the problem of the intent of the persons raising the issue of national control. As Mr. Chief Justice Taft says in the First Coronado Case, " It is clear from these cases that if Congress deems certain recurring practices, though not really part of interstate commerce, likely to obstruct,

[26] *Ibid.,* 541.

restrain, or burden it, it has the power to subject them to national supervision and restraint." [27] Congressional designation of the practice answers any question of the intention of Congress and renders unnecessary any inquiry into the intention of the persons whose practices are designated. Practices may be regulated by Congress because of their requisite effect on interstate commerce, and it cannot matter from the standpoint of the commerce clause that the persons whose acts are regulated are not evil and designing men. The scope of the commerce power is not restricted to the punishment of something that accords with a Puritanical conception of sin. If practices do sufficiently affect interstate commerce, they fall within the commerce power of Congress and can claim immunity from particular exercises of that power only by invocation of some protection derived from constitutional restraints on the mode or degree of exercise of the power in question.

Nothing suggestive of moral evil or of human misconduct was involved in *Railroad Commission* v. *Chicago, B. & Q. R. Co.*,[28] which Mr. Chief Justice Taft invokes in the Coronado opinion for the statement now under consideration. That is the case that sanctions the power of Congress to regulate intrastate rates to maintain a general level between them and interstate rates. The issue in the case was whether an interstate railroad should obey a federal or a state command with respect to its intrastate

[27] 259 U. S. 344, 408. The cases referred to include *Railroad Commission* v. *Chicago, B. & Q. R. Co.*, *infra*, note 28, and *Stafford* v. *Wallace*, *infra*, note 30, and also the Sherman Law cases of *Swift & Co.* v. *United States*, note 6, *supra*, and *United States* v. *Patten*, note 19, *supra*. The statement above quoted should be confined to the cases not arising under the Sherman Law. It is followed by sentences referring to " plan " and " intent " which are appropriate for the Sherman Law cases.

[28] 257 U. S. 563 (1922).

rates, whether what is intrinsically within state control may be removed from state control to national control because of its practical relation to matters predominantly or exclusively within national control. Congress was allowed to set new standards of intrastate conduct because that conduct was sufficiently related to interstate commerce. Congress was not forbidding naughtiness. It was merely setting desirable standards of interrelated behavior. " The affirmative power of Congress in developing interstate commerce agencies is clear," [29] says the Chief Justice. Congress must have a comparable power to develop, promote, and restore interstate commerce generally.

If this were not so, it would have been inappropriate for Mr. Chief Justice Taft to cite a transportation case along with trade cases in making a general statement on the scope of Congressional power over practices not really a part of interstate commerce. In the Coronado Case he had before him an alleged restraint of interstate trade by acts that prevented manufacture. To bring such acts within the Sherman Law there must be the requisite design to affect interstate commerce. Congress, however, has power to deal with recurring practices on the basis of their effects on interstate commerce without regard to human motives or designs. This is true, whether Congress is dealing primarily with transportation or with trade. The only difference between national power in the one case and in the other is the possible difference between practical effects in one case and in the other. The nexus between local and interstate transportation is physical as well as economic. The nexus between intrinsically local affairs and interstate trade may be economic only. The economic nexus is enough if it is close enough.

[29] *Ibid.*, 590.

The issue of degree will always be present whether we are concerned primarily with transportation or with trade.

The case sustaining the Transportation Act's regulation of intrastate railroad rates is cited in *Stafford* v. *Wallace*,[30] which also is cited in the First Coronado Case, thus again intertwining the law on transportation with the law on trade. In all three cases Mr. Chief Justice Taft wrote the opinions. The Stafford Case sustained the Packers and Stockyards Act of 1921 under which wide powers were vested in the Secretary of Agriculture to supervise charges and practices of packers notwithstanding the fact that many intrinsically local matters were thereby subjected to national regulation. The Chief Justice pointed out that the relation of these practices to interstate commerce had been affirmed in the Swift Case and that Congress had framed this more explicit regulatory statute in keeping with the principles announced in that case. " The Act deals with the same current of business, and the same practical conception of interstate commerce." [31] The point of the opinion to be especially noted is that which dispenses with the necessity of intent on the part of persons actually affecting interstate commerce when Congress itself clearly makes the actual effect the supporting basis of its commands:

Of course, what we are considering here is not a bill in equity, or an indictment charging conspiracy to obstruct interstate commerce, but a law. The language of the law shows that what Congress had in mind primarily was to prevent such conspiracies by supervision of the agencies which would be likely to be employed in it. If Congress could provide for punishment or restraint of such conspiracies after their formation through the Anti-trust Law, as in the Swift Case, certainly it may provide

[30] 258 U. S. 495 (1922).
[31] *Ibid.*, 520.

regulation to prevent their formation. The reasonable fear by Congress that such acts, usually lawful, and affecting only intrastate commerce when considered alone, will probably and more or less constantly be used in conspiracies against interstate commerce, or constitute a direct and undue burden on it, expressed in this remedial legislation, serves the same purpose as the intent charged in the Swift indictment to bring acts of a similar character into the current of interstate commerce for Federal restraint. Whatever amounts to more or less constant practice, and threatens to obstruct or unduly to burden the freedom of interstate commerce is within the regulatory power of Congress under the commerce clause, and it is primarily for Congress to consider and decide the fact of the danger and meet it. *This court will certainly not substitute its judgment for that of Congress in such a matter unless the relation of the subject to interstate commerce and its effect upon it are clearly nonexistent.*[32]

This last sentence, taken at its full face value, would bring within the commerce power of Congress almost every conceivable regulation that Congress would be likely to venture upon, if to any discernible extent the regulation affected purchasing power. No one could say that the relation between purchasing power and interstate trade and transportation is clearly non-existent. It might be hard to trace the relationship if we had to consider merely the purchasing power of a few isolated individuals, though even so it seems inconceivable that none of the drops would trickle on to enter the channel of interstate commerce. If, however, we have before us regulations affecting the purchasing power of millions, then we know and can prove the incontestable relationship between this power and interstate commerce. The nation-wide character of a slump in buying capacity affects interstate commerce more directly as well as more greviously than would

[32] *Ibid.*, 520-521. Italics are author's.

a small segregated slump. The Supreme Court has recognized that " recurrent local practices " may have on interstate commerce an effect that would not be contributed by a single local act. So must ubiquitous local conditions have on interstate commerce an effect that would not be imposed by a few scattered symptoms. When we see the same thing occurring all over the country we are compelled to believe that the uniformity is the product of interrelation and interaction. It must require the strongest proof to demonstrate that any part is unrelated to the rest.

The judgment that the wide-spread character of an economic situation is significant in determining the interrelation between things local and things interstate finds support in the opinion of Mr. Chief Justice Taft in *Board of Trade* v. *Olsen* [33] which sustained Congressional regulation of exchanges on which grain futures are bought and sold. After discussing the Patten Case, he said:

If a corner and the enhancement of prices produced by buying futures directly burden interstate commerce in the article whose price is enhanced, it would seem to follow that manipulations of futures which unduly depress prices of grain in interstate commerce and directly influence consignment in that commerce are equally direct. *The question of price dominates trade between the states. Sales of an article which affect the country-wide price of the article directly affect the country-wide commerce in it.* By reason and authority, therefore, in determining the validity of this act, we are prevented from questioning the conclusion of Congress that manipulation of the market for futures on the Chicago Board of Trade may, and from time to time does, directly burden and obstruct commerce between the states in grain, and that it recurs and is a constantly possible danger. For this reason, Congress has the power to provide the appropriate means adopted in this act by which this abuse may be restrained and avoided. [34]

[33] 262 U. S. 1 (1923).
[34] *Ibid.*, 39-40. Italics are author's. See Robert L. Stern, " That

What affects country-wide price directly affects country-wide commerce. So what affects country-wide buying power must directly affect country-wide commerce. The link between the several local parts of country-wide commerce is interstate commerce. Congress with authority over the link may deal with what sufficiently affects and is sufficiently affected by that link.

The economic significance of this link of interstate transportation may be more vividly appreciated if we were to assume its destruction. When Congress passed an embargo on foreign commerce, the languishing was not confined to those closely connected with foreign trade. If Congress should impose an embargo on all interstate commerce, the resultant stagnation could not leave all the barbers and the cleaners unaffected. A boycott in New

Commerce Which Concerns More States Than One," 47 *Harvard Law Review*, 1335, for a consideration of the proceedings in the Constitutional Convention showing that the commerce clause was designed to carry out a prior resolution that the Federal Government was "to legislate in all cases for the general interests of the Union . . . and in those in which the states are separately incompetent." Mr. Stern points out that the adoption of the test of "movement" has a tendency to narrow the original conception of the commerce power. This is for psychological rather than for logical reasons, since the possibility of movement between the states is the reason why matters in one state affect matters in another. Mr. Stern concludes his article by saying:

"The history of the commerce clause, both in the Constitutional Convention and in the decisions of the Supreme Court, makes it clear that no hiatus between the powers of the state and federal governments to control commerce effectively was intended to exist — that it was not intended to leave the people of the United States powerless to combat the play of destructive economic forces. The Court has a number of times regarded the possibility of creating such a situation as strong reason for avoiding a decision which would hold a particular course of conduct exempt from federal control. The Court can avoid the possibility of placing the nation in a defenceless position by returning to the original conception of the commerce clause — by allowing federal control of those business transactions which occur in and concern more states than one and which the individual states are separately incompetent to control."

York on stone from Indiana will affect Indiana barbers as well as Indiana stone-masons. The link of interstate transportation makes economic conditions in one state inevitably affect economic conditions in other states and the link itself is affected when conditions in one state affect conditions in another. Congress in its regulation of interstate commerce does not have to deal directly with the link that makes commerce interstate. It may deal with boycotts, strikes, and corners. The test in the Sherman Law cases is not the effect on transportation but the effect on conditions in other states or the design to have that effect. Such effect should be the test of Congressional power of country-wide treatment of country-wide conditions.

Unless such a view is adopted, the central government of the United States will lack the power possessed and exercised by the central government of every other comparable nation of the globe. This would not be material if our Constitution commands national weakness instead of national strength. It is material if our Constitution leaves the issue open for determination in the light of a practical judgment upon present-day conditions. With the issue one of practical judgment, the practical judgment of other comparable nations is not to be disregarded. To the practical judgment of other nations we may add the practical judgments of the national legislature and the national executive. Without asking the Supreme Court to follow election returns, we may invoke the fact that the problem of national recovery is widely regarded as a problem for the nation to deal with rather than for the several states. State executives and state legislatures are not subjected to responsibility for the depression or thought to have powers adequate to its cure. National economic integration is an assumption of political parleying if not yet of constitutional law.

We shall have a lop-sided system of government if our commerce power is not recognized as co-ordinate with our other national powers. State lines which have lost significance in economics have never had significance in determining the scope of national power over bankruptcy, over currency and banking, over taxation and spending. These powers do not have to stop to consider the relationship of conditions in one state to conditions in another. They are free from the limitation that restricts the commerce power. This restriction upon commerce power must be respected so far as the facts inexorably require. If Congress or delegated authorities invoke the commerce power to deal with matters that do not through the link of interstate commerce affect conditions in different states, it is the duty of the Supreme Court to call a halt. To find an entire absence of such an effect will be difficult if not impossible. In determining what degree of effect shall be deemed sufficient, the court can in last analysis apply only its own conception of what ought to be our political system. Here is the place for great deference to the judgment of political authorities and to the proper scope of the commerce power as the handmaid of our other national powers.

It is obvious that the views here asserted are not the product of lawyer's deductions from the Supreme Court decisions which have been induced in their support. The same views would be held if the Supreme Court had not sanctioned Congressional regulation of strikes and corners and stockyards and grain exchanges. Had the decisions on those matters gone the other way, the issues under consideration would not have been foreclosed. A widespread national emergency reveals relationships if it does not create them. Far-flung national action deals with re-lationships more clearly than does a single prescription for a single symptom. States have a practical competence to deal with strikes and corners and stockyards that finds no counterpart when faced with country-wide stagnation. In such a crisis the need for broad powers in a single government is manifest if we expect effective governmental action. Only an unusually self-confident judge could be bold enough to say that the directing organs of governmental policy had transgressed the boundaries of what is related to the general situation.

The weighty argument against the contentions here advanced is that they go too far and that their acceptance would mean a fundamental alteration of our federal system as we have thus far known it. Such alteration is already an established fact by the vast exercise of other national powers than the commerce power. It is an established fact by the vast exercise of the commerce power over manufacturers who compete with each other in interstate commerce and whose conduct affects interstate commerce so directly that there can be no question of their subjection to Congressional power. The alteration has come about by the alteration of the conditions of economic enterprise whereby matters once independent of each other have become interrelated. With national power dependent for its scope upon a judgment on questions of fact, the permissible scope will change with changing facts. Practically this means an expansion of national power, but it is an expansion for which the Constitution left room. The limits of the expansion may be set by the Supreme Court, but the fact that an exercise of national power goes beyond anything we have known before is no argument against its legitimacy.

Of course there remains the question of degree. No one

can doubt that Congress ought not to try to regulate everything that affects individual purchasing power. It ought to stop far short of those intrinsically local matters whose relation to interstate commerce and to matters in other states is clearly non-existent. It does not follow, however, that the point where Congress ought to stop is the point where the Supreme Court should compel it to stop. If some relationship to interstate commerce is present, the question as to the requisite degree of relationship is essentially one of policy. Judicial views of matters of policy may be affected by judicial antipathies not germane to the particular issue. Dislike of regulation in general or dislike of a particular regulation may conceivably influence a decision on the issue of remoteness, though it has no proper bearing on such issue. Courts should be slow to put the national power in a straight-jacket when the canons of decision are inevitably more subjective than objective and the judicial instrumentality has such obvious limitations as a censor of national legislative policy.

The views of desirability here asserted are of course open to question. There are still those who say that that government is best that governs least and who therefore would endow the national government with palsy rather than with power. It is easily possible to doubt the wisdom of many of the particular prescriptions now being administered. Yet it does not follow that these considerations should move men to wish the Supreme Court to curtail the scope of the commerce power. On other national powers there is no possibility of corresponding judicial curbs. No reserved powers of the state set limits to the power of the nation to tax and to spend and to regulate the currency. Powers over banking and bankruptcy are nation-wide. Plainly 'enough, national powers will be invoked in national crises whether we like it or no. The pinch of conceded powers can be as painful as any pinch of the commerce power. One does not escape extensive national control by curtailing the commerce power. There are therapeutic possibilities in this power not possessed by its companions. Those who seek to limit it may well be blind to a narrow self-interest as well as to wider considerations of statesmanship.

The contentions advanced here are not confined in their application to the Recovery Act or to national legislation in time of distress. They extend to the regulation of security issues and stock exchanges and to efforts to bring agricultural prices to the level of other prices. Devices which may be deemed questionable twistings of the taxing power if dependent upon that power alone may derive the necessary solace or support from a commerce power conceived in the light of the economic integration of national activities. Such a commerce power needs for its constitutional support only a premise of economic fact. Grant that the conclusions from the premise involve the intervention of disputable inference and fallible views of matters of degree, no judicial assumption of infallibility can take from guesses and opinions and preferences their inherent fallibility. Only by guesses, opinions, and preferences can the Supreme Court curtail the national commerce power as thus far asserted. Judicial sanction requires only a modest appreciation that there is room for difference of opinion.

National commerce power commensurate with national needs is essential for long-range constructive planning for the future. The fear that planning may not prove effective is not a reason for denying power to plan. The fear of ineffectiveness should not induce a decree that renders ineffectiveness certain and not merely possible or likely. Wide powers are more likely to succeed than narrow powers. Wide powers are more easily wielded with wisdom in time of calm than in time of crisis. What was clear to Mr. Goodnow in 1911 is demonstrably much more clear today. Step by step events have confirmed his insight and his prescience. The trend toward the wider exercise of national powers has shown no sign of abatement. Only the most presumptuous could deny that behind this development lies the increasing interdependence of the facts of economic life. In looking toward the future we must all be in the dark as to how wide national powers should be exercised, but only the blind need be in the dark as to whether wide national powers should be possessed.

# PART IV

# CONTROL OF ADMINISTRATION

# State Control of Local Finance in Indiana

BY

FRANK G. BATES

The attention of both students of government and practical administrators has, within recent years, been attracted to what has become known as the "Indiana plan" of state control of local finance. Although unknown as such to most of the citizens of the state the term "Indiana plan" has been employed widely to designate certain specific devices for the reviews of local budgets, tax levies, and proposals for incurring longtime indebtedness by local units of government.

Many discussions of the subject have been of a polemic character scarcely calculated to assist in arriving at a clear appreciation of the real merits and demerits of the institutions under discussion. The "plan" has been hailed as a panacea for the cure of all financial ills, on the one hand, and on the other cursed as an innovation violative of cherished and sacred political rights. When viewed more impartially it appears to be neither an inspired panacea nor a sinister innovation, but rather, a variant of a general trend which is perceptible in all highly developed governments in the present generation.

When the activities of local government have expanded to perform the ever increasing number of services which modern conditions of life have demanded of the local authorities, it has been found expedient, in the interest of not only the larger social group, the state, but of the local groups as well that the state exercise a guiding and sometimes a restraining hand over the activities of the local political society.

The present century has been marked by a wide extension of state authority over the activities of its political subdivisions. This has been especially true in the realm of finance where it has been manifested in varying degree from state to state. State control in Indiana, and especially control of finance, differs from that exercised in other states only in that the state has been something of a pioneer in some directions, and that here the control has been carried somewhat farther than in most other states. For these reasons that which has been done in Indiana possesses more than local interest.

It is sometimes assumed that the struggle of the mediaeval towns for freedom from their feudal masters was actuated by a desire for a realization of the principles of political liberty and a devotion to some abstract doctrine of local self-government. A more careful study of the facts fails to reveal the presence of any such activating principle. President Goodnow has said: " It would appear that the municipal populations were struggling during the middle ages merely for a better opportunity for the transaction of the business upon which municipal life was dependent." He points out, further, that having secured the desired immunities they ceased to display any interest in liberal principles, but lapsed into oligarchy wherein the small group of merchants and traders dominated public life, quite as indifferent to the preservation of civil or political rights of the masses as had been their feudal lords before them.

The outstanding political manifestation in Western Europe from the fourteenth to the seventeenth centuries was the development of absolutism. This was due, in part, to the failure of feudal paticularism to protect the fundamental interests in the security of persons and property, and, in part, to the broadening boundaries of social and economic interests to include wider areas than those established by feudalism. With this growth of absolutism on national lines the city oligarchies were incompatible, not because of any devotion to human liberty, but because their selfish interests were opposed to the major interests of society which were becoming national in scope. Whatever measure of adherence to the principle of local liberty might be found to linger in the towns, it was in time overwhelmed by the rising tide of nationalism which went hand in hand with the growth of centralization of authority.

In the rural districts of England, local government was in the hands of the justices of the peace who derived their authority from Parliament and not from their local constituency. The parish officers had likewise lost their popular character and were the agents of the higher powers. So it had come about generally, not only on the continent but in England as well, that local units were merely administrative areas established for the purposes of the state and without autonomous powers to satisfy local needs. Their legal status has been so often and so positively stated, and so widely admitted, that reiteration or citation is unnecessary.

The nineteenth century was marked by a progressive urbanization of the population, the development of a social consciousness, and a quickening of the social conscience. These changes, together with an unprecedented rise in the standards of public living, have conspired to call forth a range of community services by government hitherto undreamed of.

The existing local units of government augmented by new creations were the obvious channels through which these new functions should be performed. The nature and range of the new activities thus inaugurated called for variety in technical training and involved an ever increasing expenditure of funds. Along with power to expend money was given the power to raise funds by taxation and to make use of public credit. Over these operations as over expenditures there was at first little control.

With governmental authorities, as with private individuals, spending is a more agreeable experience than the securing of the wherewithal to spend. Appropriations are more potent to secure popular majorities than are tax levies. Hence, the call for expenditures for services outweighed the aversion to new taxes and tax rates began to soar. Meantime credit became a popular means of meeting not only capital outlays but current expenses. Sinking funds when required by law either were never established or were diverted from their purpose, and refunding operations became an accepted means of meeting maturing obligations.

A matter which in the amounts involved transcended the criminal financial delinquencies of local officers and their unethical financial operations which avoided legal liability by a scant margin was the waste of money through injudicious expenditures. Public loss from this cause has always been difficult not only to control but even to estimate.

Consonant with the position of the localities as agents of the state, came early the beginnings of state financial control. This first took the form of some control over the local tax base and the process of assessment. As expenditures by local authorities increased, tax rate limitation and restrictions on the borrowing power followed. The regulation of fees and later of local salaries have long constituted further elements of control. More recently supervision of forms of accounting and reporting, the post-audit of accounts, and the control of budgets have appeared. Further, there have been some attempts to pass upon the fidelity with which purchases have been made as well as upon contracts entered into and carried out.

State control of local affairs of whatever kind, based in every case on constitutional or statutory warrant, may be exercised either through judicial or administrative agencies. In this country where it has been so often declared that ours is a " government of laws and not of men," and where the preservation of private rights has been the chief declared aim of government, the judicial method was first resorted to and is still the one favored in theory. Administrative control has more recently been reluctantly resorted to, but not without vigorous protests. This succession of forms of control, first judicial, later supplemented by administrative supervision, has characterized the development of financial control in Indiana.

In this development not less than four stages or phases differing from each other in some respects may be distinguished. The first phase concerns itself with the administration of the general property tax and includes the subjects of tax base, tax rates, assessment, equalization and exemptions, mandatory levies, and mandatory expenditures.

Since territorial days the chief source of revenues both state and local has been the property tax. Consequently, to protect its own larger interests the state has dictated the subjects of taxation and at times the rate as well. Whenever local revenues have been supplemented by specific taxes, fees, or other sources of income these have been levied and collected under authority of statute.

The territorial assembly, in 1799, enacted a tax law for the Northwest Territory which, with minor modifications, determined the general system of taxation in Indiana for a generation. As reenacted with its general features unchanged by the first state legislature the subjects of taxation were, first of all, lands to which were added townlots, draft and breeding animals, bond-servants, and apprentices. The revenues thus to be secured were to be supplemented by license fees on taverns and ferries. Upon each of these subjects was fixed a specific rate of taxation determined by the General Assembly. The only exception to complete state control was that the local levy on land might be varied up to a maximum of one-half that levied for state purposes.[1] To these taxes were presently added specific taxes on carriages and watches, and on the issue of writs and commissions.[2] A poll tax of a prescribed maximum was also included in this act. A year later the maximum rate upon land was by statute reduced to one-third the rate fixed for state purposes.[3]

The tax system was revised in 1835 by an act which, though not imposing a tax on all kinds of property, provided for ad valorem taxes on real estate and on specified forms of personal property. The assessment was left to be made by the local assessor, and the rate was to be fixed by the county board, but the levy for roads had to be not less than one-fifth the state rate. The county board was authorized, further, to levy a poll tax not to exceed 37½ cents per poll.[4]

Under the state's first general property tax law, enacted in 1840, counties were for the first time granted complete freedom to determine their rate of levy for county and road purposes as well as the rate of poll tax.[5] The counties might, in addition, levy license fees on a variety of

[1] Acts, 1816-17, c. 19, p. 132.
[2] Acts, 1819-20, c. 73, p. 150; Acts, 1820-21, c. 2, p. 8.
[3] Acts, 1921-22, c. 51, p. 101.
[4] Acts, 1834-35, c. 9, p. 12.
[5] Acts, 1840-41, c. 5, p. 34; *Rev. Stats., 1843*, c. 12, p. 235.

businesses including ferries, dispensers of liquors, merchants, peddlers, and traveling shows, but maxima and minima were established for these several cases. For the better part of a century after this, while the general property tax continued to be the chief source of local revenues, no limitation existed on the rate of taxes though the prescribing of maxima and minima for license fees was continued as a feature of subsequent acts.

With the diversification of the forms of property accompanying the industrialization and the urbanization of a considerable portion of the state's population, came louder and louder protests from the holders of real estate and tangible personalty against the injustices inevitably growing out of the administration of the general property tax. The state constitution called for " a uniform and equal rate of assessment and taxation." This taken with the further stipulation that there should be secured " a just valuation for taxation of all property both real and personal " was held through the years to preclude the introduction of other and more modern forms of taxation. Attempts to clear the way for these forms by constitutional amendment repeatedly failed.

As a result of the policy of relying so greatly on the general property tax it came about that at the time of the financial collapse, in 1929, about twenty-five percent of the state's revenue and fully seventy-five percent of that of the localities was derived from that source. In this situation the break-down brought home to the agricultural and real estate owning group more forcibly than ever the inequities of the general property tax.

With the coming of the depression came the movement to reduce the tax burden. This movement was directed especially toward a reduction of local taxes since ninety percent of the total proceeds from the general property tax came from local levies. It was then that another form of state control began to attract attention, viz., an accumulation of mandatory levies and mandatory appropriations. In response to a demand for a variety of local services the state had from time to time imposed on various classes of local units mandatory taxes fixing maximum or minimum rates or both to support these undertakings. In 1929 there were as many as a dozen mandatory levies in effect upon cities for various purposes and half as many more upon counties and townships. Examples of such levies are the levy of one mill for township libraries,[6] the levy of from three to eight mills for the use of city plan commissions,[7] and the levy to contribute to police pension funds.[8]

Similar in their effect in limiting the freedom of the local units to arrange their own finances were the long lists of salaries of local officers fixed by law and a series of mandatory appropriations imposed. There was on the statute-book a long list of such fixed salaries for all city, township, and county officers to which the city must conform. Likewise there were mandatory appropriations to be made for a variety of purposes, such as agricultural fair associations, protection from bovine tuberculosis, orphans' homes, children's guardians, parks and teachers' institutes. These were imposed usually only upon petition of a certain number of citizens. It is true that these all constituted but a small part of the local tax burden, but since they were usually to support some service which the locality was not of its initiative disposed to provide, they constituted real limitations upon local freedom of financial action, and were among the first costs to become objects

[6] Acts, 1901, c. 112, p. 187.
[7] Acts, 1921, c. 209, p. 561
[8] Acts, 1925, c. 51, p. 167.

of attack in times of adversity. As an early step in the direction of tax reduction all maximum and minimum rates of levy were repealed, and local authorities were permitted in their discretion to fix any rate within the minimum in each case.[9]

Not least in their effect upon finance has been the very liberal policy of the state in tax exemption not only for state but for local purposes. The exemption of public property used for governmental purposes, public securities, and property used for religious and educational purposes is well-nigh universal. Indiana has added to this list property of fraternal organizations used for fraternal purposes, a proviso construed most liberally for the benefit of such bodies. Likewise the exemption of property dedicated to a charitable use is extended to property any part of which is used for charitable purposes. Still other and lesser exemptions remove considerable amounts of property from the tax rolls. In some instances the total exemptions are so great as to limit seriously the ability of local corporations to secure funds by taxation for current use and by borrowing for capital expenditures.

In spite of the disastrous experience of Ohio under the notorious " Smith one percent law " of 1911, Indiana, like several other states, resorted to the dubious expedient of property tax rate limitation as a measure for tax relief. At the special session of the General Assembly called in 1932 especially to consider financial problems, it was enacted that the total of all taxes levied in any year in any locality for all purposes, state as well as local, should not exceed one dollar and fifty cents on each hundred dollars of taxable property. The Indiana act did, however, provide a degree of flexibility not usually contained in similar tax limitation acts. This is secured by the crea-

[9] Acts, 1931, c. 145, p. 519.

tion of "tax adjustment boards" in each county with authority to reduce rates made by tax levying authorities in emergencies to such a degree that the total levy shall come within the maximum. The state levy which is included in the maximum is not subject to revision by the adjustment board even in case of emergency.[10] This act was superseded at the regular session in 1933 by an act of similar tenor whereby the total of all taxes levied outside incorporated cities and towns was further reduced to one dollar on each one hundred dollars of valuation.[11]

The tax adjustment board, now remodeled to consist of a member of the county council and six other persons appointed by the circuit judge, and including among such appointees a representative of each class of local taxing authorities, became virtually an administrative court of appeals from the local levying bodies. A further appeal was provided from the action of the adjustment board on petition of ten taxpayers to the state tax commission. Likewise any taxing unit whose levy has been reduced may appeal for an upward revision to the same commission. The commission may affirm, revise, or reduce the total levy or any specific levy included in the total, or may reapportion the total levy among the several units in the county. In no case, however, may the result be to increase the original rate in any unit or to increase the total rate fixed by the adjustment board. The board is forbidden to reduce any levy made for the purpose of meeting debt or interest charges which were incurred prior to the date of the passage of the original limitation act in 1932.

The state has been more fortunate under this act than either Michigan, West Virginia, or Ohio in that its limitation is statutory rather than constitutional. On the other

[10] Acts, 1932, c. 10, p. 17.
[11] Acts, 1933, c. 237, p. 1085.

hand Indiana cities have not been relieved as have Michigan municipalities where by judicial decision the tax limitation does not apply to incorporated municipalities.

When the " dollar-and-a-half law " was before the General Assembly it was perceived that in but few counties could the cost of government, however carefully administered, be met by so small a levy. To compensate in some measure for the reduction in revenue inevitable under the limitation act, the state diverted a larger share of its own revenues derived from the gasoline tax and the new gross income and liquor taxes to the aid of the local governments.[12] These grants in aid for whatever purpose extended open a constantly broadening road for further state control by means of making grants contingent upon conditions to be met by the beneficiary unit.

Wherever the general property tax was adopted it was customary to delegate the duty of making the original assessment of property to local authorities in county or township. When applied in a homogeneous agricultural community, the task of ascertaining a " fair cash value " was not difficult. But even under these most favorable circumstances the omission of favored property from the assessment rolls and the unwarranted lowering of values either of favored property or of that of the whole area sooner or later began to derange the tax system and to cause concern among state officials. For half a century this subject was temporized with but with indifferent success though successive acts became more and more specific in the regulation of the details of assessment. In Indiana, county auditors and local boards of equalization were set up and their work supplemented by a state board of equalization.[13] By an act of 1891 the work of state equali-

[12] Acts, 1933, c. 50, p. 388; c. 81, p. 523.
[13] Rev. Stats., 1852, c. 35, p. 273;  Acts, 1859, c. 89, p. 145;  Acts, 1872, c. 37, p. 57.

zation was transferred to a state board of tax commissioners.[14] This agency was given authority to prescribe forms and blanks to be used in assessment; to construe tax statutes; to instruct local assessors in their duties; to report to the General Assembly on the operation of the tax laws and recommend legislation; to visit the localities to observe the work of local assessors; and to prosecute violations of the revenue laws.

Although the enactment of the law of 1891 injected vigor into the system of assessment, difficulties inherent in the system were still objects of much concern to the state. Inequalities and under-assessment were still prevalent. Under the tax act of 1919 which strengthened the control of the commission in several respects, field representatives of the commission have inaugurated the custom of holding conferences with county and township assessors to instruct them in their duties and to observe their work, and the township assessor has been required to make weekly reports to the county assessor and to the state commission.

The state commission is authorized, not only to equalize assessments between counties by horizontal increases or decreases in valuations in any county, but upon the appeal of any individual from the action of a local board of review, the commission may, in order to equalize burdens, reassess any property. This power of equalization was modified in 1921 so that if the commission finds that the assessment in any unit is improperly made as between areas within the county or as to classes of property, it may certify the fact to the county and cause the assessment to be reviewed by the local board of review. The determination of the county board is, however, not subject to further review by the state commission.[15]

[14] Acts, 1891, c. 99, p. 199.     [15] Acts, 1921, c. 222, p. 638.

State control of local finance has, in its second phase, and at a later date, been directed toward the securing of the integrity of public funds and the fidelity of their official custodians. These purposes find expression in the statutes providing for the prescribing of budgets, accounts, and reports; for a system of inspection of accounts; and for a system of public depositories for public funds.

Throughout the nineteenth century the accounts of most local offices were in a state of almost hopeless confusion. Local officials totally unskilled in the art of accounting had developed their own systems of accounts or in most cases had no system at all. They usually followed the precedents established by their predecessors who were no better informed than they. In many localities the chaos had become so complete that citizens were quite unable to determine what had been the disposition made of funds, the fidelity of their public servants, or the extent of the public indebtedness. There was a wide-spread conviction supported by occasional disclosures of irregularities that leakage and waste were constantly present, and defalcations and corruption not infrequent. Under existing conditions there was no way of checking the one nor of proving the other.

As early as 1895 and subsequently in 1897 and 1899, bills were introduced in the legislature of Indiana seeking to establish some sort of an inspection of local offices. Certain serious defalcations of state officials in the opening years of the present century gave further impulse to the demand for inspection and that it be extended to embrace both state and local offices.

The movement found fruition, in 1909, in an act " concerning public accounting and reporting and supervision thereof." [16] This act set up a governmental agency having

[16] Acts, 1909, c. 55, p. 136.

three major objectives with respect to all public offices and publicly-owned public service agencies, viz., to formulate and cause to be installed uniform systems of accounting, to secure uniform annual reports of financial operations and conditions, and to provide a periodic post-audit of all public accounts.

To administer this act there was created a " department of inspection and supervision of public offices," at the head of which was placed a chief examiner and two deputy examiners. There was also set up a " board of accounts " to consist of the chief examiner, the governor and the auditor of state, with power to formulate and prescribe the uniform systems of accounting and reporting contemplated in the act. The inspections for purposes of audit were to be performed by a force of field examiners.

Under the prevailing state of public opinion in the state, a personnel for the new department entirely divorced from considerations of politics through a conventional civil service law was impossible to secure. It was, however, clear that the success of the system depended upon the establishing of the utmost confidence on the part of the public in the disinterestedness of the administration of its work. In order, under these circumstances, to remove all suspicion of partisan bias from the audits made, it was stipulated that the two deputy examiners should belong to opposite political parties and that the force of field examiners should be divided equally between the parties. To this precaution against political " white-washing " there was added within the department the practice that every audit should be participated in by two examiners of opposite political faiths. The field examiners are appointed upon grounds of technical fitness determined by competitive examination. It may be said to the credit of the department that since its inception its work has been conducted without serious allegations having been made of political bias or unworthy motives.

Upon the basis of returns from tentative reports made and the results of the earliest examinations, forms of accounting were evolved and gradually placed in operation in all public offices state and local.

Whenever in the course of their audits the field examiners discover evidence of malfeasance or misfeasance, the procedure is first to bring the matter to the attention of the official involved giving him opportunity to explain or make good the apparent delinquency. This leniency is adopted because experience has disclosed that a very large proportion of the cases discovered arise from ignorance or carelessness rather than from criminal intent. Cases not thus disposed of are reported by the department to the governor and by him placed in the hands of the attorney general for the institution of legal proceedings. As a result of the procedure of the department very few cases reach the stage of prosecution.

Assuming to act under the grant of power to prescribe forms of accounting and reporting, the department prepared and issued a complete set of budget forms for local units of government. This action was taken contemporaneously with the first years of activity of President Taft's Commission on Economy and Efficiency, thus making this one of the pioneer efforts in the direction of budgetary reform in the United States. Although the department assumed that it had authority to send out these forms it would appear that some doubt existed on the subject since the adoption of the forms was repeatedly urged upon the local units but apparently never commanded. To remove any doubt on the subject of the department's authority in this direction in the act of 1920 amending the tax act of 1919, it was made mandatory that all local units of government should prepare budgets upon forms to be prescribed by the board of accounts, publish the same, and hold public hearings thereon before appropriations for the support of government and tax levies could be made.[17] It was from levies thus made that appeals might be had first to the county council and the next year by amendment to the state tax commission.

The magnitude of the task of inspection is indicated by the fact that more than six thousand examinations are made annually, covering transactions involving the expenditure of more than two hundred millions of dollars. The examinations cover annually ten offices in each of the ninety-two counties besides one hundred and twenty-two county institutions such as hospitals and homes; five hundred and fifty-two civil cities and towns, including two hundred and eighty-eight municipally-owned utilities; one hundred and ninety-three school cities and towns; one thousand and sixteen township trustees' offices; and the offices of five hundred and sixty-six justices of the peace. These are in addition to the examination of the several state offices, departments, and institutions. The cost of inspection in the year 1931-32 fairly chargeable to local inspections was approximately $300,000.

The advantages secured from the operation of the accounting and inspection law assume two forms. First, sums recovered which would otherwise have been lost to the public treasuries and, second, sums saved through the deterrent effects flowing from the existence of the statute. While the latter effects cannot be ascertained with any certainty, a general consensus of opinion seems to be that they are more far-reaching than the first.[18]

[17] Acts, 1920, c. 49, p. 164.
[18] The sums involved in the irregularities dealt with in the year 1931-

The system of accounting set up by the department has come in for severe criticism from public accountants—criticism directed at the administration of the statute rather than at the purpose or the adequacy of the law. It is pointed out by critics that the accounts are set up on a cash rather than on an accrual basis, that as such they do not embody proper records of encumberances or accounts receivable, and that no comprehensive inventories are provided for. The result is that no current operating statement or balance sheet can be prepared.

In passing judgment upon the merits of the system, it must be kept in mind that the statute creating the system of control was passed to correct certain specific evils, namely, the loss of public funds and the infidelity of officers financially. The very desirable purpose of showing the financial condition of the several units of government was not one of the objectives sought. It was pointed out by the chief examiner in his earlier reports that since the accounts were to be kept by persons wholly unskilled in accounting a conscious attempt was made to make the forms as simple as possible consistent with the ends sought by the law. The accounting forms were calculated to disclose information with respect to indebtedness, receipts, disbursements, and balances. In spite of the diffi-

---

32, the last complete year available, and the amounts recovered measure the results of the operation of the act with respect to the first of the above categories.

| | |
|---|---:|
| Cases pending, Oct. 1, 1931............ | $   802,977.25 |
| Irregularities charged during year....... | 628,933.39 |
| | 1,431,930.64 |
| Recoveries during year................ | 402,593.04 |
| Charges dismissed.................... | 233,092.72 |
| Pending, Oct. 1, 1932................ | 796,244.88 |

Report, Dept. of Inspection and Supervision of Public Offices, *Indiana Year Book* (1932), p. 628.

culties presented by the type of officials whose duty it is to keep accounts in some localities, it would seem that it might now be practicable to revise the forms by introducing some of the features which have hitherto been absent.

Under the terms of the public accounting act the department was given " full power to examine . . . all accounts and all financial affairs of every public office and officer, and every public institution." This broad grant of power was construed by the department itself most liberally. The chief examiner said:

Our interpretation of our duty is to check the accounts and verify their correctness, and to impartially investigate every official transaction, to the end that we may know that the official has followed the law, and that the tax-payer has had value received in necessities, comforts and privileges for which he is annually required to contribute his part.

It is our belief that to accomplish this purpose the public accounting law contemplates no limit to the scope of our investigations and recommendations. Our official acts have been based on the theory that it is our duty to do everything that, in our judgment, will aid the official and prevent waste of public funds.[19]

Here was a conception of official authority under which the state did not content itself with the prescribing of forms and the audit of books merely to determine accuracy and legality of official action, but sought to go behind the record to review the discretionary acts of local officers and the execution of public contracts. Such an interpretation of the departmental authority was not destined to go unchallenged by both private interests and local officials, but in the end was to be confirmed to a large extent by subsequent legislation.

[19] *Special Report of the State Examiner* (1916), p. 10.

Among the abuses which existed before 1909 and which gave impulse to the movement for the passage of the accounting act, were those connected with the execution of public contracts and the purchase of supplies. Besides the paying of excessive prices for supplies and the purchase of supplies in excessive quantities other practices more elusive of detection were going on. These included such matters as the sale of teacher contracts and the failure of contractors to comply with specifications set down in contracts for the construction of highways and public buildings. Short weight of metal in bridges and in school house heating installations, short yardage and inferior quality in highway materials, and inferior workmanship were complained of and too often upon good grounds. These practices were due sometimes to the carelessness or the ignorance of officials but not infrequently were traceable to official participation in fraud. False claims for goods never delivered, over-billing and padding of payrolls were not occasional but frequent. Such frauds were not discoverable by a mere audit since the books were likely, especially where actual fraud was present, to be well-kept and balanced to conceal all irregularities.

Acting under their broad interpretation of the law the examiners sought to determine the propriety of expenditures and the fidelity of the execution of public works, and when suspicion of irregularity arose investigators were sent into the field to make inquiry and investigation. If the facts found confirmed the suspicions, report was made to the governor, and he caused the attorney general to institute civil suits to recover the funds paid for which the public had not received value. This practice of investigation was adopted early in the history of the department and vigorously pursued to the discomfiture of both dishonest officials and contractors.

Although the department had from the beginning pursued this course of action, it was not called in question until 1921 in the case of *State* v. *Clamme*.[20] Agents of the department upon investigation had found that a certain highway had not been constructed according to specifications and that the public had thereby been defrauded. Suit was instituted by the attorney general to recover, and the case was carried to the appellate court. That court held that the statute contemplated only an audit of accounts " for the ascertaining the true state of the accounts and the funds involved," and that the department had no authority " to inspect any public highway after it had been improved, or any public bridge or building after it had been constructed. Such inspections are wholly outside the scope of its authority."

Had not legislation been forthcoming this decision would have terminated what had come to be an important phase of the work of the department. The results of the work of the department in this direction were so generally approved by the public that, anticipating the possible outcome of the suit, the essence of the practice was embodied in statute before judgment was entered. The department was authorized " upon the petition of twenty-five taxpayers or upon its own initiative to make tests and examinations to determine whether a public contract has been regularly performed or any public work or structure carried out according to contract." Upon like petition the department was empowered to require plans, specifications, and estimates to be submitted for correction or approval before the contract is awarded. In case any action

[20] 80 Ind. App. 147 (1923).

is discovered causing loss, waste, or damage to the public or diversion or wrongful expenditure of funds or wrongfully creating any public liability, legal proceedings are to be instituted by the attorney general to secure recovery.[21]

The attitude assumed by the department with respect to its authority supported generally by public opinion has led to the development of still further practices which are not specifically mentioned in the statute. Investigations made brought out incidentally that in some instances specifications had been drawn so that but a single firm was in a position to submit bids on a project. To eliminate this practice and to restore real competitive bidding, experts have been employed to set standards for the more common materials of construction, whereupon specifications must be drawn to conform to the standards. Likewise standard price lists were prepared for the more common articles of public purchase. Whenever examinations of accounts revealed departures from these standards the transaction was called in question and audit denied unless explanations were satisfactory. Out of this grew the practice on the part of officials of submitting for approval all contracts for public building before signing. Furthermore there has grown up the custom, quite extra-legally, that officials, before making expenditures concerning the legality of which doubt exists, consult the department upon that point.

The process whereby the power of the state's officers to conduct more than a mere audit of accounts, first by a liberal construction of its powers, and later by statutory confirmation of that construction, presents an interesting example of how administrative jurisdiction has been evolved in various directions and in many states in the country.

[21] Acts, 1923, c. 120, p. 320.

Prior to 1907 there existed in the state of Indiana no law governing the deposit of public funds. Local officials gave bond for the safekeeping of public moneys coming into their hands but the place or manner of the keeping was left to the discretion of the individual officer. In the absence of any law on the subject it was the custom for the treasurer in each jurisdiction to consider the interest arising from funds in his custody as among the perquisites of the office, so that his personal pocket rather than the treasury became the beneficiary of such increase. The official collected all funds at the earliest day and retained them in his possession as long as possible with the result that certain local offices became the most lucrative in the state. Instances were well known where local bankers actively espoused the cause of local candidates with the understanding that in case of success his bank should become the depository of public funds. The state during the whole of the nineteenth century operated under the independent treasury system.

The defalcations of state officials before alluded to called attention to the anachronisms and the abuses connected with the existing methods of caring for local funds. A movement for reform in this matter which was but a part of the movement above referred to which led to the enactment of the accounting law, led, in 1907, to the enactment of a public depository law regulating the deposit of public funds both state and local.[22] Under the provisions of this act the administrative body of each unit of local government was constituted ex-officio a "board of finance," charged with the duty of selecting for that unit depositories for its funds. The depositories must be institutions subject to Federal or state inspection, and upon

[22] Acts, 1907, c. 222, p. 391.

application by any such institution, provided it offers adequate security, it may be designated as a public depository. No institution could, except in case of emergency, be made a depository for more than a half-million dollars, and in case more than one institution should make application within the same unit deposits must be divided among them in proportion to their capital stock. The rate of interest to be paid upon deposits was fixed, and the proceeds therefrom were to be added to the funds upon which it was earned.

A modification of the law enacted in 1931, which aroused some criticism as constituting a distinct and unjustifiable advantage to the depository institutions, provided that the interest on deposits should be computed monthly on the minimum balance on deposit in any month instead of on the basis of daily balances as theretofore.[23] The depository law of 1907, which put an effectual stop to a distinctly corrupting influence in local government, has given general satisfaction throughout the state.

The closing of numerous of the smaller depository banks as a result of the financial crisis of 1929 and succeeding years placed many units of local government in serious straits and led to their defaulting on many contracts, especially for salaries of employees. In many cases the funds were only temporarily impounded and would be released wholly or in part at some later date. To prevent further losses and embarrassments an act was passed with the purpose of protecting local units of government from loss of funds deposited subsequent to January 1, 1933. By the terms of this act,[24] all interest becoming due on such funds was to be diverted to the state treasury until there was built up a " sinking fund " of three million

[23] Acts, 1931, c. 147, p. 521.      [24] Acts, 1932, c. 33, p. 141.

dollars. Whenever any public depository shall have suspended payment, the depositing authority shall be reimbursed from the sinking fund for the amount of deposit and interest thus impounded. Any funds recovered
through subsequent distributions from the delinquent
banks in payment of such deposit and interest are to be
turned over to recoup, so far as possible, the sinking fund.
Whenever the sinking fund shall have been depleted
beyond two million two hundred thousand dollars, depository interest from all institutions shall again be
diverted to the fund until it is built up to its maximum.[25]

Article thirteen of the Indiana constitution lays the
foundation for a third form of state control, by seeking to
limit the authority of political subdivisions to incur indebtedness. That article prescribes that "No political
or municipal corporation in the state shall ever become
indebted in any manner or for any purpose, to an amount,
in the aggregate, exceeding two per centum on the value
of the taxable property within such corporation."

This article was first proposed in 1873, but because of
the inherent difficulty in amending the constitution as well
as to technical objections interposed by its opponents, it
did not become effective until 1881. During the decade in
which it was pending the need for such a restriction
seemed to its advocates to be increasingly greater. It was
during this period that many cities and towns were em-
barking upon what in those days seemed extensive capital
expenditures for municipal improvements, especially in
the form of water supply and sewerage systems. During

[25] During the first six months of the operation of the law, receipts of
interest going to the fund amounted to $484,531.28, while claims paid
amounted to $334,448.46. Distributions from the assets of closed insti-
tutions back to the fund amounted to $2,424.63. Rept., Auditor of
State, *Ind. Year Book* (1933), p. 104.

the same period the state had gone in for extraordinary expenditures for a new state house, and the demand for new charitable institutions was becoming pressing. To meet not only its capital needs but also to meet a portion of its current charges the state, through a subterfuge countenanced by the supreme court, had virtually nullified the constitutional limitation on its own borrowing power and was accumulating a bonded state debt. Surrounded by these evidences of a growing tendency to spend, the voters ratified the amendment in the hope of imposing a very definite restraint upon such a tendency in the local units. That this failed to a considerable degree of realization subsequent events proved.

Unquestionably the amendment had a salutary effect upon the debt-incurring propensities of local communities, but its results would have been much greater, perhaps somtimes to the point of hampering worthy civic enterprises, had it not been for the ingenuity of successive legislatures and the courts in circumventing its operation. The devices whereby the plain intent of the amendment was frustrated demonstrate certain difficulties encountered when a policy of restraint runs counter to a strong trend of public opinion. The very persons most active in promoting the limitation as a general policy might be the first to seek to avoid its application in a particular instance. The devices of evasion were of three sorts.

The first device employed was that of multiplication of public corporations within the same area. Even before the placing of this restriction on local corporations a means had been provided whereby it might be circumvented and the local areas might go on making extended use of their credit. In 1859 there had been created in every township, city, and town a new corporation, the " school township," the " school city," and the " school town," distinct from though coterminous with the civil corpora-tion.[26] The supreme court had decided in 1874 that these new corporations were for financial purposes distinct from the civil corporations.[27] The fact of this duality now de-veloped new possibilities as a means of increasing the borrowing capacity of the community at a time when it seemed highly desirable for the financing of capital ex-penditures such as city buildings, fire protection, and water supply, or for new school buildings. This multiplication of superimposed corporations had only to be carried for-ward to new ends to nullify completely the constitutional prohibition.

This opportunity was taken advantage of in cases such as that in which, in 1913, it was enacted that when two or more municipal corporations wish to construct jointly a system of sanitary drainage within the joint area, there may be created a " sanitary drainage district," a corpora-tion with power to incur debt up to the constitutional limit.[28]

The further development of the highway system in city and country likewise called for an extension of credit which led to the employment of a second device for avoid-ing the constitutional provision. This was by the creation of improvement districts.

The principle of assessment for benefits conferred on real estate had been recognized and made use of in con-nection with street improvements as early as 1852,[29] and was later expanded to meet more modern needs.[30] The same principle was applied to the construction of rural

[26] Acts, 1859, c. 199, p. 181; Acts, 1865, c. 1, p. 3.
[27] *Carmichael v. Lawrence*, 47 Ind. 554 (1874).
[28] Acts, 1913, c. 307, p. 821.
[29] *Rev. Stats., 1852*, c. 17, p. 203.
[30] Acts, 1889, c. 188, p. 237.

highways in 1877.[31] When the demand for street and gravel road improvement began to strain both city and township revenues, the courts again came to the rescue. It was held by the court that since bonds issued for street improvements were to be paid under the statute from a special fund derived from special assessment, they did not constitute a debt of the city and therefore could not be taken into consideration in determining the capacity to borrow money.[32]

It was provided by the gravel road act of 1877 that roads were to be built from the proceeds of serial " bonds of the county," issued by the county commissioners, which were to be liquidated by a tax upon the real estate in the township wherein the improved road was located. With respect to bonds thus issued the court had already laid down the doctrine just stated in the Quill case, *supra,* with respect to cities. It was now held that the bonds did not constitute an indebtedness of the county but were an obligation of a special improvement fund to be collected from assessments made upon benefited property.[33] Likewise in a subsequent decision it was held that neither were such bonds a liability of the township.[34] Although the principle of assessment for benefits is relied on to support these conclusions, they embody a plain enough effort to circumvent the clear intent of the constitution. Should further evidence of intent be desired it would seem to be furnished not only from the fact that in each case the area assumed to be benefited was declared to be coterminous with the township, but because the benefits were assumed to be uniform for all property in the township

---

[31] Acts, 1877, c. 46, p. 72.
[32] *Quill v. Indianapolis,* 124 Ind. 292 (1890).
[33] *Strieb v. Cox, Treasurer,* 111 Ind. 299 (1887).
[34] *Board v. Harrell,* 147 Ind. 501 (1890).

without regard to vicinity or to remoteness from the improvement.

By this series of judicial decisions all restraint on this class of improvements was removed, and a program of road-building was inaugurated which gave to the state what was, perhaps, the greatest mileage of improved country roads in the country. By the year 1913 the outstanding issues of gravel road bonds was so great that the state stepped in to stem the tide. By act of that year it was forbidden to issue road bonds whenever the obligations outstanding against the property within a township should exceed four percent of the taxable valuation therein.[85] In 1923 the limit of issue of road bonds in townships was reduced to two percent of the valuation, and in the case of county roads to one percent.[86] At the close of the year 1922, in spite of the fact that many of the earlier issues had long since been retired, the outstanding gravel road bonds in the state amounted to more than fifty-five million dollars. On account of the greater restriction imposed by the act of 1923 and continued retirement of matured bonds, the amount outstanding in July, 1932, had been reduced to thirty-two million dollars. In the latter year, as a part of the program undertaken to reduce governmental costs, a moratorium on the issue of all highway bonds was declared, to remain effective until September, 1937.[37]

Still another avenue of escape from the embarrassments imposed by the debt-limitation clause was attempted through resort on a considerable scale to the formation of holding companies to carry out improvements. It was found that to secure the support of judicial opinion the

[85] Acts, 1913, c. 205, p. 604.
[86] Acts, 1923, c. 70, p. 233.
[37] Acts, 1932, c. 15, p. 27; c. 53, p. 200.

municipality must proceed with circumspection. When the nature of the dummy holding corporation was too manifest the court could not bring itself to close its eyes to the fact and the arrangement was declared to be a mere subterfuge and an evasion of the constitutional mandate. Likewise when a municipality had reached the limit of its borrowing power and had pledged itself to pay annually to the bondholders a fixed sum either from the proceeds of the operation of the plant or from taxation, it was held that a debt of the city was created in violation of the constitution.[38]

In 1921 an act was passed whereby a city might issue bonds to finance the purchase or construction of a utility plant payable solely out of revenues derived from the operation of the plant. Such bonds were not to be considered a debt of the city, and hence do not constitute a violation of the constitution.[39]

A more successful attempt to employ the principle of the holding company to finance a utility was one wherein a private water company was created to build and operate a plant in which a city subscribed for about a third of the stock and from which it agreed to purchase a definite amount of water at an agreed price. When these proceedings were attacked it was held that since the city was not proposing to raise by taxation a sum more than to retire bonds which it was competent to issue nor to mortgage or pledge its property nor to pledge any of its income, there was no violation of the constitution.[40] The use of the holding company device was specifically authorized for certain cities in an act of 1927.[41]

[38] *Voss v. Waterloo Water Co.*, 163 Ind. 69 (1904).
[39] *Fox v. Bicknell*, 193 Ind. 537 (1923).
[40] *Bollenbacher v. Harris, Mayor*, 196 Ind. 657 (1925); Acts, 1925, c. 25, p. 133.
[41] Acts, 1927, c. 103, p. 269.

The General Assembly had, meantime, manifested in still another and a fourth direction its willingness to come to the assistance of municipalities which were embarrassed by the constitutional limitation. A school township in which a school building had been condemned as unsanitary and unfit for use found itself unable constitutionally to borrow sufficient funds to build a new structure. By act of 1917 it was enacted that under such circumstances the coterminous civil township might, within the bounds of its borrowing power, issue bonds to augment the funds of the school township.[42] The same permission was later granted to cover certain other contingencies specifically enumerated.[43] The court in sustaining this legislation rested its decision in part on an old statute which authorized the use of school buildings for public gatherings and for civic, social, and religious purposes.[44] It was recognized by the court in this opinion that the practice of multiplying overlapping corporations held the seeds of serious abuses. Yet, subordinating, as it had done in the past, actualities to legal fiction, it held that the court was powerless to supply the wholesome remedy provided in some states by specific constitutional provision.

The sympathetic attitude evinced by the General Assembly and by the courts as demonstrated in the acts and opinions recounted left to these units wide latitude in the use of their credit. This they had so freely availed themselves of that by the year 1922 the total bonded indebtedness of all local units in the state had reached more than one hundred and fifty-seven million dollars.

It is to a certain extent as a sequel to the policy of excessive debt accumulation displayed by local political

[42] Acts, 1917, c. 174, p. 684.
[43] Acts, 1919, c. 42, p. 94.
[44] Acts, 1859, c. 119, p. 181; *Follett v. Sheldon,* 195 Ind. 510 (1904).

units as described above that the latest phase of state control developed. This consists of two related institutions which have been thought of as together constituting the " Indiana plan." Both institutions should be examined in the light of their history.

The first part of the " plan " provides for the review under certain circumstances by the state tax commission of local budgets and tax levies.

Within the period 1900-1918, during which there was no limitation by law upon local budgets or tax rates, assessed valuations increased but sixty-four percent although the actual increase in wealth was very much greater. This was due to the weakness of the decentralized system of assessment of property. In 1919 a general revision of the tax law was enacted having as one of its purposes an improvement in the methods of assessment. It then became probable that since the revised act would result in greatly increased valuations there would be made in some localities strenuous attempts to reduce or increase local rates unduly. To meet this contingency authority was given to the state tax commission to increase the levy in any taxing unit upon a showing that a necessity existed and that otherwise the local levy would be insufficient to procure funds necessary to meet the requirements of that unit. The commission was further given power on its own initiative, or upon the petition of any taxpayer affected, to reduce any levy " whenever it shall appear that more revenue is about to be raised than the requirements of government, economically administered, warrant." [45]

As a matter of fact property valuations did increase in the first year under the new act to the extent of one hun-

[45] Acts, 1919, c. 59, p. 198.

dred and fifty-seven percent. In spite of the fact that the tax commission during that year reduced levies to the extent of more than eleven million dollars, taxes collected increased during the year more than seven million dollars.

The centralization of authority in the state commission and the reductions made by its order provoked such protest that the General Assembly, in special session in 1920, removed the power of review from the tax commission and vested it in the county council, the tax levying body of the county.[46] By the terms of the new act appeals might be made to the county council upon petition of twenty taxpayers. Thereupon, after hearing, the council might increase or decrease the rate of levy. The results of the transfer seemed to justify the position of the sponsors of the state control feature of the act of 1919. Under the new law review was obtained only upon petition and the taxpayers failed to avail themselves of the privilege. At once local levies, freed from central control, rose fifty-three percent within the year. In fairness to those who demanded the return to local control it should be said that this enormous increase in local spending was due, in part at least, to the rising costs of commodities and labor as well as to unusual demands for capital expenditures in order to overtake building needs postponed during the period of the war. The lesson was, however, so obvious that there was a general demand, especially among the agricultural classes who were already feeling the pinch of depression, for a return to some measure of state control. As a result the General Assembly, in 1921, revived the act of 1919 with respect to local levies so that when a levy had been fixed by the local authority the matter might be appealed to the tax commission upon petition of ten

[46] Acts, 1920, c. 49, p. 164.

taxpayers. The commission must then review the rate at a public hearing held in the territory affected and affirm or decrease it or any part thereof. The action of the commission was made final.[47]

Under the terms of the act the power of the commission extended only to the confirmation or the reduction of the rate of levy. Subsequently the power of the commission was extended to a review of the budget upon which the contested levy is based. If a reduction in the levy is ordered the board must indicate not only the amount of the reduction but upon what items of the budget this reduction shall fall.[48]

In the ten years ensuing after the reenactment in 1921, reductions in local levies amounted on the average annually to from a million to a million and a half dollars. The amount rose in 1927 to more than three and a half millions and the total reductions for the period were something more than twenty-one million dollars.[49]

The second part of this latest phase of state control is concerned with the limitation of the power of localities to contract indebtedness.

It was perceived in the discussions which preceded the passage of the tax act of 1919 that one effect of the expected increase in valuation of property would be an increase in the capacity of local governments under the constitutional provision to make use of their credit. To meet this probability the General Assembly reversed its earlier sympathetic attitude toward local spending. It took the precaution of inserting in the statute a provision to check the borrowing and the consequent orgy of spending which would probably follow the increase in valuation. It was

[47] Acts, 1921, c. 222, p. 638.
[48] Acts, 1927, c. 95, p. 247; *Zoercher v. Alger,* 202 Ind. 214 (1930).
[49] Rept. Board of Tax Commissioners, *Indiana Year Book* (1931), p. 633.

stipulated that thereafter no municipality might issue any evidence of indebtedness without first securing the approval of the state tax commission.[50] It was the intent of the act and it was so construed by the commission that that body should, in acting upon a proposed issue of bonds, take into consideration not merely the capacity of the unit to borrow but likewise review the question of policy involved in the expenditures to be made from the proceeds of the issue.

Although this restriction on the power of local units was sustained by the supreme court,[51] this extreme measure of control shared with the section of the act which placed limitation on the power to levy taxes general popular disapproval. Consequently, as in the case of contested tax levies, the power of review was at the next legislative session taken from the tax commission and placed in the hands of the county council,[52] to be exercised upon petition of twenty taxpayers of the area affected.

Again experience justified the predictions made as to the effects of tax act. The fact was once more demonstrated that a locally elected body was not to be depended on to stem the tide of local demand for the expenditure of public funds. So, again, the authority to review bond issues was returned to the tax commission at the following session of the General Assembly.[53] This act provided that upon the petition of ten or more taxpayers any bond issue in excess of five thousand dollars should be taken on appeal to the commission. That body might, after a hearing held in the locality affected, approve, modify or reject the proposed issue. Unlike the original act of 1919 but in accord with that of 1920 was the feature that

[50] Acts, 1919, c. 59, p. 198.
[51] *Van Hess v. The Board*, 190 Ind. 347 (1920).
[52] Acts, 1920, c. 49, p. 164.
[53] Acts, 1921, c. 222, p. 638.

appeals were to originate with the taxpayers. This as well as the provision for hearing within the district concerned was a concession to the sentiment for local self-government.

During the period in which this act has been operative down to October, 1931, bond issues to the amount of $73,000,000 had been appealed. Of this amount, $30,-000,000 were disapproved.[54]

As has been said, these measures with respect to tax levies and budgets and to the issue of local evidences of indebtedness, originally incorporated in a single act, were hailed as innovations. In the light of the policy of Indiana in common with many other states toward the financial affairs of their political sub-divisions it can, however, scarcely be properly said that they were innovations. It did constitute, nevertheless, a substitution of administrative for judicial control applied at a new point. Even this substitution was scarcely in itself an innovation since the administrative method of control had been inaugurated with respect to local assessment and equalization as early as the act of 1891 which created the state tax commission. The novelty, it is asserted, consists in removing from the local authority the determination of financial policy with respect to taxing, spending, and borrowing. But even there the novelty is one of degree and of application rather than one of principle. The determination of the tax base, the imposition of mandatory levies and mandatory appropriations, the setting of statutory salary scales, and the fixing of a constitutional debt limit were quite as truly determinations of local policy as are the measures under discussion. Partaking of the same character are the more recent limitations on tax rates in the state. Though brought into prominence by recent

[54] *Rept. State Tax Commission,* 1931, p. 637.

drastic applications of the practice in several states, such limitations are as has been suggested wide-spread and of long standing. Criticisms of the particular manifestations of state control which are included in the " Indiana plan " fall into two groups: those based on theoretical and those based on practical grounds.

The chief theoretical objection is that these measures violate the right of local self-government. It is not clear why similar objection has not been as vigorously expressed against the earlier and more wide-spread forms of local control such as those above mentioned and others pointed out in the course of this discussion.

The development of the doctrine of local self-government as a right is typical of the development of political doctrines generally. The factors of distance and the difficulties of travel fixed upon the colonies and the earlier states a decentralized form of government. This was of a kind to find favor with the self-reliant temper of the frontier and was in harmony with the more advanced conceptions of democracy. Having become institutionalized these forms of self-government acquired a character of sanctity and of finality. An idealized picture of local institutions as thus developed was rationalized, and the product invested with universality emerged as the doctrine of the inherent right of local self-government, a dogma quite at odds with the status which the law had meantime assigned to local units of government. So when, under changed conditions, the state found it expedient in the interests of the whole people to institute an increasing measure of centralized control through administrative officials, the steps taken to accomplish this were looked upon as tyrannical invasions of a natural right.

The doctrine of local self-government assumes that, whatever other powers the state may exercise, there is a field of purely local concerns in which the local community has a moral right to act as it sees fit. It is assumed, further, that it is possible to assign every situation leading to political action to one or other of these categories. By what test shall it be determined whether a given act falls in this or in that category? The test is whether the matter is one of purely local concern. Who shall apply the test? Obviously it must be the state since the locality cannot decide concerning interests outside its own, but as a matter of fact the locality assumes this function itself.

The advocates of the doctrine ignore the fact that with the lapse of time matters which yesterday were of purely local concern may today have become of wider interest. The shift in major interest from locality to state in the field of education, of transportation, and of public utility matters are cases in point.

So, then, with respect to matters of local finance. Any condition or policy which places an undue economic burden on any local community in the long run affects the state adversely. This is made plain in cases where a local unit, having managed its finances badly, finds itself in time of stress unable to support properly its schools or its burden of poor relief, and hence must have recourse to state aid. It may be fairly concluded that although the grant of a greater or less degree of self-determination in financial and other matters should so far as expedient be conferred on local subdivisions, this cannot be conceded as a moral right. If the above conclusions are valid, then it is from their practical working and effectiveness that these devices of control should be judged.

We may turn, then, to the second category of objections to these forms of state control, those based on practical grounds. It is claimed that the results of the operation of the statute setting up control in matters of tax levies and bond issues has failed to a considerable degree to accomplish its purpose, and that in some instances actual harm has been done. It is charged that the review of budgets by the tax commission does not envisage the whole local picture since it concerns itself with the financial problem of receipts and expenditures alone, and that the social needs of the community are lost sight of. It is further charged that the review does not take into view even the whole financial scene since it does not include and make assured proper provision for sinking fund and debt obligations. It is pointed out that tax reduction may not be synonymous with cost reduction when it results in a mere shifting of burdens to other forms of revenue; that the rejection of proposed issues of bonds for necessary capital expenditures means merely a postponement rather than a permanent saving, and that the justice of an order reducing a budget can be determined only upon the basis of cost studies for which no provision is made in the present procedure.

Some of the criticisms are probably well founded although it must be said that the specific good accomplished by the measures instituted has, in the last fifteen years, been very great. To determine the extent to which the strictures directed against its practical operations are justified would necessitate a more elaborate study than has yet been undertaken. That there should be defects in the statutes and inadequacies in the machinery of administration is inevitable from the circumstances under which these institutions came into being.

The statutory provisions in question were not designed to set up a completed " plan " of financial control as the unfortunate use of that term would imply, nor were they thought of as permanent measures at all. They were isolated measures designed to meet an emergency without thought of the future, but having seemed to accomplish a desirable end were perpetuated. If they have attracted a considerable measure of attention, and some criticism on both theoretical and practical grounds, it is to a large degree because they apply control at new and unaccustomed points, restrain popular impulses, and involve to a large degree the use of administrative discretion.

It is evident that these institutions which have developed in Indiana, the appeal features of the state's tax limitation law, and the centralization of supervision over assessments which has proceeded farther in some of the states than in Indiana are all symptomatic of a trend toward greater state control not only in financial matters but in other directions as well. If this be the case attention might well be directed in these days toward the development of administrative machinery of control more adequate than is now existent in any state. Such an organ of government should, perhaps, consolidate supervision of all local agencies of general administration but should not have jurisdiction over local service functions.

The present central control in Indiana of matters of general administration is restricted to matters of finance alone. It is scattered among three distinct agencies, the department of inspection commonly spoken of as the board of accounts, the tax commission, and the board of finance. The first two of these have other and important duties commanding a large share of their attention; the third is an ex officio body laboring under the weaknesses inherent in such bodies. No more common mistake is made in our states than to fail to provide adequate means of enforcing supervisory and regulative legislation. This has been the case with the Indiana department of inspection and especially so with respect to the tax commission. Neither of these has either the statutory authority or the administrative staff to enable it to perform in the best manner the important functions committed to it.

Recognizing the good services hitherto performed by existing agencies in spite of their imperfections, it is time to establish a state department of local government, perhaps along the lines blazed by North Carolina, perhaps in some other form. Such a department should administer a statewide personnel system. It should include a central purchasing organization for local units which should set standard forms for orders, bids, contracts, and specifications; test supplies and materials; purchase or give advice to local purchasing agencies—thus giving to the localities the benefits of expert knowledge and skill in merchandising. In the field of finance such a department should take over the present activities of control and in some directions expand them. It should have complete authority to prescribe forms of accounting and reporting and to inspect local accounts as at present; to appoint and supervise local assessors and to review their action; and to regulate the custody of local funds and ensure their security. It should have the authority and be equipped with a proper technical staff to supervise the preparation of plans and contracts for public works and to approve or reject such work when completed. It should be equipped to make such investigations and studies as would enable it to pass intelligently, not merely upon such cases as are appealed to it, but upon all local budgets, tax levies, and proposals for incurring bonded debt.

Such a course of action would but integrate and round out the present established policy of state control and make of it a consistent whole. The administrative form of control would avoid on the one hand the inflexibility of a legislative control enforced by the judiciary and, on the other, the waste, the blunders, and the disasters attendant upon a policy of *laissez faire* in local government.

# The Inadequacies of the Rule of Law

BY

CHARLES C. THACH

It may well seem, indeed, that anthropology, with its concentration on primitive man and embryonic social institutions, is a far, a very far, cry from such contemporary questions as administrative discretion, delegation of legislative power, and state irresponsibility. But there is sound truth in the Aristotelian thesis that the nature of the embryo is the fully developed and perfect form, with its complementary injunction to study origins.

It will perhaps prove helpful, then, to turn for a moment to the dubious days of human pre-history, to glimpse, as best one can, the beginnings of this human institution, government, in order to understand its present day operations and particularly the deficiencies of that operation.

It would seem, so we are told by competent anthropologists, that man, since he has been *homo sapiens,* and before, has formed territorial groups. On the one hand, like the dogs of Constantinople, he had his range, his source of food supply, his hunting territory. On the other, he felt towards his neighbors in this territory that sense of neighborliness, of "we-ness" which in a developed, not to say exacerbated, form appears today as nationalism. In such communities, such states *in posse,* there was as yet no government. Instead, there was only law; or, at any rate, there were rules, rules which were obeyed, if not enforced; rules which defined, in gross, the social relations of group member to group member, which set those external conditions of action and forbearance which alone made communal existence possible.

So far, we may conclude, there is only territorial community and customary rule. There is no state, or rather there is only an embryonic state, for there is as yet no government. But why does this government arise? Frankly, we are here largely in the realm of hypothesis. But the political theorist may perhaps be permitted to hazard a reconstruction.

We are familiar with the primitive institution of the blood feud and the *wergeld*. Perhaps we may be allowed to wonder what its significance is. Is it far-fetched to infer that here is a rather evident lack of obedience, uncoerced acceptance of necessary communal rules on the part of some, at least, of the community? Is it not equally possible that the blood feud proved an extremely unhappy solution of the problem whenever one group, weakened by internal strife, came into conflict with a neighbor group not so afflicted?

In other words, it is here suggested that the state as a territorial community, that nationalism as a tribal sense of neighborliness, is as old as man and that government, as a comprehended relationship of the few who rule and the many who obey, comes into being—and continues to exist—primarily as a means, in the apt words of Professor MacIver, for the maintenance of the external conditions of social order.

Law, then, in the widest sense of the term, is the body of rules which determine the action and forbearances which make community life possible. Government is to be thought of as originally a law enforcing and not a law-making agency. It is thus not accidental that the legislature, in the modern rather than the etymological sense of the word, is a late evolution in political history.

That this concept of political power and of law is the dominant one in the mediaeval age has been amply and ably shown by Sir R. W. Carlyle and A. J. Carlyle in their monumental and authoritative history of mediaeval political theory. "The fundamental principle of the Middle Ages," they write, " was that the law was the expression, not so much of the deliberate and conscious will of any person or persons who possessed legislative authority, but rather of the habits and usages of the community."[1]

Probably, as these authorities point out, the Bologna revival of civil law study with its emphasis upon the cardinal concept of Roman jurisprudence that the will of the prince has the force of law, is the literary source for the appearance of a new idea, or, if you please, the reappearance of an old one. But it was primarily due, we may believe, to social and political conditions that the concept of the supreme monarch arose to correct the manifest evils of an all but complete lack of central political authority and the resultant social disorder, so fatal to the increasingly important commercial interests of the later Middle Ages.

A second force that worked for the birth of the principle was of course increasing contemporary resentment with the principle of international control by an ecclesiastical group, which not only claimed for its locally domiciled members immunity from political control but also claimed and exercised a supervision over secular authorities in their secular capacities.

Freedom from external control and the subjection of all to the law of the land were thus the proximate goals of princes. It remained for political philosophy to furnish a rationalization of the practical ends. And it was an English philosopher who most expertly and satisfactorily performed the task—Thomas Hobbes.

[1] R. W. and A. J. Carlyle, *History of Mediaeval Political Theory*, vol. V, p. 50.

Reviving with consummate skill the Roman concept of legal personality, he centered his philosophy in the concept of the omnipotent body politic whose personality was borne and wielded by the completely representative, and hence, in equal degree, omnipotent sovereign. The state and the sovereign who, in contemplation of the law at least, is the state, became the law making, the law uttering state and sovereign. Law is again command, is will. The maker of the law is above the law. There are no rights against the law maker because he is the body politic. Liberty " lyeth therefore only in those things which in regulating their actions the Soveraign hath praetermitted." [2]

This change from the mediaeval attitude that law is primarily the community's way of looking at its social obligations and rights to the modern concept that law is the command of the state, which has the final legal and ethical right to command is a fundamental one. The test of whether a rule is or is not a rule becomes purely formal. Has the properly authorized organ of the body politic spoken? The test of legality for an executive act is the same. Is the act an application of a command of the state, that is, of the law of the land?

The possibilities of arbitrary government implicit in this doctrine of sovereignty as enunciated by Hobbes are too evident to need elaboration. It is to the everlasting glory of the Puritan rebellion that it successfully insisted that only the King in his High Court of Parliament could speak the will of the commonwealth and so utter law. It is to the equal glory of the British courts that they could and did evolve that characteristically British doctrine, the rule of law, of which Professor Dicey has, of course, given us the classic definition. Absence of arbitrary power

[2] Thomas Hobbes, *Leviathan* (Everyman ed.), p. 112.

of government officers and subjection of every man, including every government officer, to ordinary law administered by ordinary tribunals is of its essence. But, and the insistence is justified, the rule of law is only a refinement of the doctrine of the sovereign state. Nor can we hold that it has solved—rather it has obviated the necessity of finding a solution for—the greatest of all problems of law enforcement, the interpretation of general rules, couched in general terms, to individual cases, no two of which, as it has long since been observed, are or can be alike.

For it is an inevitable failing of language that it is not explicit, not accurate, in the sense that, for example, the microscopically determined blood count is explicit. In general, an attempt to find a mechanical standard to measure human actions proves a failure. One half of one percent by volume as a definition of intoxicating liquor is manifestly absurd. The question immediately arises, intoxicating to whom? But, in general, the criminal law sticks to the general and so the indefinite, term, law, that is to say, must be couched in terms of " intoxicating in fact," with the fact determined by twelve good men and true. The assumption of the analytical jurist is, to speak shortly, false. Not even criminal law consists of a body of certain rules, whose content is determined finally and absolutely through the use of rigorous legal logic by a body of infallible thinking machines, the judiciary. Whether the jury is or is not the judge of the law as well as the fact, there is no possibility of denying that determining the purport of general terms necessarily is part of its actual function.

But it may well be claimed that to criticize the rule of law for the fact that human language is defective is scarcely convincing. This is of course true. But the objection overlooks the true purpose of the criticism. The fact is that the system of representative assembly, independent judiciary, habeas corpus, and trial by jury has proved a reasonably satisfactory means of solving the problem raised by the concept of the sovereign state, but only in that field where the concept finds its only excuse, the field of the police state.

It is a truism to point out that the police state has passed into, has been merged into the service State. The keystone assumption of police state philosophy, namely, the isolated, asocial individual, has crumpled. And with its destruction the whole edifice has come tumbling down. Today the state touches human life and purpose at more and ever more points. And what, in these new circumstances, becomes of the rule of law, of that lawyer-made bit that was forced between the teeth of the sovereign state in order that there be no Bastille and no *lettres de cachet* on, at least, British and American soil?

Is it to be wondered that the rule of law, and all that it infers, is no longer found an effective means for, on the one hand, the satisfactory accomplishment by government of its necessary duties, on the other for the prevention of arbitrary action particularly on the part of administrative underlings, dressed in a little brief authority?

We need advert briefly to only a few aspects of the matter to maintain the point. Under the new dispensation of things political, it seems too patent to need elaboration that the laws which emanate from the representative assembly must be steadily more, not less, general in character. That is to say, the terms used in the underlying statute must of necessity be of the character of standards, of norms, whose detailed content must be subsequently somehow filled in. The impossibility of detailed legislation with respect to most of the matters concerning which modern statutes must deal is apparent enough. On the one hand, the information, the special knowledge of a representative body cannot extend to technical details. On the other, the attempt to govern minutiae by the statute would result in placing administration in a hopeless straitjacket.

The result of this situation is the patent necessity for supplementary administrative ordinances. No longer is it possible for the meaning of general language to be left to the uninformed and unspecialized judgment of twelve laymen. An important part of the function of the petit jury in the interpretation and enforcement of the criminal law thus passes perforce into the hands of administrative officers when the police state changes into the service state. The conclusion seems irresistible that a part, at least, of the true significance of the law must nowadays rest on the judgment of the enforcing agency itself.

But at this juncture we come all too forcibly face to face with a major defect of the rule of law, old style. In the United States it is always possible to attack the grant of ordinance power as in fact a grant of legislative power itself. But, to all realistic intents and purposes, such an attack will prove fruitless save in most extreme cases, for the good and sufficient reason that most such grants are plainly a necessity.

Normally, the court, called upon to judge concerning the *ultra vires* character of an ordinance would proceed with the utmost caution in determining the matter in an adverse sense. It may be assumed that it is only in cases of the most obvious ignoring of the sense of the language of the underlying statute would the ordinary judicial agencies feel called upon to intervene. That is, the voice of the officer is the voice of the state—and so above good and evil. Any other course would, in terms of reality,

result most often merely in the substitution of a manifestly unspecialized, if not (the suspicion is sometimes at
least possible) definitely biased judgment of the meaning of the general language of the statute for a sup-
posedly trained one, which is in direct contact with the
facts. Such a result is, as facts have amply demonstrated,
radically bad.

The problem of the application of the statute as elabo-
rated by the supplementary ordinance to the individual
case remains for consideration. Here our courts have been
less willing to keep hands off. Granting that the original
statute is constitutional and that the terms of the " com-
pleting" ordinances are within the four corners of the
statute, the question is posed, shall the meaning of such
ordinances in terms of the individual case be left to
uncontrolled administrative agents?

The difficult question is perhaps somewhat illuminated
by a realization that here again is a matter that could be
left to the petit jury where the final question to be decided was whether an act by a private citizen came within
the prohibition of a statute. But is there need to stress
the point that with respect to many, if not most, matters
of legislative interest the judgment of twelve average (or
below average) laymen is totally inadequate to the point
of being irrelevant, while the judgment of the ordinary
court of law, while more intelligent, must share some of
this lay character. But, on the other hand, the lack of
control over ordinance enforcing administrative officers is
highly dangerous. In view of the situation, the administrator is really a law giver.

Why, then, should not, the ordinary judiciary intervene
to prevent at least arbitrary and truly illegal applications
of ordinances? The point at issue here seems to be one
primarily of practicality. No one who believes in the

orderly processes of government can maintain a brief for arbitrariness. On the other hand, the insistent demand on modern government is to *get things done*. The plain truth is that we can no longer afford the luxury of the law's delay. Administrative action is demanded in no uncertain terms. The possibility of delay, if nothing more, is an insuperable barrier to this solution of the problem.

Perhaps a practical illustration will serve to illuminate the dilemma in which we find ourselves. Let us imagine that a relief law is passed to the effect that every able bodied man willing to work but unable to secure employment shall be given a cash dole, the administration of the law being assigned to a special department of public relief headed by a director. Evidently the terms " able bodied," " willing to work," " unable to secure employment " require further elaboration by ordinances drafted by the authority of the director. Such rules would set up, so far as possible, detailed tests for the guidance of social workers in applying the law. Now, if the rules so set up have any reasonable relevance to the norms included in the law, it is practically impossible successfully to impugn them in a court of law. The sole guarantee of their wisdom, save in extreme cases, thus is the ability of the director, a matter which normally will be determined only by the chief executive. And if, as in case of valuations for rate making purposes, the court substitutes its judgment concerning the true meaning of these norms for that of the director, where is the real gain? Is it not evident that we have here only the substitution of an uninformed for an informed opinion, and the introduction of an indefinite consideration, namely the court's judgment, with a resultant impossible slowing up of the performance, a vitally necessary function?

The application of these standards by specific relief

workers remains to be considered. On the one hand, there is necessitated much difficult, unspectacular investigating work by stair-climbing agents. On the other, lack of sympathy, delay, officiousness, are all too likely to manifest themselves. Indeed, at the worst, callousness and arbitrariness may easily develop. But can the individual whose case falls into the hands of an unworthy worker really get effective assistance from the courts? The delay, the expense, to say nothing of the uncertainty of the outcome, would generally serve as an insuperable barrier. But, waiving this, what could the court do in the way of sanely controlling the agent? The truth is that the disparity in respect of information would place the court at a hopeless disadvantage, and certainly the decree of an uninformed judicial body has nothing about it that would make it *ipso facto* wise.

The inadequacy of the rule of law, at least of the rule of law as at present understood, in the present situation is further evidenced by a consideration of the fact that, not even in the field of criminal law, have the courts succeeded in devising an effective, positive means to force executive officers to perform their legal duties. That this must be so is apparent from a consideration of the basic jurisprudence on which the rule of law rests. When any officer of government acts in his official character, he is acting not in his own name, not by virtue of any personal authority, but in the name and by the authority of the state. Of course, if it were possible actually to make all administrative duties strictly ministerial the difficulty would not arise. The governing rule has been lucidly summarized by President Goodnow: " If the duty, in the performance of which the act causing the damage was done, is discretionary in character, the general rule is that executive and administrative officers may not be held responsible since the courts do not like to interfere with the discretion of the administration." [3] Such discretionary action being of a *judicial* character, the officer is exempt from all responsibility by action for the motives which influence him and the manner in which such duties are performed. [4]

It seems, therefore, safe to say that the civil courts are really without power to enforce positively the performance of important duties, that indeed, where it is a case of discretion and its method of exercise, they cannot salve injured rights. And yet it is apparent enough that it is of the very essence of the present governmental problem to secure efficient performance, which at the same time is law abiding performance of administrative tasks.

The collapse, not only of parliamentary government, but of government by law [5] in contemporary Germany should perhaps give us cause to remember that we must find a way whereby things can be done, not a way to prevent action. The introduction of the unholy system of Nazism in the unhappy land of Germany was due, we may believe, in no small part to the belief entertained by no inconsiderable portion of the population that the Weimar Republic was an inadequate means to the accomplishment of ends felt to be the *sine qua non* of a bearable existence. The truth or falsity of such belief is not at issue. The point, rather, is that if an opinion comes to prevail that the traditional constitutional method of organizing political control is an unsatisfactory means of producing ends which are deemed essential, the whole

[3] F. J. Goodnow, *Comparative Administrative Law.* (Students' edition.) II, p. 168.

[4] Goodnow, *loc. cit.*

[5] See Dorothy Thompson, "The Record of Persecution" in *Nazism* (Van Paasen and Wise, ed.), *passim.*

doctrine runs great danger of collapse. And there is no little reason to fear that even the application of the rule of law in the criminal field may go down to destruction in the ruins. Assuredly, the phenomenon of the concentration camp in a modern civilized community may extend as significant a lesson as does the Bastille.

Fortunately, however, such an institution seems as yet a possibility fairly remote to the United States. It is not the President who is above criticism but the sovereign state which is above suit. It is just this fact, however, that constitutes one of the most serious practical defects in the operation of the rule of law in the broadened field of present day governmental activity. That it is a natural inference from its basic theory cannot be denied. If the state makes the law, the state is above the law. If the state officer, whatever his capacity, acts in accordance with his legally defined competence, he is acting as an organ of the state. If he acts in an illegal fashion, he no longer acts as an organ of the state. Doubtless there is an historical explanation for this theory, which eventuates in the theory of the personal responsibility of the officer for all his illegal acts.[6] But the position is logically impeccable, as is demonstrated by the argument of Mr. Justice Holmes when he held that " there can be no legal right as against the authority that makes the law on which the right depends." [7]

But what is the practical result? The only redress that is open to the private individual injured in respect of his rights by arbitrary and illegal action on the part of an administrative officer is a suit against such officer as a private, and probably impecunious, individual. The full significance of this is revealed when we observe that a

[6] Goodnow, *op. cit.*, II, p. 163.

[7] *Kawananako* v. *Polyblank*, 205 U. S. 349 (1907).

prominent bonding company refused, in 1927, to continue bonding officers for suits against illegal arrest on the grounds that too great damages were incurred by peace officers.[8] It is quite evident that the individual officer was not as a rule able to respond to a reasonable claim for damages, and that even in the field of criminal law there was sufficient cause for action. Indeed, the same news item presented the information that $3,765.00 damages had been collected for arrest of a married couple for " petting " in a Cleveland park!

The matter is further complicated by the American rule that normally the rule *respondeat superior* does not apply to matters governmental. Certainly, if the superior's order be illegal on its face, it will not serve as a protection of the inferior. A leading opinion, written by Marshall himself, is that of *Little v. Barreme*,[9] which was an action in trespass against a naval officer who had seized, upon the high seas, a ship, in obedience to an order of the President which the President did not have legal authority to issue.

I confess, [said the great Chief Justice] that the first bias of my mind was very strong in favor of the opinion that though the instructions of the Executive could not give a right, they might yet excuse from damages. I was much inclined to think that a distinction ought to be taken between acts of the civil and those of military officers; and between proceedings within the body of the country and those on the high seas. The implicit obedience which military men usually pay to the orders of their superiors, and which indeed is indispensably necessary to every military system, appeared to me strongly to imply that those orders, if not to perform a prohibited act, ought to justify the person whose general duty it is to perform them and who is

---

[8] *New York Times*, October 2, 1927.
[9] 2 Cranch 170 (1804).

placed by the laws of his country in a situation which in general requires that he should obey them. . . . But I have been convinced that I was mistaken, and I have receded from my first opinion. I acquiesce in the opinion of my brethren, which is that the instructions cannot change the nature of the transaction, or legalize an act which without them would have been a plain trespass.

Again, in the case of *Campbell v. Sherman*,[10] the court applied the rule of individual responsibility very stringently. A state court had ordered a vessel to be seized, and in pursuance of the court's orders the sheriff had taken possession. Subsequently the comomnwealth law under which the court had acted was declared to be unconstitutional and the court to be without power to issue such an order. However, while the vessel was in the hands of the sheriff, it burned. The question involved was whether or not the sheriff could be held personally liable for damages. The court held that he could be, using the following language:

Did the warrant thus issued in a cause over which that court had no jurisdiction, afford any protection to the officer for acts done in its execution? Where the subject matter of the suit is within the jurisdiction of the court, yet jurisdiction in the particular case is wanting, there is certainly reason and authority for holding that an officer who executes a process fair upon its face shall be protected. But a clear distinction exists between that case and a proceeding in which the process itself shows that the court has exceeded its jurisdiction. The rule is stated by Mr. Justice Smith in *Bagnall v. Ableman*, 4 Wis. 163, in the following language:

"When the process is fair on its face, and issued by a court or magistrate of competent jurisdiction, it is a protection to the officer. But if it be not fair or regular upon its face, or its recital

[10] 35 Wisconsin 103 (1874).

or commands show a want or excess of jurisdiction in the court or magistrate issuing it, the author is not protected in its execution."

But it is said that this rule imposed upon the officer in the present case the duty of determining in advance of any decision of the courts of the state the validity of an act of the legislature. How can it be expected, it is asked, that a mere ministerial officer could decide such a question, and thus find out that his process was void for want of jurisdiction in the court which issued it? The maxim "ignorantia juris non excusat" in its application to human affairs, frequently operates harshly; and yet it is manifest that if ignorance of the law were a ground of exemption, the administration of justice would be arrested, and society could not exist. . . . It is further said it was the duty of the officer to obey the mandate of the warrant and seize the identical steamboat which he did attach, and that he had no alternative but to obey. If the act which the writ commanded him to do was a trespass, he was not required to perform it. Nor would he be liable in that case to the plaintiff for refusing to execute a process void for want of jurisdiction.

The evident injustice that often results from a strict application of the principle of personal responsibility has resulted in a modification in favor of the officer acting in good faith. As has been stated in a comment on the case of *State v. Godwin*,[11] which laid down the general rule that an officer enforcing a statute subsequently held unconstitutional should not be held responsible:

The case seeems to be correct in principle, although there is a direct conflict of authority on the question. Many jurisdictions hold that when a legislative enactment proves to be invalid it is for all legal purposes, as if it had never existed; and before it has been declared unconstitutional by the courts, acts done or duties neglected by a public officer bona fide believing it to be valid

[11] 123 N. C. 480 (1898) ; cf. 12 *Harv. Law Rev.* (1898), 352.

and in reliance upon it, are, according to the general rule, not excused by his ignorance of the law. . . . The better and more just doctrine however appears to be that the officer is protected unless the statute relied upon appears on its face clearly unconstitutional.

Willoughby's comment on the command of a superior as a valid defence in a suit for illegal action on the part of an officer is pertinent:

Generally speaking, no officer can defend an *ultra vires* or otherwise illegal act by setting up his official position or exhibiting the command of a political superior. This last statement as to the non-applicability of the principle of *respondeat superior* is, however, subject to this qualification, that the order of an administrative superior, *prima facie* legal, though in fact not legal, may be set up as a defense of an act commanded by military superiors. The result of the doctrine last stated is, as will be seen, that an act is defended for the performance of which in fact no legal authority can be produced. Simply the color of authority on the part of the superior giving the command is held to be sufficient defence. Clearly common justice and the practical necessity of administration justify the rule, yet, inasmuch as it does in fact protect an act essentially illegal, the doctrine is one that is kept within the narrowest possible bounds. Only where there is present no fact which would put the subordinate, as a man of ordinary intelligence, upon his guard, or where the practical necessities of the case leave little or no opportunity for individual judgment in the matter, should the rule be applied. In all other cases, it is to be repeated, the public official is able to defend his act only by showing some existing legal authority for it. The necessities of the case require the foregoing doctrine with reference to the military arm of the government. There not being the same urgency for immediate obedience the doctrine does not prevail in civil matters.[12]

[12] W. W. Willoughby, *Principles of Constitutional Law* (Students' edition), p. 544.

However, Goodnow states a more liberal rule as the correct one: [13]

> A second limitation which the courts have placed upon their control over the act of the administration through their power to delimit its sphere of competence, is to be found in the rule, that purely ministerial officers will not be held responsible for damages where they have followed instructions which are legal on their face and contain nothing which will apprise the subordinate that they have been issued illegally, and are not within the jurisdiction of the superior who issued them. The weight of authority seems to be further for the rule that a ministerial officer is relieved from all responsibility for the execution of orders fair on their face, even if he is satisfied that there are illegalities back of them.

Evidently we have a conflict here between the desire to relieve the office holder of responsibility incurred through an action taken in perfect good faith and with all the appearance of legality and the opposing desire not to leave the private individual without any redress at all.

Such, then, is the situation. Need we wonder that loud cries of unhappy protest should arise, and particularly from the legal fraternity? But, in the light of the observable facts, is an insistence on the strict application of the existing rule of law to all administrative acts a cure for the failure of that very rule to work? Rather, it is submitted, the rule of law must be revitalized. In the same sense that habeas corpus was perfected as a concrete procedural means for ensuring that the police state properly performed its fundamental function of keeping the peace, the insistent need today is for a concrete, procedural means by which the new state, the service state, may be reined and bitted.

[13] Goodnow, *Comparative Administrative Law.* Vol. II, p. 166.

May it not be suggested that the trained legal talent of this country might explore the possibilities of special administrative courts, such as the Customs Court, to achieve this purpose? Might not political scientists do well to consider the potentialities latent in a " question and answer " period devoted by the representative assembly to queries concerning arbitrary and illegal acts of administrative officers? There seems little to be gained in making loud and rhetorical complaints against bureaucracy, against administrative tyranny, against, in short, the total highly unsatisfactory condition of things. Such protests will actually achieve but little. The evident answer is, yes, the rule of law has broken down, in a field for which it was never intended. But the true problem is, what are we going to do about it?

# Forms of Control Over Administrative Action

BY

MARSHALL E. DIMOCK

With the rapid increase of governmental responsibilities and the corresponding growth in the number of administrative services, the question of controlling modern bureaucracies in the public interest assumes urgent as well as perennial significance. Heretofore it has been customary to think of bureaucracy chiefly in terms of suspicion and instinctive resistance, but this motivated prejudice is an unwarranted and an unfruitful attitude for the person who approaches administrative problems with a rational and a constructive viewpoint. It is inevitable that a constantly growing percentage of the population should be employed in the public services. All over the world the ranks of civil servants engaged in the older political departments have been swollen—and in some cases outnumbered—by the adhesion of semi-governmental staffs employed in socialized industries. The gulf separating the formal civil service from the citizen body therefore tends to close in, while at the same time the problems of tenure, discipline, coordination, and comparative rewards assume greater complexity.

In approaching the question of the forms of control over administrative action, therefore, we should not predicate a constant clash of interest between government employees and the members of society. This emotional, prejudiced view of the journalist, or of the business community, is not taken seriously—except as it poisons people's minds. We are not dealing with a subversive, liberty-destroying element, but with ordinary citizens who happen to work in public business rather than in private industry.

Our purpose is to analyze the methods of external and internal discipline that are in use at the present time and to weigh the respective forms of control in considering future needs. In attempting this, to be sure, it will be necessary to assume certain criteria—standards of social and professional conduct. These assumptions should be clearly revealed to the reader. The objects of control over administrative action may be said to be these:

1. To prevent the formation of a deepening gulf which may separate the public employees from the citizenry.

2. To carry on public administration within the letter and the spirit of the law, excluding arbitrary or prejudiced action.

3. To test every action of an individual officer by its reaction upon the prestige and the integrity of the public service.

4. To obtain efficiency and *esprit de corps* as a result of positive standards and through corporate responsibility, rather than by fear of the taskmaster or by means of external compulsion—in other words, progressively to supersede the necessity of external controls by developing the internal or corporate disciplines.

By way of further delimiting the scope of this essay, it should be pointed out that we are concerned with administration as a going concern, not with the removal of individual officials by election, recall, or impeachment.[1] In other words, we are not considering the punishments which remove an unpopular employee from office, but rather the forms of control over his actions and conduct while he is in that office.

[1] These remedies have been evaluated in an article by Florence E. Allen entitled "Remedies Against Dishonest or Inefficient Public Servants," (1933) 169 *The Annals*, 172.

The methods of control over administrative action which will form the subject-matter of this paper are these:

1. The investigation of administrative officials by legislative committees.

2. Judicial control as effected by suits or by the application of remedies such as certiorari, habeas corpus, and mandamus.

3. Administrative hearings by higher officials and the exercise of disciplinary action upon subordinates.

4. The professional standards and activities of employees' associations as a means of guiding and regulating individual conduct.

5. The establishment of objectives and of canons of conduct for administrative officials by dictatorships, such as the Italian, German, or Russian.

Very rarely in the past have these forms of control over administration been considered in juxtaposition—as a complete pattern. The artificial categories separating public law and public administration have been largely responsible for this result. It should be stated emphatically, therefore, that the processes of control are not exclusive or incompatible, but that each is part of the broad problem of making administration more principled, effective, and impartial. These interrelations should be carefully investigated, and the peculiar merit of each should be clearly understood. At the same time it is undoubtedly true that, as the problems and the characteristics of administration change, some methods of control will be found more useful than others. By emphasis on alternative forms of control it may be found that the older means of keeping officers on the straight and narrow path are not so productive of good results and of *esprit de corps* as are some of the less developed methods of control. On the other hand, it may be possible that the relative merits of different forms of control cannot be fairly measured, because the peculiar function of each undoubtedly differs in important respects.

### Legislative Investigations of Administrative Conduct

In his treatise on administrative law, Goodnow has referred to legislative investigations as one of the methods by which the actions of departments and of officials are controlled. Writers on public administration—for example, Leonard D. White in his *Introduction to the Study of Public Administration*—also analyze the effects of investigating committees on the conduct of the public business. White has concluded that in some cases this form of control is undoubtedly beneficial, *i. e.*, really constructive, but Goodnow expressed skepticism and reserved judgment. Largely because of Goodnow's interest in the subject, one of his students wrote a study of Congressional investigations.[2] Since then studies on state investigations have appeared,[3] making this an opportune time to reevaluate the significance of legislative investigations in the framework of control over administration.

Since 1792 Congress has conducted nearly 400 investigations, and the majority of these have dealt, directly, or indirectly, with executive departments or offices. In every state and community there have been, in varying frequency, legislative investigations of administrative conduct. Thus, in 1931 the legislatures in 39 states authorized

[2] Marshall E. Dimock, *Congressional Investigating Committees*, Baltimore, 1929.

[3] John A. Fairlie, "Legislative Committees and Commissions in the United States," (1932) 31 *Michigan Law Review* 25; Herwitz and Mulligan, "The Legislative Investigating Committee: A Survey and Critique," (1933) 33 *Columbia Law Review* 4.

237 committees and commissions to sit and investigate after adjournment. In legal theory legislative investigations are upheld on the ground that they are a necessary and proper step in lawmaking, present or future.[4] It will be seen that this rule affords the legislative body great latitude. In reality most important investigations are definitely for the purpose of examining the conduct of some officer or department; in many cases the immediate purpose is to correct an abuse or to examine situations which excite suspicion. Alteration of the law or the passage of a new one is frequently never accomplished, nor really intended. Usually the idea appears to be the one suggested by John Stuart Mill as the most important function of a legislative body, *i. e.*, " to watch and control the Government; to throw the light of publicity on its acts; to compel a full exposition and Justification of all of them which anyone considers questionable; to censure them if found condemnable. . . ."

Investigations naturally occur more frequently when dishonest or incompetent administrations are in office. The greatest number of federal inquiries took place during the Grant and Harding periods. During the Hoover administration there were very few investigations of the executive departments. In the period between December 3, 1928 and July 16, 1932 only one Congressional investigation, the leasing of Post Office buildings, was aimed directly at the executive departments. This inquiry disclosed a reprehensible situation of long standing, and cleared the way for reforms which are urgently needed.[5] Unlike the Teapot Dome investigations, this inquiry did

---

[4] The leading case is *McGrain* v. *Daugherty*, (1926) 273 U. S. 135; Dimock, *op. cit.*, Ch. VI; Herwitz and Mulligan, *op. cit.*

[5] 71st Congress, 2d session, *S. R.* 244; 72d Congress, 1st session, *Senate Report* 971.

not lead to judicial action against members of the federal administration.

The Senate's investigations of the naval oil leases have since led to the important decision in *Sinclair* v. *United States,* which adds to the law as laid down in the *Daugherty* case (273 U. S. 135). In the *Sinclair* case the Supreme Court held, in answer to whether Congress has the power to compel testimony and to make investigations regarding naval petroleum reserves, and as to whether the question of the validity of an oil lease is a proper one to propound to the lessee, that " The Committee's authority to investigate extended to matters affecting the interest of the United States as owner as well as to those having relation to the legislative function." [6] If the legislative resolution is skillfully drafted, there would appear to be no question that a Congressional investigation of almost every conceivable question would be sustained by the Supreme Court.

In the state governments the character of the investigations and the law relating thereto differ rather considerably. One of the most interesting cases of recent years arose out of the inquiry into the official actions of Mayor Hague of Jersey City. In the appeal to the Court of Errors and Appeals it appeared that the Senate and General Assembly of New Jersey had created an investigating committee for the purpose of inquiring into " the conduct of any state official, state department, commission, or body. . . ." This was a clear-cut instance of a legislature's determination to exercise control over administrative officials. By joint session of the two houses a warrant was authorized to hale the petitioner, Mayor Hague, before the joint session. When the mayor refused, contempt pro-

[6] *Sinclair* v. *United States* (1929) 279 U. S. 263, 297.

ceedings followed. This was the issue which arose: Was it lawful to order a warrant for the arrest of Mayor Hague and to bring him before the legislature? The Chancery Court declared the joint session and the joint resolutions illegal,[7] but the Court of Errors and Appeals reversed the lower tribunal on this point. However, by a tie vote of 6-6, the appeal court refused to reverse the decree granting a writ of habeas corpus. This conclusion was based on the ground that the investigating committee was completely political—that it was composed entirely of Republicans who were interested in the candidacy of Hague's opponent.[8] No doubt this point was well established, but such arguments are not the usual ones employed to defeat a legislative investigation. When judges go off into what is politically actuated, they assume a grave responsibility, and arbitrary decisions are inescapable. The reasoning of the United States Supreme Court is clearly preferable.

A much more satisfactory judgment is that afforded by the case of *Attorney General* v. *Brissenden.*[9] In 1930 the General Court of Massachusetts directed the Attorney General to make an investigation of the activities of one Garrett as a member of the Boston police department. The police department of Boston is under the general control and management of a police commissioner for Boston, appointed by the Governor. On the refusal of a witness to testify, two issues were raised in the Supreme Judicial Court: Does the legislature possess power of amendment and modification of the statutes touching the Boston Police Department, and, secondly, as an incident to its power to legislate, has the General Court the power to make investigations in order to ascertain facts as a

[7] (1929) 104 N. J. Eq. 31.
[8] (1929) 104 N. J. Eq. 369, 145 A. 618.
[9] (1930) 271 Mass. 172, 171 N. E. 82.

basis of legislation and for that purpose to summon witnesses and compel them to testify? Both questions were
answered affirmatively. The court pointed out that, because of the governmental set-up, " the police department
of Boston is peculiarly subject to the legislative department of government so far as concerns its establishment
and regulation." Therefore, the General Court has ample
power of amendment and modification of the statutes
touching the police department of Boston. Although
there is no express grant of this power in the Constitution, the legislature may subpoena witnesses as " an attri-
bute of the power to legislate," and it is " an essential
implication of that power." [10]

In some cases state courts have evidenced greater latitude toward legislative inquiries than did the United
States Supreme Court in early cases. For example, in
*People ex rel. McDonald* v. *Keeler,*[11] the New York
Senate adopted a resolution ordering its committee on the
affairs of cities to investigate the department of public
works in New York City. In a contempt case which resulted from the committee's activities the Court of Appeals held that it was immaterial whether the questions
which the witness refused to answer were proper or not;
his refusal to remain and submit to further examination
was a contempt of legislative authority. The inquiry per-
tained to legislation. The relator was not guaranteed the
right to have counsel, for he was not on trial, nor was
he a party; he was merely a witness.

In some instances, however, the state courts have ob-

[10] In the early case of *Lowe* v. *Summers* (1897) 69 Mo. App. 637, it
was held that " either house of the General Assembly has the inherent
power to punish as for a contempt an obstinate and refusing witness."
In this case the legislature's right to exercise control over the Kansas City
Police Department was upheld.

[11] (1885) 99 N. Y. 463, 2 N. E. 615.

structed the investigatory activities of state legislatures. Examples of this will be found in *State ex rel. Robertson Realty Co.* v. *Guilbert*,[12] which involved the control of city government and especially the commissioners of waterworks, and *Ex parte Caldwell*,[13] an investigation of the Governor of West Virginia.

As an effective method of orderly control over administrative conduct, the legislative investigation cannot begin to qualify. Investigations are sporadic and incomplete, and only too frequently are they motivated by callous partisanship and legislative jealousy. Yet they are not merely " a scavenger of the private drains responsible for public malady," and they sometimes do more than " clean out dirty corners." The benefits of legislative investigations are that they help to acquaint law-makers with the needs and the processes of the administration—they provide a link between the legislative and the executive branches; they are a means of bringing wrong-doers to the bar of justice; and they provide the legislature with knowledge which sometimes results in administrative reform and a reallocation of functions. At the present stage of our governmental development it would be a loss if investigations of administrative conduct should drop completely out of the picture. Nevertheless, they are an extraordinary remedy which can be dispensed with in a responsible government—controlled by trustworthy administrators. Experience in Great Britain, where investigations once abounded and where they have now disappeared, proves that other controls are more effective. As interest

[12] (1906) 75 Ohio St. 1, 78 N. E. 931. A single branch of the legislature has no power of independent legislation, and hence no power of independent investigation.

[13] (1906) 61 W. Va. 49, 55 S. E. 910. A single branch of the legislature cannot investigate after adjournment. The reasoning in both this and the above case appears indefensible.

in government increases, as more reliable leaders are obtained, as the framework of government is more satisfactorily coordinated, as positive controls over administration replace the old negative inquisitions, the legislative investigation should gradually fade out of the picture.

## The Courts and the Official

The realm occupied by judicial control of administrative action is so vast that we can merely attempt to relate it to the general problem and draw certain observations and conclusions therefrom. This phase of the subject has received more attention from writers on public law and administration than have any of the others, and for that reason the substantive law will not be examined in detail. We are here concerned only with judicial control of official conduct, as a means of preventing arbitrary or unlawful action, and not with the jurisdiction of courts over problems such as fair value, reasonable return, and other moot questions of administrative law. In other words, this is the general category entitled " faute personelle " in the French *Droit Administratif*.

In a round-table on " Le Regime Administratif " which was held at Congrès International de Droit Comparé, the French representatives proposed a resolution which ran somewhat as follows: " That the action of every official and of every service should be in, by, and through law; and that no arbitrary or prejudiced act should be countenanced by any government." From later discussion it appeared that " administration through law " means, in the continental view, that some judicial tribunal should have declared what constitutes lawful procedure, and that the aggrieved individual should be free to appeal to a court whenever he thinks his rights are being violated. This assumption underlies a great deal of American thinking, with the result that judges are frequently thought of as the only suitable custodians of administrative honor and decorum. Proponents of public administration have naturally revolted against this authoritarian notion. By what strange process do judges become more trustworthy than career men in the civil service? Is it reasonable to expect that lawyers should understand the intricacies of modern administration as fully as do those who come in daily touch with these problems? Hence, the current of American opinion has begun to flow in the direction of control exercised over minor officials by higher administrative officials. Most writers on public administration assume that appeals to courts should be discouraged whenever possible and that judicial intervention usually creates, for all parties concerned, more difficulties than it does solutions. The realistic analyses of Jerome Frank, Charles G. Haines, Walter Wheeler Cook, and others have emphasized the essentially human character of judges, thus stripping courts of the mystical prestige with which they have been uncritically adorned.

The common law remedies which the citizen can employ against an administrative official are, like investigations, extraordinary in their nature. A very small percentage of administrative acts ever comes before the courts. Moreover, judicial control comes into operation only when an individual complains of the deprivation of some right or the sufferance of damage to person or property. Court control is not adapted to the improvement of efficiency, method, or attitude. Judicial control of administrative conduct is hence largely retroactive and compulsive. Court decisions create standards regarding property rights, but techniques, methods, and employee attitudes fall almost completely outside of judicial competence. The effect of judicial control is therefore more personal than institutional, more negative than positive. The most serious faults of administration are the accumulations of petty grievances, such as discourtesy, inadequate explanations, impatience, officiousness, and carelessness. These complaints rarely come before the courts. They are not clearly unlawful, and the expense involved in going to the courts serves as an effective deterrent. Minor complaints may be dealt with more advantageously by other means.

An appreciation of the limits of judicial control is a matter of great importance, because superficially it would appear that all aspects of administrative conduct are covered by the scope of common law remedies. If misunderstanding is not to result, it is necessary to concentrate upon the processes and the faults of administration, rather than upon the types of judicial relief which, under the proper circumstances, are available to the citizen. The traditional administrative law, *i. e.,* the case law made by judicial decisions, is built into the body of the common law, the core of which consists of individual rights (largely property rights) and duties. The new administrative law must commence with a new starting-point—the nature and the needs of administrative processes. On this foundation the faults of administration can be inductively analyzed, and a resulting compromise between individual and social rights can then be worked out. Within the framework of the new administrative law, administrative justice constantly tends to replace court adjudications.[14] Efficient administration demands a fusion of adjudication and administration; the prerogatives must be placed in the same department and frequently in the same hands.

[14] John Dickinson, *Administrative Justice and the Supremacy of the Law*, Cambridge, 1927; Marshall E. Dimock, " The Development of American Administrative Law," (1933) 15 *Journal of Comparative Legislation*, 35.

Only by this development, moreover, can the accumulations of petty grievances be effectively dealt with.

Judicial remedies are, and will no doubt continue to be, one of the most important forms of control over administrative action. The above discussion was merely designed to show the limitations of court control, and the nature of the contribution which may be expected from that quarter. The comprehensiveness of legal remedies indicates the scope of judicial intervention. The jurisdiction of administrative officials may be challenged by habeas corpus, certiorari, injunction, or quo warranto proceedings. The action of the administrator may be prevented by prohibition or by injunction. He may be forced to perform a duty by an action for mandamus. If he has invaded personal rights or has acted maliciously, he may be sued for damages. Hence, the governmental employee may be forced to act, prevented from proceeding, have his jurisdiction questioned, or be punished for having proceeded in an unlawful manner.

The practical effectiveness of common law remedies is limited by several important factors. The administration of justice generally is slow, costly, and uncertain. When to this situation is added the fact that actions brought against administrative officials do not usually involve large sums of money or very important interests, it is only natural that most cases involving administrative dereliction or incompetence never get before the courts at all Our public service commissions, industrial accident commissions, tax and other administrative tribunals afford speedier and cheaper relief in many fields of administration, but court actions involving the non-feasance or tort of most classes of officials must be heard in the ordinary courts. If justice is to be brought within the reach of many to whom it is now denied, and if dispatch and low cost are to be obtained, a system of special administrative courts similar to those found in Europe would seem to be clearly indicated. The American judicial system does not function as efficiently, on the whole, as do the administrative services. The extraordinary remedies are not generally understood or easily employed. Quo warranto and prohibition are almost never brought into operation any more. Mandamus, certiorari, and injunction are enmeshed in legal quibbling regarding degrees of discretion or the availability of other remedies. Experienced administrators who know some comparative law and some legal philosophy, but who have not been immersed in legal sophistry, would be the best candidates for our proposed administrative courts.

The Anglo-American doctrine of non-liability for damages sustained in the performance of " governmental " acts has caused immeasurable hardship to thousands of persons, and has impaired the administrative services by transferring a liability to a government employee which in many cases should have been borne by the community. Our courts have held officers liable in damages, even to the extent of confiscating their property, in spite of the fact that there appeared to be no personal fault; but damages could be awarded in no other way.[15] Negligence, malice, or prejudice on the part of the specific official

---

[15] For example, in the case of *McCord* v. *High*, (1868) 24 Iowa 336, the court declared, speaking through the famous Dillon, C. J.: " . . . Although the injury done the plaintiff is a direct invasion of his rights of property, and actionable in its nature, he is without remedy, unless it be against the defendant. In such a case, upon principles of justice, the action should, I think, be held to lie against the public officer. And the principle involved in this holding, and which, upon the whole, I believe to be sound, is this: That where a public officer, other than a judicial one, does an act directly invasive of the private rights of others, and there is otherwise no remedy for the injury, such officer is personally liable, without proof of malice and intent to injure."

being sued need not invariably be proved if the court finds that the plaintiff has sustained a tort and that compensation should be made. In some cases, to be sure, legislative bodies have reimbursed officials who have borne the brunt of official liability. But random inquiries which have been made prove that—particularly a generation or so ago—conscientious employees have been literally ruined because of successful damage suits on the part of a taxpayer or a corporation. The deterring effect of this situation on capable men who might have entered the public services and the sense of injustice felt by employees must have had a serious result on the efficiency of administration. The bonding of employees has helped to correct the evil, but justice will not be established until full governmental responsibility, like that found in France, has been won in this country.

Fortunately considerable progress has been made in recent years toward redefining governmental immunity, and a group of indefatigable workers in the legal profession has awakened some of the legislatures and also Congress to the necessity of more liberal legislation.[16] In several states, for example, legislation has been passed acknowledging liability in the operation of publicly owned vehicles. Legislative withdrawal of sovereign immunity, and specific provision for damage suits and compensation, must be relied upon chiefly for relief to both administrators and future litigants. The pending federal tort claims bill would considerably extend the national government's liability, but, as Professor Borchard has pointed out, it leaves much to be desired. In certain south-

[16] Edwin M. Borchard, "The Federal Tort Claims Bill," (1933) 1 *University of Chicago Law Review*, 1; "Governmental Liability in Tort," (1925) 34 *Yale Law Journal*, 1, 129, 229, by the same author; for recent cases and tendencies see Marshall E. Dimock, "American Administrative Law in 1931," (1932) 26 *American Political Science Review*, 894.

ern states, notably Florida, governmental non-liability has been altered by judicial decisions,[17] but it is too sanguine to hope that this practice will be widely followed. Nevertheless, it is reasonable to expect that as public opinion becomes more fully informed regarding the injustice of sovereign non-liability to both citizens and employees, and if other jurisdictions follow the progressive example of the Florida courts, something tantamount to the " faute de service " principle may in time become deeply rooted in American government.

Reforms such as those which have been suggested would take care of only flagrant cases of official unlawfulness, negligence, or some form of arbitrary action. There would still remain the problem of making judicial relief more democratic, by making court actions speedy, cheap, and informal. Again we return to the thesis that the most important problem of control over administration arises from the large number of disciplinary cases which lie outside of judicial competence, or which might be dealt with more advantageously by special administrative courts. Then, too, it needs to be constantly reiterated that we are more likely to make administration " lawful " by making it good, and this seems to suggest that self-regulation, or reform from within, may be the most fruitful means of creating the norms, the behavior patterns, and the corporate traditions which are the strongest assurance of impartial, public-spirited administration.

## Administrative Self-Regulation

In the next chapter of the history of American institutions self-regulation will probably be found replacing

[17] *City of Tallahassee* v. *Kaufman* (1924) 87 Fla. 119, 100 So. 150; *Wolfe* v. *City of Miami*, (1931) 103 Fla. 774, 134 So. 539, Rehearing, 137 So. 892; *Chardkoff Junk Co.* v. *City of Tampa*, 102 Fla. 501, 135 So. 457, (1931).

wholesale reliance on outside compulsion. Corporate responsibility is one of the substantial foundations of the social edifice. Self-regulation has assumed new prominence in many fields of endeavor, some of the notable evidences being the guild control of professions, commercial arbitration, the self-governing bar, and trade association codes which have been created under the Industrial Recovery Act. After ambitious experiments with prohibition, anti-trust laws, and similar enactments, the American people are learning that there is no magic in government, law, or enforcement agencies; law and obedience are built upon social solidarities and upon an adequate tradition and machinery of government.

Our present interest is in the governmental factor—in the control of civil servants by means of disciplinary measures administered by higher officials. This relationship is more than the ordinary employer-employee formula of industry—it is a corporate device which may become the means of making other forms of control largely unnecessary. Official discipline and the next form of control we shall discuss—i. e., the norms of employees' organizations —are obviously closely related.

The potentialities of administrative self-regulation and self-discipline are not, in the United States, widely appreciated or extensively put into practice. The necessity of appeals to courts has been dispensed with in many instances, to be sure, by the substitution of appeals to higher administrative authorities. The most notable examples of this are immigration, revenue, customs, land office, tax, tariff, education, banking, insurance, and public utility cases. In these jurisdictions, however, substantive rights rather than employees' faults are usually the problem under consideration.

Then, too, financial control, exercised through a budget

21

director, a comptroller, or a director of finance has become an important means of regulation and control within administrative departments. This, one of the most important forms of control, has been given a great deal of attention by other writers. In reorganized administrations questions of efficiency, fault of service, and improper action on the part of employees are increasingly brought within the jurisdiction of those who are concerned with general administration. This is an extremely important and recognized method of self-regulation. Moreover, agencies responsible for personnel questions, such as civil service commissions and bureaus of efficiency, frequently possess the power to keep a record of, admonish, or penalize, employees who fail to observe accepted standards of conduct and efficiency.

Our consideration of the existing forms of administrative control is made complete by reference to the oldest relationship of all—that of the head of the department and the employee. In addition to the superior officer's authority to advise and direct the work of his subordinate, he exercises disciplinary power in the form of a reprimand, demerit rating, loss of seniority, imposition of fines, demotion, suspension, or removal. In most cases the exercise of drastic measures of discipline is limited by the requirement that the civil service commission, police commission, or some other reviewing body must be consulted by the officer imposing the punishment.[18]

The machinery and the standards for administering discipline have not been worked out in the United States to anywhere near the same extent they have in Europe. Outside of Anglo-American countries, special disciplinary tribunals are usually found as a part of the formal frame-

---

[18] Leonard D. White, *Introduction to the Study of Public Administration*, New York, 1926, Chapter 15.

work of administration.[19]  As a rule there are departmental disciplinary tribunals from which appeals may be
taken to a national disciplinary court.  In some countries
all of the members of a disciplinary tribunal are chosen
from the higher positions of the Civil Service, but in
others judges of national courts are added to the membership.  In Germany, for example, the president and at least
two other members out of the seven members of the
disciplinary chambers—or court of first instance—must
be members of a regular law court.  The disciplinary
court, to which appeals are taken, consists of 30 members,
of which less than half are usually administrative officials;
the balance are judges.  In Italy a disciplinary commission
is attached to each ministry; it consists of three employees
engaged in such ministry.  In Switzerland the Federal
Council is the supreme disciplinary authority for civil servants; it may delegate its disciplinary power to the departments which are subordinate to it.  Most of the
systems adopted by other countries approximate one or
another of those which have been mentioned.

The jurisdiction of disciplinary tribunals differs slightly
in all countries.  Uusally, however, they may impose warn-
ing, reprimands, minor penalties such as fines, reduction
of salary, disciplinary transfer, retirement with a reduced
salary, and discharge.  The constitution of Austria's disciplinary courts provides for exclusion from salary advance-
ment; and in Poland, civil service privileges, such as free
travel, may be withdrawn.  In Sweden the higher civil
servants are not subjected to disciplinary punishments, but
they are brought before a court of justice and punished
according to criminal law.  From the decisions of depart-

[19] Leonard D. White, *The Civil Service in the Modern State*, Chicago,
1930.

mental disciplinary commissions there is an appeal to the highest administrative court in Sweden.

The general effect of creating this disciplinary machinery in various countries has undoubtedly been beneficial. The discernment and severity with which the several systems have operated have differed rather considerably. Where a dictatorship has been established, the disciplinary court has proved a ·convenient instrument in obtaining absolute conformity. It cannot be said categorically that the representation of judges has produced results which are either strikingly better or noticeably worse than those where administrative officials alone administer the system. Germany is clearly a good example of the former, but Switzerland and Sweden afford good illustrations of what may be accomplished through purely administrative heads. In Austria, members of the disciplinary commissions are appointed by the director of the central office from among the professional officials and those with legal training; this compromise may be the most satisfactory solution of the personnel problem. If the purely administrative character of the process is altered too much, the danger is that the tribunal will be slow to act and extremely formal, with the result that only serious charges are likely to come before it.

The nature of the penalties imposed raises some very important problems. Some punishments undoubtedly impair the employee's morale to such an extent that the remedy is worse than the disease. For example, the penalty of perpetual disbarment from promotion is clearly unwise, if for no other reason than its effect on the service; discharge would plainly be the more desirable course. The imposition of a fine usually produces an unfortunate result on the morale of employees. This form of discipline, once widespread, has largely disappeared from industry, and should have very limited application in the public services. At one time a national postal organization experimented with fines on careless telegraphers, the administration hoping thereby to increase efficiency. Restlessness and discontent became so widespread that the method was given up after a short time. "Docking pay" is usually a mistaken disciplinary measure.

The most fruitful part of disciplinary systems is the creation of positive standards of civil service conduct and ethics. A standard is better than a half dozen controls; a norm of conduct is the most effective form of regulation. In a few countries disciplinary codes have been drafted by administrative authorities; in other countries this power exists but has not been used. The principal source of information is the body of decisions handed down by disciplinary courts. In Germany very complete rules of official conduct may be gleaned from this source. Standards of obedience, respect, veracity, impartiality, punctuality, candor, courtesy, dignity, moral behavior, incompatible employment, official secrecy, and political activity have evolved and have become an integral part of the employee's make-up.[20] The touchstone of all conduct is

[20] Herman Finer, " The Civil Service and the Modern State: Discipline and Rights," (1929) 7 *Public Administration*, 323. The writer is indebted to Dr. F. Marstein Marx, formerly Regierungsrat, Hamburg, Germany, for the following interesting excerpts from decisions of disciplinary tribunals: The office embraces the whole personality of the civil servant; never is he only a private citizen. The obligation of the civil servant to show deference to his superiors requires that he should also greet them outside the office. Women civil servants are not supposed to greet first. In his whole mode of life the civil servant must prove himself worthy of his profession. He must not endanger his health, *e. g.*, through excessive drinking. He is not allowed to borrow money from his subordinates or from private citizens with whom he comes in touch through his official activities. Extramarital intercourse is generally not a disciplinary offense, but as a rule adultery is. Civil servants must show the utmost reserve in their dealings with the women employed in the same department. The civil servant must

the prestige of the service; any action which diminishes it must be disciplined. The employee's behavior and attitude must be designed to improve public satisfaction with the quality of service rendered.

Greater attention undoubtedly needs to be given to the improvement of disciplinary measures in the United States. An adaptation of the disciplinary tribunal, in the light of experience in many countries, would appear to be desirable. We should insist upon true administrative self-regulation and not permit the legal profession to control the process. The benefits to be expected from a system of disciplinary tribunals are rather far-reaching. The ill-defined relationship existing at present between employer and employee would be superseded by a more representative system, in which greater fairness should be expected.

The corporate responsibility of the administrative service for its own conduct would be given concrete recognition, and the necessity of legislative and judicial interference should be appreciably diminished. Finally, of greatest importance, the way would be opened to the evolution of concrete standards of professional conduct and of a comprehensive code of ethics. This is the direction from which the most promising future developments in administrative regulation may be expected.

### Conduct Codes of Employees' Organizations

The reestablishment of authority, discipline, and standards of conduct appears to be one of the functions which may be performed by the guild organization of society—this trend which is assuming world-wide significance. Neither individualism nor the authoritarian state alone has proved able to maintain a satisfactory equilibrium in the

not tolerate an activity of family members belonging to his household which is not compatible with the esteem of the civil service.

machine age. A combination of planning and control, emanating from the state and carried out by organized bodies of government employees, trade associations, and labor organizations, is the modern formula of contemporary developments in the United States, Italy, Germany, Spain, Russia, and, to a certain extent, in Great Britain. In the N. R. A. program, for example, codes of competition and ethical standards of remuneration are the core of national policy. If present tendencies in the United States continue, the economic likenesses between the N. R. A. and the Italian Corporative State will be very striking. The guild concept involves a close collaboration, but a division of responsibility, between the government and the organized interests. The government prepares the master plan, sanctions agreements, composes differences, coerces non-conformists, and modifies corporate relationships in the light of experience; capital and labor form responsible organizations, propose the rules of the game, advocate their respective policies, and attempt to obtain conformity on the part of member organizations entering into the agreement. This is not self-regulation, in the old sense of the expression; it is corporate legislation and enforcement under the aegis of the state.

The development of corporate initiative and responsibility in public employees' organizations has been a significant feature of recent years. Its extension and increased importance may be expected. The motive will probably be largely defensive. Government remuneration has been drastically slashed. Existing associations of employees have been powerless before the onslaught of business organizations wielding the economy axe. Judging from past experience, the adjustment of salaries in the public service will lag far behind the increase in the cost of living. Moreover, as larger concentrations of power arise in the business world, the bargaining power of public employees' associations progressively shrinks. As experience in Germany and elsewhere has proved, if government employees do not develop a united front, acting through a few major associations, their prospects will become progressively worse.

Because of the struggle for existence, and the resulting preoccupation with union activities, the public employees' organizations will be likely to overlook the importance of policies which would improve the administrative services, create better public relations, and bring about effective control of official conduct through their own *esprit de corps,* standards, and disciplinary measures. " Despite one or two brilliant exceptions," Professor White has concluded, " Whitleyism is hardening into civil service unionism, and the life and spirit of Whitleyism are being absorbed in the energy and aspirations of the union." [21] It will require determination as well as statesmanship if the constructive work which might be done by organizations of public employees in the United States is not to be swept aside because of the constant struggle for better wages and conditions of service. If constructive policies are followed, quick and permanent improvement of American administration is more likely to come from organizations such as the Civil Service Assembly of the United States and Canada, the United States Conference of Mayors, the International City Managers' Association, the Municipal Finance Officers' Association, and leagues of municipalities, than from any other quarter. Suggestion from the outside is important, but lasting improvement of administration is ultimately controlled by those who perform the actual work.

[21] *Whitley Councils in the British Civil Service* (Chicago, 1933), 348.

These organizations of public employees engender prestige, *esprit de corps,* standards of efficiency. A man comes to think of his standing in a profession, and as the guild becomes older and more powerful, this attachment transcends the employees' relation to a particular job. The city manager profession is the best illustration of this point in the United States, but examples abound in Great Britain and on the Continent.[22]

It is not necessary that an association of government employees should establish codes of conduct or ethical standards before the corporate control may be said to exercise an important influence over employee behavior. Few organizations of public servants have adopted written standards of professional conduct, although the practice is common in most forms of industry.[23] A code of conduct, as Heermance has pointed out, is almost always a creed and not a law. By the mere act of association, and the feeling of professionalism which results, powerful stimulants and standards are put into operation. A tax official, for example, desires to be regarded highly by his confrères and receives inspiration from being thrown into association with men of greater experience and prestige. These factors are positive, lasting, and cumulative. There is no reason why their effect should not be as great, in course of time, as that of professional standards upon the judge or the physician. As a matter of fact, the International City Managers' Association probably achieves a higher standard of ethics than any other profession in the country.

Codes of conduct are usually found only when almost the entire profession or trade has been brought within a common organization. Exclusiveness is a condition pre-

---

[22] Carr-Saunders and Wilson, *The Professions, London,* 1933, 239-250.
[23] E. L. Heermance, *Codes of Ethics,* Burlington, Vt., 1924.

cedent. Nevertheless, it appears desirable that definite standards should be created as soon as it appears feasible to do so. Men are essentially religious in the sense that they crave creeds by which to guide their lives. Prestige and fraternalism are also nourished by credal formulations. Views will differ as to the practical result of ethical standards upon individual conduct. Generally speaking, it may be said that hypocrisy is more likely to be avoided and consistency to be obtained when the association is professional rather than social or general. The physician and the Rotarian are cases in point.

The code of ethics of the International City Managers' Association may be taken as an example of what has and can be done within the public service. "In order that city managers might maintain a high standard of professional conduct," the following code of ethics was adopted by the International City Managers' Association on September 25, 1924:

1. The position of city manager is an important position and an honorable position, and should not be accepted unless the individual believes that he can serve the community to its advantage.

2. No man should accept a position of city manager unless he believes in the council-manager plan of government.

3. In personal conduct a city manager should be exemplary, and he should display the same obedience to law that he should inculcate in others.

4. Personal aggrandizement and personal profit secured by confidential information or by misuse of public time is dishonest.

5. Loyalty to his employment recognizes that it is the council, the elected representative of the people, who primarily determines the municipal policies, and is entitled to the credit for their fulfillment.

6. Although he is a hired employee of the council, he is hired for a purpose — to exercise his own judgment as an executive in accomplishing the policies formulated by the council; and to

attain success in his employment he must decline to submit to dictation in matter for which the responsibility is solely his.

7. Power justifies responsibility, and responsibilty demands power, and a city manager who becomes impotent to inspire support should resign.

8. The city manager is the administrator for all the people, and in performing his duty he should serve without discrimination.

9. To serve the public well, a city manager should strive to keep the community informed of the plans and purposes of the administration, remembering that healthy publicity and criticism are an aid to the success of any democracy.

10. A city manager should deal frankly with the council as a unit and not secretly with its individual members, and similarly should foster a spirit of cooperation between all employees of the city's organization.

11. No matter how small the governmental unit under his management, a city manager should recognize his relation to the larger political subdivisions and encourage improved administrative methods for all.

12. No city manager should take an active part in politics.

13. A city manager will be known by his works, many of which may outlast him, and, regardless of personal popularity or unpopularity, he should not curry favor or temporize, but should in a far-sighted way aim to benefit the community of today and of posterity.[24]

Although all of the above precepts contain important suggestions, points 6, 7, and 12 deserve our special attention. It goes without saying that the real test of a city manager's loyalty is when he will resign his position rather than violate the ethics of the profession or compromise his own standing by engaging in political controversy.[25] Impressive evidence of the compelling effect of definite standards of professional conduct is found in

---

[24] (1933) *City Manager Yearbook*, 269-270.

[25] John N. Edy, "Conditions under which a City Manager Should Resign," (1932) *City Manager Yearbook*, 109.

the fact that seven managers resigned in 1932 because the council interfered with appointments, and another resigned in 1932 because the council interfered with appointments, and another resigned because he was made an issue in a council election.[26]

In the past our thinking about government has been distorted because of over-emphasis on restraint, on agencies of external control. This approach is probably explained in large measure by theological assumptions which have created a general " climate of opinion." Perhaps we are now on the threshold of a new era, in which positive, inspiring standards of professional conduct will progressively replace uncertainty, apprehension, and the sporadic inquisitions which have emanated from the legislative and judicial branches of the government. The most reliable guarantee of honest, efficient, intelligent, public-spirited administration is a corps of professional administrators. No amount of outside pressure can make an incompetent, unprincipled employee fulfil high standards of conduct.

## Administration in the " Geist " State

The term " geist " (spirit or concept) state is used to distinguish the purposeful, party-controlled state—like that found at the present time in Italy, Russia, and Germany—from the laissez-faire, non-interventionist state which characterized the nineteenth century. The designation is not important. Like all classifications, it is suggested merely because it appears to possess utility for certain purposes. The writer would be the first to admit the shortcomings of the term. For example, how should the United States be classified since 1932? Is the philosophy represented by the N. R. A. eagle our *geist?* Objection may be made to using the term *geist* in connec-

[26] (1933) *City Manager Yearbook*, 304.

tion with regimes which, like those previously mentioned, have been established by, and depend so largely upon, force. This criticism contains validity, but it is nevertheless true that in all of these dictatorships definite philosophical premises have been formulated, and concrete objectives are pursued. In the respective ideologies of the corporative and the proletariat state, therefore, are afforded effective instruments of inspiration and discipline for the government employee.

Under the authoritarian or dictatorial regime, several important changes take place in the civil service situations which obtain under republican administrations. The line separating policy formulation and law execution is largely obliterated. The democratic assumption regarding the non-political status of government employees is discarded. Officials who do not actively support fascism or communism are replaced by those who will. Even this does not suffice. Devoted work in the service of the state becomes the highest ethic, the state religion. Being a religion, zeal is the normal expectation; the party creed is the guide to action, and non-conformity is severely punished. Rigid rules regarding the conduct and the ethics of the bureaucracy do not need to be promulgated; every act is judged by the loyalty, enthusiasm, and skill with which party objectives are carried forward. Ethics and judgment supplant a strict legalism.

In Soviet Russia there is no distinction between party members and administrative officials, nor between the political and the economic functions of the state. "The rôle of leadership of the party," Samuel N. Harper has written, "extends to all fields of economic life." [27] Party members are divided into "active" and "passive" elements, the former holding administrative posts. An offi-

[27] *Civic Training in Soviet Russia*, Chicago, 1929, 34.

cial may be assigned to any kind of position and in any part of the Union, and he must accept the appointment. This system guarantees that zealous workers will carry their enthusiasm to all parts of the country. Those who have the strongest fervor belong to the " cult of Lenin." All members of the party must pay dues, and " one of the positive obligations of party membership is a minimum of public activity."

The disciplinary measures adopted by the Communist Party are exceedingly interesting. According to Paragraph 51 of the Statutes, " The most strict observance of party discipline is the first duty of all members of the party and of all the party organs. The orders of the central authorities of the party must be carried out promptly and implicitly. The discussion of all conflicting problems within the party is permitted only until a decision has been adopted, when all discussion must stop." N. N. Alexeyev has written as follows:

Failure to execute the orders of the party authorities entails various penalties, beginning with censure and ending with exclusion from the party. For the purpose of enforcing discipline, the party has special bodies, the Control Committees, established to strengthen its unity and authority. These committees consist of from three to five members, with a party stage dating from before March, 1917. The party statutes explain the importance of these committees in the following way: ' The prestige of the party among the masses depends, not only upon its achievements, but also on the behavior of each separate member. The Communists, as the vanguard of the laboring masses, must display exemplary conduct not only in public matters but also in their private lives. If a member of the party indulges in drunkenness or abuses the privileges of his position to live in luxury, he dishonors not only his own prestige but also the prestige of the party. If a member of the party goes to church, he undermines the entire work of the party, which endeavors to disclose the fundamental unsoundness of religion. If a member of the party infringes discipline, he disrupts the party itself.[28]

Professor Harper's statements regarding methods of control over Soviet officials are so revealing and suggestive that they deserve to be set forth rather fully:

The discipline within the party is enforced by a system of penalties. The most extreme penalty is that of expulsion from the party. The names of expelled members must be published in the party press for general knowledge. It is impossible to determine what the attitude of the non-party element of a community is toward an expelled member of the party, but it would seem that such persons would not be elected to any responsible position in the Soviets or other bodies. Other penalties are party censure, public censure, and temporary removal from responsible positions either in the party or in a Soviet institution. This last form of penalty is a real punishment because the individual is kept under discipline of the party and must accept any minor tasks which may be assigned to him. The grounds for expulsion or other penalties are numerous, the more general being " acts recognized as being criminal by the public opinion of the party." Thus, there have developed a whole series of acts which are considered unbecoming the conduct of a Communist. A type of Communist morality has been evolved, very specific in many respects. Habitual drunkenness or wife-beating will lead to expulsion; frequently steps are taken to help the erring member reform. Abuse of the law on marriage and divorce is also punishable. Bullying, or even 'commanding,' methods of admin-

---

[28] In P. Malevsky-Malevitch, *Russia U. S. S. R. — A Complete Handbook*, New York, 1933, 215-216. Continuing, Alexeyev says: " From the day of its accession to power, the party has kept close watch on the discipline of its members, combatting not only external infringements of this discipline but also departures from the principles of policy periodically laid down. The so-called ' cleanings ' occur frequently. Thus, between January, 1928, and June, 1929, the party excluded — for various offences, including ' political heresy ' — 34,000 members. From June, 1929, to February, 1930, 7,300 members were called to account by the Control Committees for various disciplinary offences; of these 3,500 were rehabilitated and reinstated."

istration by Communists holding official positions are now being actively combatted by the party, with the effective sanctions of the party discipline. Where Communists holding responsible positions in state institutions are found guilty of dishonesty or corruption, they are more severely punished. It is not clear on what basis the judicial authorities impose the more severe penalty when the guilty party is a Communist. One of the first questions asked of a person brought before a Soviet judge is whether he or she is a member of the party. The judges of the higher tribunals are, almost without exception, Communists, and as such under the dictation of their revolutionary conscience may impose the higher penalties provided by the law where the crime has been committed by a citizen with a conscious responsibility. Where a party member is expelled for a specific crime, the fact must be officially reported to the administrative and judicial authorities.[29]

In Italy the employees of the state are no longer considered mere non-political beings whose permanence in office should be guaranteed by all political parties. This English theory of civil service has been cast overboard. Fascism teaches that the public employee cannot serve the state and at the same time oppose the government, for the government and state blend into each other. Consequently, if the civil servant is opposed to the government,

---

[29] Harper, *op. cit.*, 26-27. Harper adds: "There are activities positively forbidden to a Communist. A member of the party may not engage in any activity from which personal profit is derived by the exploitation of the labor of another. This is a positive regulation, supplemented by warnings against too close association in personal life with 'bourgeois' elements. Some leaders urge that Communists carefully avoid the dress and manners of the enemy class. Thus, the outward appearance of a party member should not be such as to suggest a non-toiling life or arouse the indignation of toilers, says one writer, adding that the Communist should live as nearly like the workmen have to live as possible, and particularly he should not handicap himself with the economic burden of finely equipped living-quarters. It is added by this writer that this does not mean that the Communist is to go dirty or in rags. Finally, it is considered bad taste for a Communist to marry a woman from another and alien class. Thus, personal life is not separated from party life. The interests of the Revolution and of the party are paramount. Disorderly sexual life or drinking weaken the fighter for the Revolution."

he is opposed to the state. It logically follows that under the new order the public functionary is not only the performer of certain duties for which he receives a stipend but also a political force and even an agent of propaganda in whom the Fascist state may find a servant for the support and promulgations of its doctrines. It is for these reasons that the bureaucracy plays a unique rôle in Italian civic training.[80]

From the moment that the public employee expresses a desire to enter the service of the state, his political views play an important part in his career. In order to secure an appointment he must give proof of having led a correct civil, moral, and political life! A law of 1925 provides that the government may discharge civil servants who " by reason of acts committed either in or out of office do not give full guarantee of a complete faith in their duties or who make themselves incompatible with the general political aims of the government." Since 1922 there has been a constant " purging " of government departments, as a result of which " the administration of the interior and practically all branches of the civil service were thoroughly disrupted and thrown into confusion." [81]

The Fascist party constantly emphasizes the fact that employees of the state stand in a peculiarly intimate relation to the party and therefore enjoy its special solicitude. The activities of the General Fascist Association of Public Employees are supposed to improve the morale of employees. However, employees' associations have no legal recognition, and the provisions of the Labor Charter of 1926 do not apply to them. A high official has stated that servants of the government, " being freed from the petty daily struggle for wages, can dedicate themselves to an enterprise which is vaster, nobler, and more essential

[80] Schneider and Clough, *Making Fascists*, Chicago, 1929, 129.
[81] *Ibid.*, 137.

to the future of the Italian nation and its political formation."

Fascism, like Communism, has its religious fervor, its self-denying ordinances, and its rigid disciplines, which apply with peculiar force to all members of the administration, the stalwarts of the party. This social asceticism, this political puritanism, is counterbalanced by the prestige, power, and general satisfaction which comes from affiliation with a great national enterprise. The state is creative life, is purposeful, loyalties are simple, and progress is orderly. The government employee leads a totalitarian life. In such a milieu the forms of control over administrative action do not present a very complicated problem for the student of governmental processes.

## Summary

The traditional approach to this problem has emphasized external controls over administration to the virtual exclusion of other aspects. Government should be kept in its place; most public servants were presumably bad or incompetent. Hence, clumsy devices like legislative investigations were frequently employed, usually after the thief had already escaped. The time should arrive when legislative investigations will almost completely disappear. When offences were committed against the property or other rights of citizens, court actions were brought against the official. This remedy still possesses utility, but it gets at only a small proportion of administrative faults. The government should greatly extend the right of individuals to sue the state or the particular service. Special administrative courts should be a means of dealing with administration more satisfactorily and of democratizing justice.

The surest road to administrative improvement is within

the administration itself. In several fields administrative appeals have already replaced court adjudications, and this method will undoubtedly be extended. As public administration has progressed, executive, fiscal, and personnel controls have been improved. So has the calibre of public employees, the most important factor of all. Administrative discipline and control occupy the largest part of the process of producing "lawful" administration. Definite standards have emerged from the administrative techniques of control. A modification of the European disciplinary tribunal might with benefit be introduced into American administration.

In the last analysis, the raising of levels of ability and of performance depends upon the organized interest and demands of public employees. The chief responsibility for making administrative improvements is theirs. Employees' organizations can exercise a great deal of influence and control over members. Traditions, *esprit de corps,* standards, codes of ethics constitute an essential part of the contribution to be expected from organized government employees. The success of the International City Managers' Association is a model of what may be accomplished. A creed appears to be very desirable, but there are apparent objections to the extreme cultism found in the *geist* state. The best features of this system—its devotion, spirit, and self-discipline—may, while avoiding its excesses, be emulated with great benefit to American administration.[32] The corporative principle, the theory of self-discipline, and the stimulus of a constructive philosophy of government are controls which are likely to prove of increasing importance in American public administration.

[32] On this point see Marshall E. Dimock, " The Potential Incentives of Public Employment," (1933) 27 *American Political Science Review,* 628.